SHUT UP AND EAT!

TONY LIP AND STEVEN PRIGGÉ

SHUT UP AND EAT!

Mangia
WITH FAMILY RECIPES AND STORIES
FROM YOUR FAVORITE
ITALIAN-AMERICAN STARS

BERKLEY BOOKS
NEW YORK

THE BERKLEY PUBLISHING GROUP
Published by the Penguin Group
Penguin Group (USA) Inc.
375 Hudson Street, New York, New York 10014, USA

Penguin Group (Canada), 90 Eglinton Avenue East, Suite 700, Toronto, Ontario M4P 2Y3, Canada
    (a division of Pearson Penguin Canada Inc.)
Penguin Books Ltd., 80 Strand, London WC2R 0RL, England
Penguin Group Ireland, 25 St. Stephen's Green, Dublin 2, Ireland
    (a division of Penguin Books Ltd.)
Penguin Group (Australia), 250 Camberwell Road, Camberwell, Victoria 3124, Australia
    (a division of Pearson Australia Group Pty. Ltd.)
Penguin Books India Pvt. Ltd., 11 Community Centre, Panchsheel Park,
    New Delhi—110 017, India
Penguin Group (NZ), Cnr. Airborne and Rosedale Roads, Albany, Auckland 1310,
    New Zealand (a division of Pearson New Zealand Ltd.)
Penguin Books (South Africa) (Pty.) Ltd., 24 Sturdee Avenue, Rosebank,
    Johannesburg 2196, South Africa

Penguin Books Ltd., Registered Offices: 80 Strand, London WC2R 0RL, England

The recipes contained in this book are to be followed exactly as written. The publisher is not responsible for your specific health or allergy needs that may require medical supervision.
The publisher is not responsible for any adverse reactions to the recipes contained in this book.
The publisher does not have any control over and does not assume any responsibility for author or third-party websites or their content.

PRINTING HISTORY
Berkley hardcover edition: October 2005
Berkley trade paperback edition: October 2006

Berkley trade paperback ISBN: 0-425-21177-0

The Library of Congress has catalogued the Berkley hardcover edition as follows:

Lip, Tony.
    Shut up and eat! : mangia with family recipes and stories from your favorite
Italian-American stars / written by Tony Lip and Steven Priggé.
    p. cm.
    1. Cookery, Italian. 2. Italian Americans. 3. Celebrities—United States. I. Priggé,
Steven, 1975– II. Title.
TX723.L553 2005
641.5945—dc22

        2005048062

PRINTED IN THE UNITED STATES OF AMERICA

10 9 8 7 6 5 4 3 2 1

Tony Lip's Dedication

This book is dedicated to the memory of my mother, Nazzerena,
and my wife, Dolores.

Steven Priggé's Dedication

This book is dedicated to my late grandmother, Carmela Rispoli Solla,
and my mother, Deanna Priggé, who never let me leave the house
with an empty stomach or an empty heart.

CONTENTS

CONTENTS

CONTENTS

CONTENTS

CONTENTS

CONTENTS

ACKNOWLEDGMENTS

Tony Lip

First, I'd like to express my appreciation to all of the actors and actresses who agreed to be featured in this book. I would also like to thank my good friend Danny Aiello for writing such a wonderful foreword and Chazz Palminteri and Robert Davi for their contribution and support. I would like to thank the folks at Penguin, especially Marilyn Ducksworth and my editor, Denise Silvestro. I would also like to offer my appreciation to the following people: our creative consultant/chef, John Chibarro; my agents, Ron Bard and Mitch Ducksworth (founders of the Northeast Media Group); Frank and Angela Vallelonga; Nick Vallelonga; Rudy and Ruby Vallelonga; Mark L. Beigelman Esq.; Gary M. Emmanuel Esq.; Frank Scaturchio; Craig Balkam of NIG Executive Protection; Michael Bard; Marty Grossbach; Yoshiki; the Bertolotti Brothers; Arthur Chiusano; Samir Patel; Lou and Lynn Venere; John Venere; Tony and Donna Trotta; Ginger Bisaccia; Paul Stable; Nick Miceli; Nick Dintino; Dominique Alberga; Michael J. Galluzzi; Frankie Loc; Vincent Punchetore; Vincent Toronto; Donna McKenna; Jeremiah Ferrentinos; Evonne Coutros; Larry and Margie Borgognoni; Tony Fusilo; Tom Serbak; Joe and Anne Palughi; Andy Albanese; Mitch and Ana Prodani; Anthony and Rose Gentile; Al and Fay Ioimo; Tom Collelo; Rose Virgilio; Mario Occhicone; Jeffrey Marchetti, Steven Priggé, Ed Salzano and Bruno of Bruno's Restaurant. Also, thanks to Psychic Media International and Howard Greenblatt and the National Pork Board for all their support.

Steven Priggé

I would first like to thank Tony Lip for making this project so much fun to write. I would also like to offer my sincere gratitude to all of the Italian-American actors and actresses who offered their stories and recipes for this book; without you, there would be no book. I would also like to thank Danny Aiello, who wrote a thoughtful and insightful foreword. I would like to offer my appreciation to the team at Penguin, especially David and Elizabeth Shanks; Marilyn Ducksworth; our editor, Denise Silvestro, who did an incredible job; and her helpful assistant, Katherine Day. I would like to thank the following people who helped me on this journey called writing a book: our creative consultant/chef, John Chibarro; my agent at ICM, Andrea Barzvi; Ron Bard and Mitch Ducksworth for their genuine support and friendship; Lina Hansson; Alan Priggé; Lou Massaia; Deanna Priggé; Dana Priggé; Robert Shoblock; Susan Prigge; Daniel Zinn; Anthony Edwards; Jeanine Lobell; Angel DeAngelis; John Halko; Steve Vasak; Brigitte Starr; Jerry Ohlinger; Keya Morgan; Jules Mignonac; Kevin Holmes; Richard Hart; Elio Lombardi; Loraine Scott; Anne Morea; Randy Steingeiser; Danny Ramm; Staci Gilchrist; Sal Esposito; Michael DeGeorgio; Dr. Daniel Conte; Dr. Kenneth Conte; Jamie Kreshpane; Vincenzo Cardinale; Sam Cosma; and Lynn Matsumoto. Everyone on this list believed in this project, and your support has been invaluable.

FOREWORD

When I was growing up, if you were an Italian American, chances were your mother was a great cook. And let me tell you, my mom, Frances, was the best! She was a working single mother and we didn't have much money, but every day she made sure her children were well fed. However, on one particular day, she taught me a life lesson that I have never forgotten. The day started like most. The kids in our family were awake getting ready for school and having breakfast—cornflakes, Rice Krispies, or oatmeal with milk. Like always, when we finished, our mom would clean up and make sure we were off with all our books and homework and she was off to work at a toy company on Southern Boulevard in the Bronx. She was an amazing person.

I was nicknamed Junior and I hated that name. I was ten years old and I attended P.S. 54 Elementary School. I had four sisters and one brother. My sister Anna was the youngest and I was the next oldest. As usual, I arrived at school at 8 a.m. At noon, my lunch was prepared by the school and consisted of a small container of milk, a cupcake, and a peanut-butter sandwich. Then, it was out to the schoolyard for recreation, where we would play basketball, punchball, or softball. After recess, we went back to class, and, finally, the dismissal bell rang promptly at 3 p.m.

On the way home, I stopped by a small neighborhood restaurant on Freeman Street. I almost always went there after school. Mom established a friendly agreement with the owner so that if any of her children were hungry, they could go to the restaurant and eat. My favorite was mashed potatoes with brown gravy or rye bread with butter topped off with an egg cream to drink. Our mother would pay the owner at the end of the week. On this particular day I knew to eat light at the restaurant because that night we were having my favorite dinner: macaroni and meatballs. It was an evening meal of leftovers from the day before, Sunday, and we all loved it, especially when it was a day old. Somehow, the meal tasted as good or better the second day around.

Mom arrived home at 6 p.m. to prepare dinner for us. The meatballs were great, made with egg, pignoli nuts, grated cheese, and no onions. Mom did that especially for me because I've always hated onions. We put cold ricotta cheese on the macaroni and then added the sauce made with chicken and pork. What a taste! It was outrageous. Kids used to love to come to my house. I thought they liked me and maybe they did, but I found out later that the main reason they loved coming to my house to play was because of my mother's terrific cooking.

That night, some of the food was left uneaten. It was here that I learned a life lesson. Mom said, "Remember, people in China are starving." You see, we had very little, but my mother was willing to share what little we had with others, and we always did. The very next day I arrived at school with two paper bags filled with canned and other nonperishable foods to be sent to China, for those who were starving. My mom paid for that food. She taught me another important lesson at dinner one time when she said, "If you want to share, food is a good place to start!" I love her for that.

You will learn throughout this book that many of the actors and actresses included here grew up with simple means, just as I did. However, food was the common tie that kept the family together. In the traditional Italian-American culture, the dinner table is a place where you laugh, cry, share memories, make new memories, and, of course, learn life lessons. It's the place where I've made some of my fondest memories, which I hold close to my heart. Also, if there is a person more qualified to write a cookbook, I want to meet that person. Until that time, I'll stick with the person who I think is the best—my buddy Tony Lip! He's great with food and a damn good actor too. *Mangia* and God bless!

Danny Aiello
September 2005

INTRODUCTION

by Tony Lip

❧

FIRST OF ALL, I'm gonna tell you why this is not just another Italian cookbook. For one thing, you don't have to be a gourmet chef to cook the recipes. For another, you're gonna learn a little bit about me, about my love for food, and about why you're not gonna find the recipes in this book anywhere else.

Who am I? You're probably familiar with me as Carmine Lupertazzi, the New York mob boss on the hit HBO-TV show *The Sopranos*, but I have also acted in many classic movies over my lifetime like *The Godfather*, *The Pope of Greenwich Village*, *Year of the Dragon*, *Goodfellas*, and *Donnie Brasco*, just to name a few. Over the past thirty years, on these movie sets and off, I have exchanged hundreds of Italian recipes with some of my good friends—and your favorite stars. And let me tell you, in mob movies no one ever kills anybody on an empty stomach!

In this book, you're gonna get my family's secret Italian recipes, which are out of this world. But, most important, you're gonna get another special treat—family recipes from some of the best actors and actresses who have appeared in the most successful Italian-based movies and television shows of all time. We are talking about the personal recipes of top talent like James Gandolfini (Tony Soprano of *The Sopranos*, *True Romance*, and

The Last Castle), Danny Aiello (*The Godfather, Part II; Moonstruck; Dinner Rush*), Joe Mantegna (*Wait Until Spring, Bandini; The Rat Pack*), Chazz Palminteri (*A Bronx Tale, Analyze This*), Lorraine Bracco (Dr. Melfi of *The Sopranos, Goodfellas*), and more. To them, good Italian food represents a very special kind of bonding as well as pleasure. I am honored to say that they are sharing their personal recipes for the first time in this book. And, finally, I'm gonna tell you the secret ingredient all Italians use in everything they cook that makes the food taste so damn special! Hey, but that's for later. First, you're gonna learn something about yours truly, me.

A "REAL-LIFE" BRONX TALE

MY PARENTS, NICHOLAS and Nazzerena Vallelonga, came to America from Calabria, Italy. I was born Frank Anthony Vallelonga in Beaver Falls, Pennsylvania, and within a couple weeks of my birth, my parents moved us to 215th Street in the Bronx, New York. Although it's an Italian tradition to name the firstborn male after the father's father, my mother preferred the name Anthony. Therefore, she never called me Frank like my grandfather. She always called me Tony. As for my nickname, The Lip, my younger brother, Rudy, tells the story of how I got it: "Even as a kid, Tony could out-talk everybody. He could talk anybody into doing anything, and he could talk us out of any tight situations or problems we found ourselves in. So we all started calling him The Lip."

215th Street was in a tough, rough area of the Bronx. There was the neighborhood crew of guys I hung out with: Frankie Lock, Vito Crabs, Frankie Maze, Vinnie Mole, and Joe the Hand, just to name a few. Joe got that nickname because he had a hand that was quicker than a bolt of lightning. Not only could he take your wallet, but he could take your belt off you without you ever knowing it. I had a lot of fun with the guys and the Bronx was a wonderful place to live in. Mine was a real Italian neighborhood where most of the kids ate a cannoli before they even learned how to walk. My memories of that time are filled with fun, laughter, and love. However, the most interesting and always generous characters of my colorful neighborhood were the mob guys. They usually drove nice cars, always seemed to have money, and generally tipped well. I would shine their shoes and bring them the newspaper for a dollar tip. Sometimes I would get ten dollars and that would be "a score and a half." They were always good with a buck and always protected the neighborhood, and we protected them too. In fact, when someone suspicious or strange came on our block and asked about certain local people, all of a sudden everyone couldn't speak English. We were treated right by these guys: during World War II, they brought sugar and silk stockings to people in need, sometimes not charging anyone. So why would you ever rat on them? When I was a kid, they would eat at my house and they were always generous to us. As an actor today, I call upon those experiences to portray the mob-type guys I play.

The Vallelonga family photo. (Bottom row, left to right): *me, my brother, Rudy.* (Top row, left to right): *my mother, Nazzerena, and my father, Nicholas*

My favorite thing about living on 215th Street in the Bronx was how it smelled. When you walked down my street, the smells of homemade Italian cooking—the meat gravy, grilled sausage and peppers, fresh-baked Italian bread, and delicious Italian pastries—filled the air as their delicious fragrances floated out from the kitchen windows of all the homes on the street. My mouth is watering just thinking about it. But of all the Italian "mamas" on the

My mother, the best cook who ever lived!

block, my mother was, without a doubt, the best cook. I know that everybody says their mother was the best. However, I'm telling you that my mother's cooking was unbelievable. She made everything from soup to nuts. Hell, she probably made soup with nuts! Honestly, she was able to make everything. No matter what time of day it was, my mother was always cooking something spectacular and everybody in the neighborhood knew it. My house was always filled with friends and family sitting around the table, eating my mother's cooking. Of course, we would always start talking and that's when my mother would say, "Shut up and eat!" I don't care what culture you're in, when it comes time to sit down and have a meal and people are still talking, the mother always says, "Shut up and eat." So that's where the title of this book comes from.

I learned at a very young age that the key to great cooking is the freshness of the ingredients you put in every recipe. Everything my mother made was fresh because my father grew everything in our garden, which was really more like a little farm. Yeah, you heard me right. We had a little farm right there in the middle of the Bronx. We had cherry trees, apple trees, pear trees, plum trees, and peach trees. We grew tomatoes, lettuce, fresh basil, and peppers. We raised lambs, pigs, chickens—you name it! My father made his own salami, prosciutto, cheese, beer, and wine. I'm telling you, the food was incredible. It was so good that when my cousins got married, the only gift they wanted was for my mother and father to make the dinner for their wedding reception. My parents agreed and they made the very first buffet dinner in the neighborhood. Here is my mother's recipe for one of the dishes we had on the menu at that wedding buffet way back in the 1940s:

SCALOPPINE AL MARSALA

1 pound veal scallops, sliced ⅜-inch thick and pounded very thin

1 teaspoon salt

1 teaspoon pepper

2 cups flour

2 tablespoons butter

3 tablespoons olive oil

1 (10-ounce) box white mushrooms, sliced thin

1 cup dry Marsala

1 cup chicken or beef stock

2 tablespoons butter, softened

Season the veal scallops with salt and pepper. Then, dip them in the flour and vigorously shake off the excess. In a heavy 10- to 12-inch skillet, melt the 2 tablespoons of butter with the oil over moderate heat. When the foam subsides, add the veal, 3 or 4 slices at a time, and brown them for about 3 minutes on each side. After they have browned, transfer them from the skillet to a plate.

Sauté mushrooms in the same pan until light brown. Add the Marsala and ½ cup of chicken or beef stock, and boil the liquid over a high heat for 1 or 2 minutes. Scrape in any browned fragments clinging to the bottom and sides of the pan. Return the veal to the skillet. Cover the pan and simmer over low heat for 10 to 15 minutes, basting the veal now and then with the pan juices.

To serve, transfer the scallops to a heated platter. Add ½ cup of stock to the sauce remaining in the skillet and boil briskly, scraping in the brown bits sticking to the bottom and sides of the pan. When the sauce has reduced considerably and has the consistency of a syrupy glaze, taste it for seasoning. Remove the pan from the heat, stir in the 2 tablespoons of soft butter, and pour the sauce over the veal.

SERVES 4

OFF TO THE ARMY I GO

MY MOTHER'S COOKING was so good that I never ate in a restaurant until I went into the army. I got drafted during the Korean War and was eventually stationed in Germany. One day, I got into an argument with one of the sergeants and they threw me into the stockade. They also punished me by taking two-thirds of my pay as a fine. So, when I got out, I was flat broke. Anyway, living up to my nickname, The Lip, I bullshitted all the officers into believing that I was an expert chef and became the head cook for the entire platoon. All of a sudden, I was in charge of cooking breakfast, lunch, and dinner for a couple hundred men. I didn't have a clue where to begin. So I decided to ask the only real expert I knew—my mother. I sneaked into our captain's office and called her on the telephone daily. She would give me the recipes right over the phone, and that's how I first learned how to cook. I got so good that I started charging the officers seven dollars a head for

Me as a cook in the army

specially prepared Italian dinners, totally outside of the usual menu. Everybody loved my cooking. I think we ended up having the fattest platoon in the American army. I guarantee you that my mother's recipes made these guys feel like they were getting a real home-cooked meal. After a couple years, and hundreds of great dinners from my kitchen, I received an honorable discharge and returned home.

When I got back, I worked for the New York City Department of Sanitation. I also worked as a bartender and I opened several small businesses including luncheonettes, pool halls, ice cream parlors, and pizza joints. I also worked as a bouncer at New York nightclubs like the Wagon Wheel and the world-famous Peppermint Lounge, where the Twist dance craze became famous. During this time, I met and married my wife, Dolores, and we had two children, Nick and Frank.

My late wife, Dolores, was another great cook and every meal was a true feast. Her macaroni and gravy was as good as my mom's — maybe even better. Oh, yeah, for those of you who tend to call it "pasta," to a *real* Italian,

Me and the love of my life, my late wife, Dolores

SHUT UP AND EAT!

My two wonderful sons (left to right), Frank and Nick

it's always called "macaroni." Rigatoni, ziti, linguini, cavattelli—it's all macaroni to us. Also, it's never referred to as "sauce." It's always "gravy." My wife would cook the gravy with meatballs, sausage, spareribs, braciole, pigs' feet—you name it. We'd always start our meals with some cold cuts like salami, prosciutto, and pepperoni, mozzarella and Parmesan cheeses, and some nice roasted peppers. Then we'd hit the macaroni, and then the meat, along with some eggplant parmigiana and chicken parmigiana. Then, we'd end the meal with a big salad. That's right, Italians eat their salad after the meal. It's good for the digestion. Then, we'd finish off with fruit and nuts, some nice pastries, maybe some homemade cheesecake, or some cannoli, and we'd wash it down by sipping a nice cup of espresso. I'm getting hungry just thinking about it.

To an Italian, the meatball is the first and most important ingredient to a happy marriage. In my day, many Italian men would call off the wedding if their fiancées couldn't get their meatballs just right. Most men would make their mothers spend hours and hours with their future brides to teach them how to make the meatballs the way their little boys loved them. Now, my mother made a great meatball. However, when I met my wife, Dolores, she didn't need any cooking lessons. Her meatballs were out of this world. In the middle of cooking our huge Sunday afternoon dinners, Dolores would make fifty or sixty mini-meatballs and feed them to all the men and the kids to hold us over before we had dinner. We would be eating her meatballs while we were waiting to eat. One taste of these meatballs, and I'm telling you, you're gonna be in heaven. Here's her recipe:

DOLORES'S MEATBALLS

3 pounds chopped chuck meat
(You can also mix veal, pork and beef)
3 eggs
1 cup parsley, chopped really fine
8 cloves garlic, chopped fine
¾ cup grated imported Romano cheese
¾ cup grated imported Parmesan cheese
1 cup plain bread crumbs
½ cup warm water
Olive oil, for frying

In a bowl or on a countertop, mix together the chopped meat, eggs, parsley, garlic, cheeses, and bread crumbs. Dolores's little secret when she was mixing it was to add about ½ cup of warm tap water.

Next, roll the mixed meat into small balls that fit into the palm of your hand, about 2½ inches in diameter. You don't have to make them perfectly round, and you don't want to pack the meat too tightly.

Then, in a frying pan, pour enough olive oil to coat the pan and heat it until it's hot. Gently place the meatballs into the frying pan, leaving a little breathing room between each one. Once the pan is full, let the meatballs brown gradually. Slowly turn them as they're browning, making sure they don't stick to the bottom of the pan. When they're done, remove them to a plate lined with paper towels, which will absorb the excess oil. Now, they're ready to be added to your tomato sauce (gravy), or you can eat them as a snack just the way they are (or even make a sandwich on some nice Italian bread).

SERVES 6

THE COPA

AFTER A YEAR on the road as a bodyguard for a concert pianist, and with a deep desire to be closer to my family, I began working at the world-famous Copacabana nightclub in New York City, where I worked as a supervisor and eventually as a maitre d'. Throughout the sixties and early seventies at the Copacabana, I had the pleasure of working alongside some of the top entertainers of the era, including Sammy Davis Jr., Bobby Darin, Tony Bennett, Louis Prima, Johnny Mathis, Nat King Cole, and Diana Ross and the Supremes—just to name a few. When Bobby Ryan and I were the head maitre d's and singer Tom Jones performed, we used to have to sit beside him to lit-

Me and Tony Bennett at the Copa in 1973

erally protect him from the women. The girls would throw Tom their panties, scream, cry, and even try to rush the stage. One night, a girl was standing on her table and tried to jump on Tom Jones. Luckily, I caught her in midair. We would have to watch Tom all night to make sure he didn't get hurt. The cook at the Copa hated when Tom Jones was there—women just wouldn't eat while he performed. They only wanted to eat Tom Jones!

Here I am with the "lady killer" Tom Jones at the Copa in 1966

The Copa was so popular that sometimes the members of the audience, which included major political figures, movie stars, business tycoons, and mobsters, were more famous than the acts they were watching. One time at the Copa, Frank Sinatra came in to see a show, and when he was leaving, he almost forgot his hat. He came up to me and said, "I forgot my hat." I went to the coatroom and found it. When I handed it to him, he gave me one hundred dollars for a tip. He could have bought a new hat for the hundred bucks! I tried to squeeze another hundred out of him by saying, "Let me take a closer look at that hat, Frank. It's a little dirty. I think something got on your hat." But he didn't buy it.

Sinatra was a strong tipper, but so were the mob guys. I won't mention their names, but many mob guys were bigger tippers than Sinatra. They would give you two hundred dollars like it was nothing. They would peel it off a stack of new bills as if they printed it. Who knows? Maybe they did. Just kidding.

Since I used to see big stars at the Copacabana every night, it took a lot to impress me. What can I say? I got spoiled. However, I was thrilled when I met the great baseball legend Joe DiMaggio. I have always been a huge New York Yankees fan, and I think Joe DiMaggio was the best ballplayer who ever lived. I remember that I approached him and said, "Hi, Joe. It's a pleasure to meet you. I've been a big fan of yours for many, many years—ever since I was kid. You are undoubtedly the greatest ballplayer who has ever lived." Of course Joe liked what I said. How could he help but like it? He smiled and shook my hand, and he had a grip

I am proudly standing next to "Yankee Clipper" Joe DiMaggio at the Copa on August 8, 1964

just like a gorilla, strong as a bull. At the end of the show, I was standing in the back of the lounge, and Joe DiMaggio actually came in there to look for me. He looked straight in my eyes and clearly said, "It was a real pleasure to meet you." I will never forget that moment because many people had told me Joe DiMaggio was tough to get along with. However, when he came over looking for me to say good night, it made my evening. Actually it made my year!

One thing was for sure. The Copa had one of the best kitchens in the city. I learned a lot about food there. In fact, when I was working as a supervisor at the Copa, I was taught French service, which is tableside serving with a spoon and fork in one hand. Once, when I was just learning this style of service, I hosted a table full of mob guys. They ordered spareribs and I just couldn't do the stupid French service. I was trying to serve with one hand, but I was dropping spareribs all over the table. Finally, I said, "Screw this!" I picked up the ribs with my hands and threw them on the plates. The wiseguys all started laughing and said, "Now that's the way you serve ribs!" But I personally loved the Copa's chicken cacciatore and thought it was amazing. Here's their recipe:

CHICKEN CACCIATORE ALLA COPA

1 frying chicken (about 4 pounds), cut up

Salt and pepper to season chicken

1 cup flour

5 tablespoons olive oil

4 small onions, sliced thin

1 clove garlic, chopped

1 large green pepper, sliced lengthwise

1 cup red wine

1 cup canned chopped tomatoes

1 cup sliced mushrooms

Salt and pepper to taste

SHUT UP AND EAT!

Season chicken pieces with salt and pepper and roll lightly in flour. Heat oil in a skillet and brown chicken on all sides, about 10 minutes. Remove chicken from skillet and place on a dish lined with paper towels. Add onions, garlic, and peppers to skillet and sauté for two minutes, or until onions are translucent. Take skillet off the heat and add the wine. Return to the heat and cook for about 3 minutes. Add the tomatoes and the chicken. Cover and simmer slowly for 40 minutes. Then add mushrooms and simmer 15 minutes more, or until mushrooms and chicken are tender. Add salt and pepper to taste.

SERVES 6

BOBBY DARIN—MY FRIEND FOR LIFE

I KNEW BOBBY Darin since he was a young kid who grew up not far from me in the Bronx. Before I worked at the Copa, I worked at the Peppermint Lounge, which was what I called a "bust-out joint" back then because there were usually one-shot customers like soldiers, sailors, and marines with hookers chasing them. Military police and shore patrol were also on the scene. It was a very bawdy atmosphere. I had to break up three to four fights every night in the place. When we would close late at night, a group of friends and I used to eat at a Chinese restaurant on West Forty-eighth Street between Sixth and Seventh Avenues in Manhattan. It was this little twenty-four-hour joint and that was where I used to take Bobby Darin to eat. Bobby was broke at the time and didn't have a dime to his name. The other guys would always say, "Why are you always bringing this guy Bobby along? He never has any money." I would

Tony Lip, Bobby Darin, and maitre d' Bobby Ryan at the Copa in 1968

always say, "Relax. I got it. I'll pay for his food." You see, I always liked Bobby Darin, and I saw something special in him. He was a good kid from the Bronx, and I respected that he was trying to make it as a singer. A lot of people felt he was never going to be successful, but I liked him as a person.

When I started at the Copa, I hadn't seen Bobby in a long time. Then he came as a headliner to perform there. When Bobby saw me, he ran up to me and I literally caught him in my arms. Bobby never expected to see me at the Copa and we had a wonderful reunion. It was just like old times. I was so happy for him when he finally made the big time. I was really proud after he made "Splish Splash" and all the other hit records. I remember that I said jokingly to him, "Bobby, you're making all of this money now. Are you gonna do the right thing by me or what?" Bobby began laughing. After the show, he came down to the lounge where I was working. Bobby walked up to me and handed me a blank check and said, "Thanks for believing in me, Tony. Make it out for whatever you want!" I kept the check as a memento of this great guy and never, ever filled it out or cashed it. That was the kind of good friend he was.

Bobby Darin appeared at the Copa often, and when he did, I always had a special treat for him. Bobby loved my wife's cooking, and before I left home for work, my wife would prepare a special plate of whatever good Italian dish we had had for dinner. I would bring it to Bobby to eat before he went onstage. Now, Bobby really loved everything my wife cooked, but he especially loved her stuffed calamari. He kept asking for it one night and I promised Bobby that I would bring him some the next day. That day, there was an incredible snowstorm. I was living in Jersey at the time and there was no way I could make it to New York to go to work because the streets were covered with snow. So, I called in and told them that I needed the night off.

Well, that didn't go over so good with Bobby. You see, he was really superstitious. At that point, there were almost seven hundred people jammed into the Copa. They had battled a blizzard to make it there to see the great Bobby Darin perform. Believe it or not, Bobby was refusing to go onstage until he had my wife's calamari! Well, luckily I had some pull with the mayor of my New Jersey town. I called him and told him what was going on. So he sent a snowplow to get me out of the snowdrifts on my suburban street. Then the plow and a couple cop cars escorted me and the calamari to the George Washington Bridge. From there, I drove downtown to the Copa and delivered my wife's stuffed calamari to Bobby. He quickly sat down with a nice glass of Chianti and ate the whole plate. When Bobby finished, he said, "Lip, your wife's a helluva cook!" Then he went onstage and gave one of the greatest shows anybody has ever seen at the Copa. Hey, I guess when a guy's gotta eat, he's gotta eat! Here is my wife's recipe for Bobby Darin's favorite stuffed calamari:

STUFFED CALAMARI

6 garlic cloves, diced

1 medium-size onion, diced

6 tablespoons olive oil

1 cup bread crumbs

½ teaspoon salt

½ teaspoon black pepper

½ cup Italian parsley, chopped

6 tablespoons fish stock (or water)

2 cans tomato sauce

1 dozen baby calamari

Preheat the oven to 350 degrees. Sauté the garlic and onion in the olive oil on medium heat. When the onion turns translucent, add the bread crumbs and sauté. Add the salt and pepper. When the bread crumbs turn a light brown, add the parsley. Sauté for a minute more, and then turn off the heat. Add the fish stock (or water) and mix. Stuff the calamari with this bread crumb mixture. Pour the tomato sauce into a 9 x 12 baking pan. Lay the stuffed calamari on top of the sauce, spooning a bit of sauce over the calamari. Cook in the oven for 10 to 15 minutes and that's it!

SERVES 4

BREAKING BREAD WITH THE BEST

IT WAS ALSO at the Copa where acclaimed movie director Francis Ford Coppola and his casting executive, Louis DiGiamo, met me and asked me to play a bit part in their film *The Godfather*. It was great. I worked in all the wedding scenes and even got my kids into the movie. The thing I remember about it most was that all the food and wine you see in those wedding scenes was real. It was like being at an Italian wedding every day for a week. Some days, people were eating and drinking and having such a good time they didn't even know the cameras were rolling. Then, during breaks, Coppola would cook these great Italian meals. He cooked up a storm. I was invited and joined Marlon Brando, Al Pacino, James Caan, Robert Duvall, Richard Castellano, Richard Conte, Talia Shire, and the rest of the cast as we feasted on Francis's dinners.

On the set with the boys from Donnie Brasco:
(left to right) James Russo, Bruno Kirby, Johnny Depp, Tony Lip, and Al Pacino

Even though it was only a small part, I loved the experience I had making *The Godfather* and decided that I wanted to pursue acting as a career. After I performed in several plays, things took off for me during the 1970s, and I appeared in dozens of films including *Cops and Robbers, The Taking of Pelham One Two Three, The Stone Killer, Crazy Joe, Dog Day Afternoon, Across 110th Street, Marathon Man, The Super Cops,* and *Fighting Back.* In the 1980s and 1990s, I continued acting and had the privilege to work with top directors and actors while appearing in many more films, including *Raging Bull, The Pope of Greenwich Village, Year of the Dragon, Lock Up, Goodfellas, Innocent Blood, Who's the Man?, Donnie Brasco,* and *In the Kingdom of the Blind, the Man with One Eye Is King.* I got to be friendly with many of the stars of the movies I worked in, and many times I would cook for them. I'm fortunate to be able to say that I've shared meals with lots of celebrities—even with legends like Frank Sinatra when he used to hang out at Jilly's, Frank's favorite restaurant and bar in Manhattan. Jilly's was owned by Jilly Rizzo, Sinatra's best friend. The story I heard about how they met was that one night two guys were

trying to strong-arm Frank on Fifty-Third Street. Jilly saw the commotion from his apartment window up above, ran downstairs, and beat the shit out of both of the guys at the same time. After that, Frank and Jilly became friends for life. Jilly's was a great place to hang out 'cause you never knew what would happen there. It was always unpredictable.

I have broken bread with many big shots. In fact, I recently ate with New York City Mayor Michael Bloomberg.

Me and Hollywood's infamous bad boy Mickey Rourke. That's me on the cake!

He tried sticking me with the check, but I straightened him right out. No, just kidding! Today, when I'm hanging out with a bunch of friends like David Proval, Frankie Gio, Vinny Pastore, Frank Vincent, Steve Schirripa, Vince Curatola, and Vinny Vella, I'll sometimes just make something from whatever I can find in the fridge. I believe in homestyle cooking, where you can look in your refrigerator or pantry and whip something up with whatever you find there. That's the fun of it for me—just sitting around and making a nice meal for family and friends in an unplanned way. In fact, when I was living with actor Mickey Rourke in LA for three months, he loved my homestyle cooking. We had dinner together almost every night, including my fiftieth birthday. Mickey Rourke absolutely loved my pasta fagiole. Here is the recipe I used to make for the infamous Hollywood bad boy:

PASTA FAGIOLE

2 cups medium shell or elbow macaroni

1 tablespoon salt

¼ cup olive oil

1 cup chopped red onion

1 cup sliced (¼-inch) carrots

½ cup sliced celery

2 garlic cloves, minced

8 ounces fresh green beans, trimmed and cut into ½-inch lengths

1 can (19-ounce) white kidney or cannelloni beans, rinsed and drained

2 tablespoons chopped Italian flat-leaf parsley

Generous grinding of black pepper

½ cup grated Parmesan cheese

Cook the pasta in plenty of boiling salted water for 5 minutes (the pasta will be undercooked). Place a colander over a heat-proof bowl and drain. Reserve 3 cups of the pasta cooking liquid. Set pasta aside until ready to use.

Heat the oil in a large, wide saucepan; add the onion, carrots, and celery; sauté until tender, but not browned, about 5 minutes. Stir in garlic; sauté 2 minutes. Add the 3 cups pasta cooking water and green beans. Cook, covered, over medium heat, until the vegetables are very tender, about 15 minutes.

Stir in the reserved pasta, kidney beans, and parsley. Cover and cook over low heat until pasta is tender and has absorbed enough liquid so that the soup is very thick. Season to taste with salt and pepper. Sprinkle each serving generously with Parmesan cheese.

Serves 4

THE SOPRANOS AND BEYOND

Unfortunately, in 1999, my wife, Dolores, passed away. At that point I decided to slow down my acting career, preferring to spend time golfing, fishing, and cooking great meals with my two sons. But my idea of slowing down didn't last long. During the third season of the critically acclaimed HBO-TV series *The Sopranos,* I got a call from the show's casting directors. I went in and met with them and the show's creator, David Chase. We hit it off and I appeared in one episode as Carmine, the New York mob boss. I guess that I did okay because in season four, Carmine became an important part of the story line. Working on the show was a great experience because it was really like working with family. Once again, like true Italians, the best part of the day for all of us is when we break to eat. David Chase really knows how to feed his people.

I've had a lot of good times in my life. Like I said, at this stage of the game

James Gandolfini and Tony Lip on the set of The Sopranos

I enjoy dining at home with family and friends and cooking a good meal. There are only a few restaurants where I'll make an exception and go out to eat. In New York City, I love to eat at Bruno's on Fifty-eighth and Second, Patsy's on West Fifty-sixth Street, and, of course, my friend Frank Pellegrino's place, Rao's, on Pleasant Avenue and 114th Street, where the food is out of this world. In New Jersey, I love Rivoli's in Toms River, Tutta Pasta in Hoboken, and Vincenzo Martino's Market & Restaurant in Hackensack.

Me cooking some great meat sauce with the owner of Rivoli's

SHUT UP AND EAT!

Me with the owners of Martino's

EGGPLANT PARMIGIANO

MARTINO'S
107 LODI STREET
HACKENSACK, NJ 07601
201-342-9077

1 large eggplant

Salt and pepper to taste

1 cup seasoned bread crumbs

2 eggs

½ cup all-purpose flour

1 lb. mozzarella cheese, cut into 12 slices

1 cup vegetable oil, for frying

1 (12 ounce) can crushed tomatoes

½ cup grated Parmesan cheese

SHUT UP AND EAT!

Preheat oven to 350 degrees.

Peel and slice eggplant into 12 round slices. Salt each slice on both sides and let stand in a colander for 30 minutes. This will take some of the water out of the eggplant.

In a bowl, beat eggs. Add salt and pepper. Place flour in a pan or flat dish, and place bread crumbs into another pan or dish. Dredge each eggplant slice in flour, then dip in egg and then coat with bread crumbs. Heat oil in a large skillet. Fry eggplant slices on medium heat for three minutes on each side, or until golden. Be careful not to crowd the pan (you may have to fry the eggplant in a couple of batches). Place eggplant on a dish layered with paper towels to absorb some of the oil.

Put half of the crushed tomatoes in the bottom of a 9x13" baking pan. Place eggplant slices in on top of the tomatoes, trying not to overlap the slices. Top each eggplant slice with a slice of mozzarella cheese and spoon remaining tomatoes on top. Sprinkle with the Parmesan cheese and bake for about 20 minutes, or until the mozzarella is melted and bubbly.

SERVES 6

Dining at a great restaurant with good friends is always fun, but there's nothing I enjoy more than cooking some nice Italian food for people who love food. As a matter of fact, just recently, I was cooking some sausage and peppers at my New Jersey home when there was a knock on my door. There were about six teenagers, all *Sopranos* fans, who came around asking for autographed pictures. They must have smelled the sausage because they asked me what I was cooking. The next thing I know, they're all sitting at my table and I'm feeding them. There wasn't even enough food left for me. But I didn't mind. I was glad the kids enjoyed it. Well, word got around in my neighborhood, and now I have kids knocking on my door almost every night asking me what I'm making for dinner!

SHUT UP AND EAT!

Me and Danny Aiello cooking with the owner of Tutta Pasta, Fortunado DiNatale

The next step is throwing in the tomatoes!

SHUT UP AND EAT!

Hey, we like it well done, what can I say?

I've been blessed with many great experiences in my life, but by far my favorite memories are the ones that have taken place with family and friends sharing great meals together. That's why I wanted to share these recipes with you. They are recipes from my mother, my wife Dolores, and my acting friends. Nothing fancy. Just good home-cooked Italian meals. Whether it's Danny Aiello's lentil soup, James Gandolfini's osso buco, or Dolores's stuffed calamari recipe, you've got to promise me that you're going to share it with your friends and family. Get a group of your friends together, put on your favorite music (Frank Sinatra, Dean Martin, and Tony Bennett recommended), and feast on one of the Italian recipes from the stars of your favorite films and TV shows.

Okay, I told you that I would let you in on the one special ingredient that goes into every Italian recipe—the one ingredient that only you can put into the meal you are cooking—LOVE. My mother and my wife, taught me that when you cook with love, it makes all the difference in the world, and they were right! I love cooking for people. It relieves me of all my daily problems and relaxes me. It makes me feel that I'm giving something back to all the people I care about. I love to see friends and family enjoying my cooking and hear them say, "Tony, this is great. How the hell do you make it?" I always kid back and say, "It's a secret. I ain't telling you nothing. So, just shut up and eat!"

*(Left to right) David Proval, Tony Danza, me, Joe Palughi, Tony Sirico,
an unidentified guest, Vincent Pastore, and Ronald Maccone*

CHAZZ PALMINTERI

I GREW UP in the Bronx in a very Italian neighborhood, just like in the film I wrote and starred in called *A Bronx Tale*. I lived on 187th Street and Arthur Avenue in a walk-up apartment building. My grandmother lived on the second floor and we lived on the fifth floor. On Sundays, the whole building smelled like tomato sauce. When I came into the building on my way up from the ground floor to the fifth floor, I would have to stop by my grandmother's apartment on the way to my family's apartment. She would give me a meatball on a fork with a fresh piece of Italian bread.

Then, I would dunk it in some gravy and leave. There was also a very nice woman who lived on the fourth floor, and I would stop by her place and she would give me a fresh piece of sausage. So, by the time I got to the fifth floor where my own mother was cooking up a storm, I would be totally full!

I had a wonderful, wonderful childhood filled with great people and great food. I can't say enough good things about it. Even today, it's great to go back to my old Bronx neighborhood. I still go shopping there once a month. I love to go to Mike's Deli in the Arthur Avenue Market, which is the best deli in the whole world. They definitely have the best cold cuts. While I'm waiting there, David Greco, who runs the deli for his dad, Mike, usually gives me a glass of wine and makes me a little sandwich. And you know what? David doesn't just do that for me because I am a celebrity. He does that for everyone that comes into the store. That's the way you can tell how somebody really is as a person—when they treat everyone the same. That's one of the reasons why I love it there. Then, there's Addeo Bread, which is also on Arthur Avenue in the Bronx. Addeo has the best bread in the world. It is very hard to get great bread and Addeo bakes the best. It's just like eating cake. You don't even need any butter for their bread. It is that wonderful!

When I think of food in movies, *The Godfather* automatically comes to mind. Every time I watch *The Godfather*, I have to go out and eat an Italian meal. There are so many great food scenes in that film that it makes me hungry just watching it. Also, there are so many wonderful Italian-American actors in the film.

When I play "tough guy" Italian-American roles, I like to play the parts with humanity. If you look closely at the "tough guy" characters I've portrayed throughout my career, you'll see they are not buffoons. I always want them to have various levels. For instance, Sonny, a part I portrayed in *A Bronx Tale*, was a tough guy, but he was also like a father to the young boy, Calogero. Sonny had heart and he was very human. In *Bullets Over Broadway*, the character I played, Cheech, was a stone-cold hitman, but he was also a brilliant playwright. In *Analyze This*, my character, Primo, was the head of the mob, but he was also extremely funny. In *Faithful*, my character, Tony, was another stone-cold hitman, but he also wanted to find the reason why men and women stay together. All these characters had unique human qualities to them, and that is what I wanted to try to bring to these types of roles I've played.

Nowadays, in between acting roles, I love to cook. I am not a gourmet chef, but I am a good cook. I can make a great sauce. My wife, Gianna, is truly a great cook, but I have to say that my sauce is getting very good! She even lets me make the sauce on Sundays if she's busy. And I really enjoy doing it. My wife and I believe that it's very important to instill our Italian heritage in our children, Dante and Gabriella. For instance, our family must have homemade tomato sauce on Sundays. No matter where we are, or what part of the world I am in, I will somehow find a way to make sauce on Sundays. Even if I am on the road and I have to walk into a local restaurant and ask someone to let me make sauce there, I will make it. It is a proud tradition with me and my family. I sincerely believe that Italian cuisine is one of the most family-driven cuisines in the whole world. Sunday dinner was always a warm and wonderful tradition in not just my own family, but in so many Italian-American families in my neighborhood. My fondest memories are being at my house, where my parents and all my aunts, uncles, and cousins would sit around a huge table filled with macaroni, meatballs, sausage, and salad. I am going to pass along two of my favorite recipes from my loving grandmother that have been handed down from my mother to me. Enjoy and God bless!

CHAZZ PALMINTERI possesses the rare talent of being able to portray the combination of sheer intelligence in tandem with street smarts on stage or screen. Born and raised in the Bronx, New York, Palminteri pursued his acting aspirations by taking classes at the world-renowned Lee Strasberg Institute. In 1988, after years of struggle, Palminteri wrote and starred in a play entitled *A Bronx Tale,* an impressive one-man stage production in which he vividly depicted his New York childhood. Eventually, Robert De Niro became interested in turning the show into a major motion picture. De Niro decided to make *A Bronx Tale* his directorial debut and also star alongside Palminteri. The movie went on to amass critical and commercial success. Palminteri has gone on to play impressive movie roles in films like *Faithful,* which he wrote and acted in opposite Cher and Ryan O'Neal; *The Usual Suspects,* with Kevin Spacey and Gabriel Byrne; *Analyze This,* acting alongside Robert De Niro and Billy Crystal; *Hurlyburly*, with Sean Penn and Kevin Spacey; Woody Allen's *Bullets Over Broadway,* which got him a Best Supporting Actor Oscar nomination, and many more major motion pictures.

PASTA BOLOGNESE WITH TURKEY MEAT

¼ cup olive oil

1 medium-size onion, finely chopped

4 garlic cloves, minced

3 carrots, finely chopped

3 celery stalks, finely chopped

2 (6-ounce) cans tomato puree

½ cup white wine

½ pound ground turkey

½ pound ground beef

4 (16-ounce) cans plum tomatoes

6 fresh basil leaves

Salt and pepper to taste

1 pound ziti (or your choice of pasta)

In a large pot, heat olive oil on medium heat. Add the onion and garlic and cook until onions turn translucent. Add the carrots and celery and cook for 5 minutes. Then add the tomato puree and sauté for 3 minutes, stirring constantly. Add the white wine, stir, then add the turkey and beef. Add the plum tomatoes and basil and bring to a boil. Reduce heat and simmer over medium to low heat for approximately 1½ hours, or until the sauce is thickened to your liking. Add salt and pepper. Meanwhile, cook the ziti al dente according to the directions on the box. Drain, and serve pasta with the sauce.

SERVES 8

LEMON CHICKEN

⅓ cup olive oil
⅓ cup freshly squeezed lemon juice
Salt and pepper to taste
3 garlic cloves, finely minced
2 boneless, skinless chicken breasts
2 cups fresh bread crumbs

Preheat oven to 350 degreees. In a small bowl, mix olive oil, lemon juice, salt, pepper, and garlic. Set aside.

Cut each chicken breast in half lengthwise. You will now have four thin cutlets. Place the chicken in a 9x13" baking pan and pour the olive oil mixture evenly over it. Coat the top of the chicken with bread crumbs, and bake in the oven for 35 minutes.

SERVES 4

James Gandolfini

WHEN I WAS growing up in Park Ridge, New Jersey, the town had many Italian immigrants living there. In fact, my own mother and father were born in the northern part of Italy and emigrated to New Jersey. My mother was originally from Milan. I have had many great visits to Milan, but haven't been back for about fifteen years. I'd like to go again, but, unfortunately, I never seem to have the time. When I get the chance to visit again, I hope to bring my son, Michael, if he wants to go.

Growing up, I, along with my family, would spend our vacation time at the Jersey Shore. But wherever we were, my mother cooked all kinds of great Italian dishes. My two favorites would have to be her osso buco and polenta, which I am going to give you the recipes for. I've got to say that my father was talented in the kitchen as well. I loved all of his spaghetti and pasta dishes. The funny thing was that we didn't use a lot of tomato sauce because my family didn't like it. Tomato-based sauces are a tradition of southern Italy and my parents came from the north, so we enjoyed meat-based sauces instead. My mother was a lunch lady in the local school cafeteria, so I also ate a lot of hot dogs and grilled cheese sandwiches.

When Tony Lip asked me to be a part of this book, I immediately said "yes." He's a great guy. Tony has a very interesting and colorful past from his real-life offscreen. He always tells us great stories and I could sit and listen to him for hours. It is nice having a man who has the actual real-life credentials to go along with the part. As an actor, I find it's easier to defer to him. We bust each other's balls and make each other laugh, and I really enjoy working with Tony.

I've got to tell you that the prop Italian food on *The Sopranos* is terrific. If I look like I'm enjoying the food on the show, that's because I am. (Our prop guy used to get the food from an Italian deli in Park Ridge—my old hometown.) I like the prop food so much that I eat it in between takes as well as on camera. I just love good Italian food! Since my schedule is so hectic these days, I don't get a chance to cook that often. I love to go to this little Italian restaurant called La Cucina Italiana on the corner of Jane and Hudson Streets in Manhattan. I feel at home

A typical street sign in New Jersey, home of The Sopranos

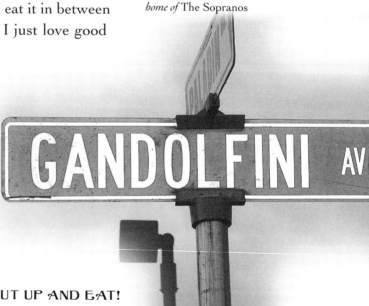

there and the food is always very good. But when I do cook, I love to make these two dishes that were first introduced to me by my mother during my childhood. I loved them as a kid, and I still love them today!

EVERYBODY KNOWS James Gandolfini as Tony Soprano, the fictional New Jersey mob boss on *The Sopranos*, for which he has brought home two Emmy Awards for Outstanding Lead Actor in a Television Drama Series. The "Gandolfini momentum" really started rolling when he received the 2000 Golden Globe for Best Performance by an Actor in a TV Series Drama. However, audiences also recognize him from a wide variety of other roles in over twenty motion picture productions. There were memorable tough-guy parts that he played in *Get Shorty* and *True Romance* (where he was very intimidating, playing a henchman for lead mob villain Christopher Walken). Gandolfini began his acting career in New York theater, making his Broadway debut in the 1992 revival of Tennessee Williams's *A Streetcar Named Desire*, with Alec Baldwin and Jessica Lange. Gandolfini's film credits also include the Coen Brothers' *The Man Who Wasn't There*; *The Mexican*; *The Last Castle*, in which he played opposite Robert Redford; and *Romance & Cigarettes*, written and directed by John Turturro.

POLENTA STUFATA
(Baked Polenta)

9 to 10 cups water
2 teaspoons coarse salt
3 cups coarsely ground cornmeal
2½ tablespoons olive oil
½ pound Italian pork sausage, casings removed
16 ounces freshly cooked or 2 (8-ounce) cans tomato sauce
Pinch crushed red pepper
Salt to taste
⅔ cup grated Pecorino cheese
¾ cup grated Parmesan cheese
4 tablespoons butter

Bring the water to a boil in a large, heavy pan; add coarse salt and sprinkle in the cornmeal, stirring continuously with a wooden spoon to avoid lumps. Continue cooking over a moderate heat, stirring frequently, for about 50 minutes, or until the polenta comes away cleanly from the sides of the pan. Turn it onto a marble slab or a large wooden pastry board. It will shape itself into a dome. Let sit until quite cold.

While the polenta is cooling, prepare the sauce: Heat the oil in a pan, add the sausage, and fry, crumbling it with a fork, until it begins to brown. Pour in the tomato sauce and season to taste with the red pepper and salt. Simmer for 10 minutes.

Preheat the oven to 350 degrees. Cut the cold polenta into slices about ⅛-inch thick using either strong thread or fine wire. Mix the cheeses. Grease a 9x13" baking dish and fill it with alternate layers of polenta, sauce, and the grated cheeses, dotting each layer of cheese with a few slivers of the butter. The top layer should be one of polenta sprinkled with cheese and butter. Bake for about 1 hour, by which time the polenta will have formed a golden crust. Serve hot.

SERVES 6

SHUT UP AND EAT!

OSSO BUCO
(Stewed Shank of Veal)
WITH RISOTTO ALLA MILANESE

6 veal shanks (2½- to 3-inches thick)

1 cup all-purpose flour

Salt and pepper to taste

6 tablespoons butter

1 medium carrot, cut into ¼-inch-thick pieces

1 celery stalk, chopped into ¼-inch-thick slices

1 small onion, chopped

2 tablespoons chopped thyme leaves

2 cups dry white wine

1 (16-ounce) can Italian peeled tomatoes

2 cups chicken stock

1 clove garlic, finely chopped or minced

Grated rind of ½ lemon

4 sprigs Italian parsley, finely chopped

2 anchovy fillets, soaked in milk and finely chopped

Roll the shanks in flour, and season with salt and pepper all over. In a large pan, fry the shanks in butter at high heat, turning them once or twice to ensure even browning all around. Remove shanks from frying pan and reduce heat to medium. Add the carrots, celery, onion, and thyme, and sauté until golden brown and slightly softened, 8 to 10 minutes. Pour the wine over them, and cook for 15 minutes at high heat. Then add the tomatoes and chicken stock, and season to taste with salt and pepper. Cover and cook for 2 hours over a low heat, or until the meat is so tender it almost falls off the bones. If necessary, some additional hot stock or water may be added during cooking.

Prepare a gremolata: Mix the garlic, lemon rind, parsley, and anchovy mixture together. Sprinkle this over the shanks a few minutes before serving, and turn them once to distribute the flavor of the gremolata.

SHUT UP AND EAT!

Risotto alla Milanese

7 tablespoons butter

1 small onion, thinly sliced

2 tablespoons bone marrow (removed from veal shanks after they are cooked)

3 cups Arborio rice

½ cup dry red or white wine

About 6½ cups boiling meat stock

Generous pinch saffron, soaked in water

¾ cup grated Parmesan cheese

Melt 3½ tablespoons of the butter in a large, heavy pan, and sauté the onion and bone marrow gently until the onion is transparent and golden. Stir in the rice, and sauté gently until it begins to brown. Add the wine and cook until it is absorbed by the rice.

Pour in 1 cup of boiling stock and stir. Continue cooking until the liquid has been absorbed, and then add another cup of boiling stock. Continue to cook the rice in this manner, stirring carefully, until all the liquid has been used up and absorbed.

When the rice is almost ready, after about 20 minutes, add the saffron and stir into the rice to color it. (If all the rice does not change color, this does not matter.) A two-color risotto is very effective. Turn off the heat, and gently but thoroughly stir in the remaining butter and the cheese. Cover the pan and let the risotto settle for 2 minutes. Serve at once, offering grated Parmesan to those who want it.

SERVES 6

TALIA SHIRE

I love to eat, but I also love the preparation of food. Cooking is a true art form. It involves intuition and then that sort of leap of faith when you are putting a dish together. There are people who cook by absolute measurement, and there are others who are more passionate and creative. The knowledge of preparing food is also about chemistry. It's about mixing together the right amounts of ingredients to get the desired result.

I've always loved cooking and have many wonderful memories of preparing meals with my mother. I grew up in Long Island, New York, and we always had a sense of food and celebration in our house. I remember that we had a Ping-Pong table in our home, but I never remember playing Ping-Pong on it. We were too busy eating around the Ping-Pong table because it was so loaded with food. Food was a big part of bringing aunts and uncles, cousins, and grandparents together.

One thing that has been a constant factor in my family over many years is that the men all cook. The men in our family love to put meals together, and they are all great at doing it. My uncle Mikey makes the greatest chicken cacciatore ever! My brothers are excellent cooks as well. Of course the women also got involved, and I recall that my mother would make an incredible Italian dessert of dough, honey, and colored sprinkles called strufoli.

My father told me that it's important to have a diet high in vegetables, and because of that, I've always leaned toward a vegetarian diet. My father was always eating escarole. Or for lunch, he would often have something as simple as asparagus with a hard-boiled egg. He would even enjoy pepper and onion sandwiches all by themselves, without the sausage. My uncle Mikey would make a simple meal of fresh Italian bread with cannellini beans and Parmesan cheese on it. Then, he would bake it in the oven for a little while, and that would be his whole meal. It's a version of pasta fagiole, but my uncle used bread instead of macaroni. I especially love zucchini and eggplant. Our meals were always healthy, with lots of vegetables.

While I was in Italy, I ate many delicious Italian vegetable dishes. Italy is a breathtaking country, and I don't mean just the geography. The art and the people are breathtaking too. The eating style is very different from here. Meals in Italy are festive events, and I like the fact that the biggest meal of the day takes place in the afternoon. While I was there, they had long lunches that went from twelve to two in the afternoon. There was a wonderful feeling of the family coming together, and a sense of tremendous well-being during those early afternoon siesta-type breaks from the day's routine. It was a nice and a relaxed time before people went back to work. I haven't been back to Italy in a while, but a trip is always in the works. I'm constantly collecting frequent flyer miles and I long to visit there again. I have to say that I fell in love with all the cities, and I found Sienna to be especially lovely.

Holidays always were and still are a big affair in my family. I really enjoy Christmas, and because my son Robert was born on December 24th, it's a very special holiday in more ways than one. Holidays always mean big gatherings of friends and family with plenty of food. There is always the excitement of seeing everybody, but there is also the all-day cooking marathon, which is almost just as much fun.

I believe that it is important to share Italian traditions with my children. I want to preserve the rituals, customs, and memories that are their heritage. So it's important to me to continue to share the foods I grew up with. These dishes have been passed down from generation to generation, although through the years interesting variations have been added to them. I want my children to eat and smell the foods that were an important part of my childhood. Smell and memory go together; familiar smells can conjure up some very important memories. I can still close my eyes and recall my mother's tomato sauce with braciole. The sauce would be cooking all day, and I remember coming into the kitchen and checking on how the sauce was doing, and then maybe even dipping a little bread in it. The smell of the kitchen is so special.

A fantasy dinner for me would include that magnificent Italian actor, Marcello Mastroianni, director-actor Vittorio De Sica, Sophia Loren, and, of course, the legendary actress Anna Magnani. Magnani's presence was breathtaking. Now, I'm not talking about looks alone, I'm truly talking about her presence. My mother and Magnani shared that same kind of energy, charisma, and power.

The problem with Italian food and me is that I like everything. However, I wanted to give you my special recipe for pumpkin gnocchi. My mother and I would enjoy spending weekends where we would do experimental cooking. One weekend, we might try to master making the bagel, and there would be about a hundred bagels around the kitchen. However, we never did master the bagel. But I feel we mastered gnocchi. It can be hard, but we discovered that if you use instant potatoes, you have a better chance to make the gnocchi lighter. Add some canned pumpkin, and it is a truly wonderful dish for Thanksgiving!

BORN AND raised in Long Island, New York, Talia Shire attended the prestigious Yale School of Drama. Shire's skills and acting talents contributed to memorable performances like her role as the wife of boxer Rocky Balboa, played by Sylvester Stallone, in the *Rocky* movies. She first came to the attention of film audiences for her role in *The Godfather* and also appeared in its two sequels. She was nominated for the Academy Award for Best Supporting Actress for *The Godfather, Part II* (1974) and was nominated for the Academy Award For Best Actress for her portrayal of "Adrian" in *Rocky* (1976). In addition to her work on the big screen, Shire has appeared in many films for television. Extremely multitalented, in 1995 Shire directed the film *One Night Stand*, starring Ally Sheedy.

THANKSGIVING GNOCCHI

1 quart water
1 (32-ounce) box instant potatoes
1 tablespoon salt, with extra for seasoning
1 egg
1 (6-ounce) can pumpkin puree
2 cups all-purpose flour
½ teaspoon baking powder
4 tablespoons butter
8 sage leaves

Bring water to a boil. Add salt and the whole box of instant potatoes, following the instructions on the back of the box. Mix well, and add more water if needed. Add salt to taste. Let cool to room temperature; then add egg and pumpkin and mix well.

Sift flour and baking powder together and add potato-pumpkin mixture, mixing until a pliable ball of dough forms. Turn out onto a floured board or counter and knead gently for 5 minutes until ball is dry to the touch. Divide dough into balls roughly the size of a baseball. Roll the balls into logs about ½-inch thick. Now cut each log into 1-inch pieces. Press a fork into each piece; flick pieces off the fork with your index finger. Gnocchi should have a slight curve to it. The lines from the fork will help the sauce stick to the gnocchi.

Boil the gnocchi in batches of salted water until they float (about 1 to 2 minutes). Remove with a slotted spoon. Meanwhile, melt butter in a saucepan, add the sage and cook for a minute. Pour the sage butter over the gnocchi and serve.

SERVES 10

MICHAEL RISPOLI

I COME FROM a large Italian-American family where I'm one of eight children. I have four brothers and three sisters. My mother did all the cooking and definitely had a lot of mouths to feed. We never had a set dinnertime because my father owned his own hardware store and worked many hours each day, so many nights he would get home late. My father first opened the hardware store back in 1959, the year before I was born, so I basically grew up there. It was located in Tappan, New York, the town

I was born and raised in. It was a big store in a little town, so every kid got their first baseball glove or bicycle there. My mother was from the Bronx and my father was from Brooklyn, and after they got married, they moved to Tappan, which is only thirty minutes from New York City.

Sunday was the one day of the week when we would all sit down together and eat as a family. Our whole family would go to church and then, afterwards, come home and eat a big home-cooked Italian meal of macaroni and gravy. Some people call it "sauce," but my family called it "gravy." Gravy, of course, is one of the most important things in an Italian meal because it flavors the food. My friends and I knew who were the good cooks out of our mothers and my mom's gravy was the best.

Since my mother had to cook for ten or more people daily, we had to watch our budget. We could not eat expensive things like veal chops, so we would eat chuck steak instead because it was a cheaper cut of meat. However, my mother always made it tender and delicious. It was the same thing with fish. We never ate salmon fillets or swordfish. Instead, we ate bluefish and picked the bones out of it. But as a result I learned how to eat healthy in an inexpensive way. My mother taught me how to whip up something out of nothing. She would take a can of beans and a box of macaroni out of the cupboard, then add some spices, and all of a sudden we would have some delicious pasta fagiole. She would make it for a ton of people, and it would always be fresh and tasty.

My mother taught her children early on how to fend for themselves. We learned how to wash our own clothes, and we were taught how to cook — guys and girls. My younger brother is a chef and learned a lot from my mother. If I weren't an actor, I would be a chef, too. I remember when I went away to college, I lived on campus for the first couple of years with a group of guys and we always ate in the dining hall. By our junior year, we were thinking about moving off campus, and there was one guy, Kenny, who didn't want to move. I asked Kenny why, and he said, "I don't know how to cook." I came to realize that he didn't even know how to boil an egg. My mother made sure her kids knew how to cook, and it has served us well throughout our lives.

The tradition of having a big family is still going strong with the Rispolis. My older sister, Annette, has ten kids and seven grandchildren. My brother Vinny has three kids while my brother Ernie has four. My sister Maryann has five children; my brother Damien, who is a year older than me, has seven; and I have three children. My sister Camille is a standout in the family because she only has one child. My brother Joey just got married and doesn't have children yet. With such a large family, holidays have always been fabulous. On Thanksgiving we would, of course, have a turkey. However, we would also have some great Italian food. Before the turkey, my mother would make her delicious holiday soup. It consists of little meatballs, eggs, escarole, and broth. After the soup, we would have the antipasto. Following that, we would always have ravioli with big sausages and meatballs and then finish with the turkey. Oh, by the way, it was not just turkey. We would also have a ham and a leg of lamb as well. My sister Maryann is the only sibling in our family who married an Italian American. Everyone else married someone who's an American mix. So the first time the husbands and wives would come to a Rispoli holiday feast, their eyes would go wide because of the tons of food and wine. Even to this day, when we are serving them, they say, "We don't need that much." Of course we push it on them anyway. Why? Because we're Italian.

We would always celebrate Christmas Eve like most Italians do. There would be the seven kinds of fish on the table and pasta and antipasto, all with no meat. Then, we would sing songs and go to midnight mass. Christmas day is just as elaborate. I realize now that although everyone enjoyed the holiday, it must have been stressful to feed all of those people. When you're younger, you are excited that Mom is making all that food. Then, as you get older, you realize Mom is working very hard. These days, since our family is so big, we rent a hall and have a big Christmas party there. My uncle Theodore arranges all of it. Everyone brings a different kind of food, and there is a baking contest. We even make snowballs out of old nylon stockings stuffed with cotton and we have a snowball fight. Then, of course, Santa Claus shows up and passes out the gifts to the kids. In the summer, we always have large outdoor parties. The combination of food, family ties, and gathering together is one of the strongest traditions the Rispoli family has. We realize someone might not be around next year, so we try hard to make every occasion spent together count. Our belief is that holidays and food go hand in hand, along with love and the thankfulness that the whole family is together.

Throughout history, food has always been a sign of prosperity. Immigrants originally came here from Italy because times were tough back there. Remember, America is an immigrant country. My mother's side of the family is originally from Santa Maria La Carita, Italy, and my father's side is from Sant'antonio Abate, Italy. They packed up their families and came over here to start a new life. So today all of us in the Rispoli family believe that spending time together, happy and healthy, is a true blessing. I try to pass on our Italian heritage to the children through the food. On holidays, we explain to each child what the different Italian dishes are. To be honest, the kids look at the calamari, and you see in their faces that they would rather eat chicken nuggets. However, I keep trying to expand their minds, and I make a special point on Christmas Eve to ask my mother, right in front of the kids, to name the seven different fish we are about to eat. She names each one and the kids listen and that's how tradition gets passed along. I never lose sight of the fact that if the authentic Italian food goes away, so does the tradition. I am going to give you some recipes we eat as a family on different holidays. I'd like you to remember the Rispoli family motto: "We live in deeds, not years." That means life is not measured by how long you live, it is measured by what you do for other people.

BORN AND raised in Tappan, New York, Michael Rispoli has a true third-dimensional list of acting credits, which range from film to television to theater. After starting his acting career at the well-known Circle in the Square in New York City, Rispoli set his sights on the stage, appearing in such classic productions as *A Midsummer Night's Dream*, *Macbeth*, and *Twelfth Night*. His earliest film appearances include *Household Saints*, *Angie*, and *Above the Rim*. He went on to a steady career in motion pictures, appearing with some of the industry's top talents in top films such as Spike Lee's *Summer of Sam*; *Rounders*, starring Matt Damon and Ed Norton; *While You Were Sleeping*, starring Sandra Bullock; and *Death to Smoochy*, starring Robin Williams. Rispoli has appeared on top television shows like *Third Watch* and *The Sopranos* as well as in the Fox series *The Great Defender*, as a lead. In 2000, for his lead role portrayal of Buddy Visalo in the hit independent film *Two Family House*, he won the Best Actor award at the Verona Film Festival in Italy. His most recent feature film credits include *Mr. 3000*, starring Bernie Mac, and *The Weatherman*, starring Nicolas Cage.

SAUSAGE, CHICKEN, AND POTATOES ALLA CARMELA

Salt, pepper, and garlic powder to season chicken
10 chicken thighs and legs
10 hot or sweet links of sausage
½ cup extra-virgin olive oil
5 large Yukon Gold or red potatoes,
cut into equal eighths for uniform cooking time
1½ cups Italian parsley, chopped
Salt and pepper to taste
3 to 4 cloves garlic, chopped

Preheat oven to 400 degrees. Rinse chicken and then pat dry. Season pieces of chicken with salt, pepper, and garlic powder. Place in a large roasting pan with the skin side up. Prick sausage with a fork and cut links in half. Place sausage between pieces of chicken; drizzle a light coat of olive oil over all pieces. Place in heated oven.

Meanwhile, parboil potatoes in salted water. Drain and place potatoes in a bowl. Take the pan with the chicken and sausage out of the oven and spoon some of the juices over the potatoes. Season with parsley, salt, pepper, and chopped garlic, and then toss to coat the potatoes.

Return chicken and sausage to the oven and continue to cook. When chicken is almost done (total cooking time is about 40 minutes), add potatoes to the pan and return to the oven. Lower oven temperature to 350 degrees and continue cooking until potatoes are browned (about 20 minutes), stirring and turning mixture periodically for even browning.

SERVES 10

MUSSELS AND CLAMS CAMPANIA-STYLE

2 to 4 pounds littleneck clams

2 to 4 pounds mussels

1 tablespoon fine sea salt

2 cups cornmeal

1 cup extra-virgin olive oil

4 cups dry white wine

3 or 4 cloves garlic, chopped

1 cup flat-leaf parsley, chopped

2 cups fresh fennel fronds (green tops of fennel), chopped,

or 1 teaspoon dry fennel seeds

Red pepper flakes (optional)

Sea salt, to taste

2 tablespoons good red wine vinegar (optional)

Freshly ground pepper to taste

Scrub and debeard clams and mussels. Place in a large container. Sprinkle with sea salt and cornmeal, and add enough cold water to cover the clams and mussels. Mix to combine and let sit for approximately 1 hour. This soak is to purge the shellfish of any sand. Be sure to occasionally move them around during this time to help clean them out.

In a large pot on medium heat, add olive oil, wine, garlic, ¾ cup chopped parsley, fennel, red pepper flakes, and sea salt to taste. Cover and simmer on lower heat for approximately 5 minutes to reduce wine. Rinse clams and mussels thoroughly; add to simmering sauce and cover. Poach clams and mussels until they open (throw away any unopened shellfish).

When all the clams and mussels have opened, remove the pot from heat. Add red wine vinegar, the rest of the chopped parsley, and the freshly ground black pepper. Spoon liquid over clams and mussels, and allow to sit for about a minute to blend flavors. Serve hot.

SERVES 6

BROCCOLI RABE WITH SAUSAGE

1 bunch broccoli rabe, washed and cleaned 3 times in cold water
1 package hot or sweet Italian sausage (approximately 6 links)
3 tablespoons extra-virgin olive oil, plus ¼ cup
3 cloves garlic, lightly crushed
Red pepper flakes (optional)

Cut the end off the broccoli rabe, about 2 inches from the bottom. Remove all tough and woody stems and wilted leaves. Chop rabe into 3 parts. Bring a large pot of salted water to a rolling boil. Place rabe into water and cover immediately. Cook rabe until crisp and tender, about 10 to 15 minutes; do not overcook. Strain the rabe and set aside.

Place sausage in a skillet over a medium flame. Prick casing and combine with 3 tablespoons olive oil to brown. When browned, remove from pan and set aside. In the same skillet, over medium heat, combine ¼ cup olive oil, garlic, and red pepper flakes. Do not brown garlic, just cook until softened, when it releases its flavor into the oil. At that point, remove garlic (if you like).

Add blanched rabe to the skillet and sauté. Cut browned sausage links into thirds and add to skillet. Cover pan and cook over a very low heat for approximately 10 to 15 minutes, stirring and tossing a few times until rabe is soft, but not overcooked.

SERVES 4

JOE MANTEGNA

I FIRST TRAVELED to Italy in 1975. My dad's family is originally from Sicily and my mom's is from Bari. Nobody from my family had ever gone back to visit their native Italy, except my grandfather. It's an interesting story, starting with my grandfather and his brother coming to America at the turn of the century. His brother didn't like it here in the United States and went back after two weeks. However, my grandfather did like it and stayed. The brothers never spoke again. My grandfather's brother, my great-uncle, died, but his children knew they had this uncle in the United States, their dad's brother. Through the Italian embassy, they decided to track him down. My grandfather went back to Italy in 1974 as the patriarch of the family and reopened contact with this side of the family we didn't even know existed.

I went to Italy the next year, in 1975, when I was touring with a theater group. My wife and I decided to stop for an afternoon to visit my mother's side of the family, near Bari, in a town called Aquaviva della Fonte, which is in the province of Puglia. We were going for just an afternoon visit, and wound up staying for twelve days! Every morning it was, "Guiseppi, you must stay one more day!" On that trip, we also went to Sicily to complete the picture and discovered some of my father's side of the family. That, too, was a very exciting experience.

I have been very close to my mom's side of our family ever since that first visit in 1975. My cousin Nicola has since opened a resort there called Masseria Mofetta. It is on about fifty acres and has olive orchards and cherry orchards. However, the main attraction is the food at their marvelous restaurant. They serve an impressive four hundred people a day. It has a pre-fixe menu, and for one price they serve about seven courses. Everyone loves the food. I visited twice over the last few years and thought the resort was wonderful. I think the food from the Puglia region is the best in Italy. It is rural, natural, fresh, and fabulous.

I grew up on the West Side of Chicago. My parents were raised right there in the Little Italy of Chicago. It is referred to as Taylor Street. I have strong memories of Italian food from my childhood. I thought everyone ate pasta three times a week because that is what our family did. It was a very Italian area. It was a great neighborhood for Italian food. Actually, the popular frozen Italian food they have today in supermarkets bearing the Celeste brand name originated in Chicago. The founder of the line, Celeste, had a restaurant in Chicago not far from where I lived. I would buy Italian gravy sandwiches from there for twenty-five cents on my way home from school. It was Italian bread dipped in homemade gravy. Celeste was

a family-run place, a wonderful example of the types of places that existed where I grew up.

We lived in an apartment house, upstairs from my mother's parents, and I have vivid memories of the mouthwatering homemade bread that my grandmother used to make. I loved Christmas because the whole family would get together and we would traditionally eat seafood.

There have been many great food scenes in movies that I've acted in. I used to compliment the prop guys on *The Last Don* and deservedly so. There were a lot of special food scenes in that movie, and they made all the Italian food not only look good, but taste good. As an actor, you really don't want to pretend you are eating a good meatball when you aren't. To tell the truth, more than once I've gone to the food service area on a film set and whipped up a red sauce for the whole company.

I remember working with Danny Aiello when we did the movie *Off Key* and we traveled to Spain and France to shoot. Danny would only eat the sauce if it was pureed. He prefers tomato sauce to have the consistency of applesauce; there cannot be any chunks of tomatoes in the sauce for Danny because that's not the way his mother made it for him growing up. I respect and understand that because it is his own personal food background. Danny also doesn't like onions. In short, he is very

Joe and his wife, Arlene, outside their restaurant, Taste Chicago, located in Burbank, California

particular, but also has very good taste in his own unique way. Danny is a great guy to work with and really has a genuine love of Italian food.

One man I never ate with, whom I would have loved to, was Dean Martin. Of course, in *The Rat Pack*, I was honored to play him. The closest I ever came to eating with Dean was while I was a struggling actor in LA. I was in Hamburger Hamlet on Sunset Boulevard, and he was sitting in the booth next to me. However, I didn't have the nerve to go up to him. Dean loved La Famiglia restaurant in Beverly Hills. My assistant, Dan, a great guy who loves *The Rat Pack*, eats at La Famiglia simply because he knows that Dean loved it.

I enjoy cooking various dishes. My wife, Arlene, whom I have been married to for twenty-eight years, is a fabulous cook, and that led to her opening a restaurant, Taste Chicago, in Burbank. She opened it in October 2003 and had about eight hundred people at the opening. So far, the experience has been truly wonderful. Arlene has that ability where we will be out to eat somewhere and she will taste something, really like it, and be able to duplicate it. She can tell what the ingredients are by just tasting it. My wife is of Czechoslovakian descent and always dreamed of owning her own little restaurant. Some of her dishes at Taste Chicago are, of course, indigenous to Chicago. My favorite is the Italian beef sandwich because it is impossible to get out here in LA. There are different versions around town but not like hers. The Italian beef sandwich is to Chicago what the Philly Cheesesteak is to Philadelphia. The sandwich is unique and extremely flavorful. It's served with very thinly sliced beef that's been soaking in a sauce flavored with different things like anisette and fennel. You put it on Italian bread with roasted peppers and hot oil. She also serves delectable meatball sandwiches, Sicilian pan pizza, ribs, and Chicago-style hot dogs with poppy seed buns. There's truly something for every taste. Even though we are located in Burbank, California, this is not California cuisine. The restaurant also serves low-carb plates with just meatballs, which my wife calls the Meatball Splash. There is no waiter service, but it still is not in the category of fast food. It is similar to places on the East Coast that are family pasta and deli places where they serve fresh homemade Italian food at reasonable prices.

My children are so far ahead of the curve when it comes to Italian cuisine, much more knowledgeable than I was when I was their age. They really grew up with it because I felt it was important to instill that aspect of Italian heritage in them. My kids were into many kinds of exotic foods when they were young, like snails and other delicacies. When I was growing up, we didn't have the money to eat cuisine like that. I have given my daughters everything from caviar to pâté and everything in between. They have real international tastes. They travel a lot and we have been all over the world together, to places such as Russia, Spain, France, Italy, and Germany. As a result, they have real eclectic tastes.

When I am not in Los Angeles or traveling for work, there are a few Italian restaurants I enjoy going to. When I am in Chicago, I like to go to Rosebud, owned by Alex Dana. I know him and respect his menu. There are a few of his restaurants in Chicago, but it is not a chain by any means. I enjoy Rosebud's food a lot. When I am in New York City, I like Fontana di Trevi, which is right across from Carnegie Hall. I also like Carmine's, which serves great family-style Italian cuisine. You can go there with a group of people and order a nice bowl of pasta. The prices are reasonable, which is always a plus.

When I am not in some other city for work, I enjoy cooking at home for my family. I would like to give you two recipes, which are favorites of mine. The first recipe is from my personal family heritage and is called Mussels Mantegna. My brother, Ron, who's a great cook, lent the inspiration for this dish. Traditionally, you use the largest shell as a spoon to pluck the mussels from their shells. It's a very tasty dish and brings back a lot of great memories. The second is called Sauce Bandini. I call it this because when I was making a film called *Wait Until Spring, Bandini*, one of the Italian producers of the film made it for the wrap party. It's a very simple, uncooked sauce that can be made very quickly, and I have added my own touches. I sincerely hope that making these dishes and eating them with your family contribute toward creating some great memories for you.

CHICAGO NATIVE Joe Mantegna made his Broadway debut in *Working*, the Stephen Schwartz musical based on Studs Terkel's book of the same name. Joe catapulted to success again on the Broadway stage by winning the coveted Tony Award for his role as real estate sales whiz Ricky Roma in *Glengarry Glen Ross*. Playing a small-time hood who babysits mob fall guy Don Ameche in 1988's *Things Change*, Mantegna came to the attention of Francis Ford Coppola, who cast him in the lead of *Wait Until Spring, Bandini*, opposite Faye Dunaway. Coppola then cast Mantegna in *The Godfather, Part III* as the hot-tempered gangster Joey Zasa. That role set his career in full motion with formidable parts in pictures like *Bugsy, Searching for Bobby Fisher, House of Games, Homicide, Liberty Heights, Persons Unknown*, and two Woody Allen movies, *Alice* and *Celebrity*. Joe's original feature films for cable television include starring roles in *State of Emergency, A Call to Remember, My Little Assassin, The Water Engine, The Comrades of Summer, Boy Meets Girl, Women vs. Men, The Last Don* (which garnered him an Emmy Award nomination), and *The Rat Pack* (for which he was nominated for another Emmy as well as a Golden Globe for his portrayal of Dean Martin). In 2000, Joe completed production on his feature film directorial debut, *Lakeboat,* written for the screen by David Mamet from his original play and starring Charles Durning, Peter Falk, Robert Forster, Andy Garcia, Denis Leary, and George Wendt. The film opened at the LA Film Festival to critical acclaim and had its theatrical release in June 2001. Mantegna is also known for his stint as the voice of Fat Tony on *The Simpsons*, as well as playing Detective Will Girardi on the Emmy-nominated CBS-TV primetime drama *Joan of Arcadia.*

MUSSELS MANTEGNA

2 to 3 pounds mussels, fresh and tightly closed
1 small onion, or 2 large shallots, chopped
2 tablespoons butter or margarine
1 to 2 tablespoons olive oil
1 pound sliced mushrooms
2 to 3 cloves garlic, minced
½ cup fresh chopped parsley
2 to 4 tablespoons white wine or dry vermouth
1 (14½-ounce) can Italian-style stewed tomatoes
Salt and black pepper to taste
Fresh basil or oregano to taste (optional)

Scrub and debeard the mussels. Set aside.

In a heavy stockpot, over medium heat, sauté onion or shallots in butter and oil until transparent. Add mushrooms and garlic to onion and sauté until golden, stirring frequently. Stir in parsley and add wine to just cover the bottom of the stockpot. Add tomatoes and bring to a boil over high heat. Season with salt and black pepper.

Add mussels and cover tightly to steam. Carefully shaking the pot every 30 seconds, cook over high heat for 3 minutes. Mussels are done when all the shells are open. Discard any that do not open. Check the broth and adjust seasoning, adding basil or oregano.

Divide mussels among deep individual serving bowls. Carefully pour cooking liquid over mussels, but do not use the last of the liquid in the pot because it may contain shell fragments.

SERVES 4

SAUCE BANDINI

12 fresh roma tomatoes

8 garlic cloves

12 to 18 fresh basil leaves

1 cup olive oil

1½ pounds rigatoni pasta, cooked and hot

Salt, to taste

Slice an *X* on the bottom of each tomato. Blanch in gently boiling salted water for 2 to 3 minutes. Drain tomatoes and submerge in cold water. While the tomatoes are cooling off, peel and slice the garlic into large, thin slices.

Peel the tomato skins and discard; cut tomatos in half and remove seeds. Tear tomatoes into bite-size pieces. Slice the basil leaves into thin ribbons. Put tomatoes, garlic, and basil into a large glass jar, and stir in olive oil (more or less to taste). Screw on lid and let sit for 1 to 6 hours. Serve at room temperature over hot rigatoni pasta.

If serving the next night, refrigerate the sauce. Bring to room temperature before putting over pasta.

SERVES 6

Cook's Note: For a hot sauce, simmer finished sauce for 15 to 30 minutes. Salt as desired.

MICHAEL IMPERIOLI

THERE WERE MANY families with Italian backgrounds living in Mount Vernon, New York, when I grew up there. A bread guy used to drive his truck through my neighborhood on his rounds, and we used to buy fresh bread off the truck just like he was the ice cream man. My grandmother would buy a round loaf of Italian bread, and it was even still hot. I find that bread is an important part of an Italian meal.

We had a very strong Italian heritage, especially when it came to eating.

One side of my family was originally from Rome, and the other side was from Naples and Calabria. On Sundays, we would always have a big Italian meal that would start at two in the afternoon. We would have macaroni, meatballs, braciole, sausage, and many other traditional foods. That Sunday Italian dinner happened pretty much religiously in my family. On holidays, we would eat seven courses of food. In fact, on Thanksgiving, not only would we have turkey, but we would have lasagna, too. On Christmas Eve, our family would have tons of seafood such as baked clams, shrimp scampi, and fried baccala, and then we would even add to that by having the baccala salad or the scungilli salad. Those memories of my whole family eating together are something that I really cherish.

I enjoy cooking now; it's one of my big interests. If I'm home and I'm not working, then I'm cooking. I began cooking around six years ago when I started having my own family. I'm married with three kids and I really love cooking for them. I think that I originally began cooking because I missed eating a lot of the foods that I grew up on. My wife is not into cooking that much, and years ago, we were always rushing around getting take-out food. I honestly got sick of it and really missed a nice home-cooked meal. So I got some cookbooks and I asked my grandmother and my mother how to prepare certain Italian dishes. Soon, I found myself delving into cooking much deeper, wanting to know more and more. I don't cook exclusively Italian food. I also cook other cuisines. When I first started cooking, I stuck to the recipes and really followed them exactly. After a while, I became more daring and began to mix in some of my own ingredients to make the dishes even more exciting. I created a homemade barbecue sauce and I love it. It purely came out of improvisation in the kitchen. The sauce tastes great on pork ribs or beef brisket, whichever you prefer. Sometimes, I improvise based on what I have in the cupboard. It might be at night and raining, and I don't feel like going to the store, so I'll make do with what I have on hand and then wind up stumbling onto something good.

Whatever and whenever I'm cooking, the very fact that all of my family is sitting around the table eating a home-cooked meal is special and very important to me. I also believe that my kids really love it. Carrying on good traditions is important to children. I believe that cooking is important. It brings warmth to a home and a family. Memories from my childhood still come to me from certain food smells.

It's also great to eat with my other family on *The Sopranos*. In fact, I have a funny story. A few cast members and I shot a scene for *The Sopranos* on a Friday. In the scene we had to eat meatballs. We ended up eating meatball after meatball after meatball. In fact, we ate so many meatballs that we came to the point where we wanted to shoot ourselves in the head. The next day, the same people who were in that scene, including me, had to go to the Foxwoods Casino in Connecticut to do a personal appearance. Foxwood

Michael Imperioli with some of New Jersey's finest

SHUT UP AND EAT!

got this great chef to fly in from a top restaurant in Florida to cook us a terrific Italian meal for our big night. The chef proudly announced to all of us, "I am going to cook you the greatest meatballs you will ever have in your life." We all looked at each other and said, "Meatballs?!" It was hysterical. You couldn't have written it better.

When I went to Italy, the food there was so good that it was like I had never tasted Italian food before. In reality, when I first went to Italy, I hadn't tasted food at any of the truly great Italian restaurants in New York, restaurants like Mario Batali's where you can eat anything as good as they make it in Italy. I had been more used to the typical Italian-American restaurants here. However, in Italy, I was impressed by the quality and freshness of the produce and the meat. They really focus on seasonal stuff. Italy has one of the most diverse cuisines in the world. The north and south of Italy, as well as in between, have very different types of produce and agriculture, and that makes for unbelievable variety. For example, the cuisine in Sicily is completely different than the cuisine in Tuscany. In Tuscany, they eat a lot of meat, while in Sicily fish is more prevalent. Also, the sun is a lot stronger in Sicily so the wine tends to be more full-bodied.

It was a revelation traveling there. When I walked into the house of my great-aunt in Rome (my grandfather's sister), it was Sunday and she was in the middle of cooking macaroni and sauce. It was exactly like the atmosphere in my grandfather's house on Sunday back home in America. In fact, I soon realized that the sauce recipe was handed down from my great-grandmother, so when I tasted it, the sauce had the same exact taste.

I love Italian wine with my meal. It's something that I am crazy about. Naturally, your choice of Italian wine depends on what you are eating. With pasta, there are some great Chiantis from Tuscany. I also like Dolcettos and Barberas, which are classic red wines from the Piedmont region. If you're serving braised meat dishes or stews, I suggest a Barolo. There are some great wines from the areas of Sicily and Naples. The whites from the north of Italy are excellent too.

I'm very into cooking. But living in Manhattan, how could I not take advantage of the amazing Italian restaurants here? I like to go to Giorgione on Spring Street, Il Cortile on Mulberry Street, Roc on Greenwich Street, Patsy's on West Fifty-Sixth Street, and Manducatis and Manetta's in Queens. Also, anything Mario Batali does is amazing. After dinner, I love to go to Rocco's pastry shop on Bleecker Street, which has the best cannoli in the city. In Los Angeles, I like to go to Alto Palato.

When I am cooking at home I love to experiment with many different dishes. Spaghetti carbonara and braised short ribs are two dishes that I made recently and loved. I hope you try these recipes and enjoy them as much as I do.

MICHAEL IMPERIOLI is a multitalented actor who has appeared in almost fifty films to date. Who can forget him in one of his earliest roles as Spider in *Goodfellas*, the "gofer" who Joe Pesci's character first shoots in the foot and eventually kills for speaking out of turn. Imperioli has appeared in various popular feature films like *Postcards From America, Bad Boys, The Basketball Diaries, Dead Presidents*, and *I Shot Andy Warhol*, just to name a few. He appeared in numerous movies from director Spike Lee, like *Jungle Fever, Malcolm X, Clockers*, and *Summer of Sam,* which he also cowrote. For the last five seasons on *The Sopranos*, Imperioli has been brilliantly portraying Christoper Moltisanti, Tony Soprano's nephew. As well as acting on the show, Imperioli has written numerous episodes. Imperioli has won an Emmy Award for his work on *The Sopranos*.

BRAISED SHORT RIBS

1 cup tomato sauce
4 teaspoons butter
2 tablespoons Worcestershire sauce
3 tablespoons lemon juice
½ teaspoon finely minced garlic
2 tablespoons honey
3 sprigs Italian parsley, diced fine
1 rack spareribs (the meatier and smaller the ribs, the better)
Salt and freshly ground pepper to taste

Preheat the oven to 350 degrees. In a saucepan combine the tomato sauce, butter, Worcestershire sauce, lemon juice, garlic, honey, and Italian parsley. Bring to a boil and stir to blend. Place the spareribs on a rack, meaty side up, and sprinkle with salt and pepper. Place in the oven and bake 30 minutes, or until nicely browned. Brush the spareribs with a layer of sauce and bake 15 minutes longer. Turn the spareribs and brush with sauce. Bake 15 minutes longer and turn. Brush with sauce again. Continue baking 15 to 30 minutes longer, basting as necessary. Serve hot or cold.

SERVES 4

SPAGHETTI CARBONARA

4 eggs
2 tablespoons heavy cream
Salt and freshly ground black pepper to taste
½ pound prosciutto, cut in slivers
1 pound spaghetti
1 cup mixed grated Parmesan and caciocavallo cheeses

In a small bowl, beat the eggs with the cream, salt, pepper, and prosciutto. Cook the spaghetti according to directions on the box. When it is done, drain and return it to the pot but keep off heat. Give the egg mixture another stir and then begin to mix it gently and slowly into the spaghetti, keeping it moving all the while so that the eggs don't cook. Add the cheese and continue to toss the noodles until everything is blended. Serve immediately with more grated cheese.

SERVES 4

EDIE FALCO

I'M HALF SWEDISH and half Italian; Swedish on my mom's side and Italian on my dad's side. I was born in Brooklyn and lived as a child on Ainslie Street in the area called Greenpoint. My impression back then was that it was a very Italian neighborhood. We lived with my dad's Italian parents. His aunts, uncles, and cousins all lived on Ainslie Street as well. My memory is that the whole Falco clan lived on that same street. Then, my family moved to Long Island, and that is where my family still resides to this day. My father is one of five children, so he has a very large family. My father's side of the family comes from just outside of Naples. The concept of family is a big part of his heritage and background. My mother, being Swedish, has a very different kind of family orientation. Her side of the family is not as close, and they don't have the big Sunday dinners that the Italian side does. There is a very strong Italian identity and feeling to my immediate family.

We moved around a lot on Long Island. However, no matter where we lived, every Sunday we would travel to my grandmother's, in East Northport, for a huge Italian dinner. My grandmother is the best Italian cook in the world. To this day, nobody can make meatballs like my grandmother, who is eighty-six years old and still cooks. My family eventually moved to Northport, probably in part for the family Sunday dinners. So that move eliminated the tedious process on Sundays of packing up the car with the kids and driving there. After we moved to Northport, it was basically just a matter of going up the block to my grandmother's house for the big traditional Sunday feasts. Over the years, it has diminished a little because some people have moved away.

The memories of holidays for me are surely about food and what seems like millions of family members. It is about eventually graduating from the kids' table to the big table with the grown-ups, which is always the way it's done in Italian families. Memories include having already eaten too much food by the time the third of eight courses came out from the kitchen. I remember so many Thanksgivings with us all leaning back in our chairs totally full! Even though it is often deemed politically incorrect today, many of our family members smoked. Even in between courses, after the plates were cleared, family members would light up. Then, when everyone was done with their cigarettes, we would start the next round of food. My family also enjoyed wine, but they were never connoisseurs. They definitely enjoyed the taste of wine with a hearty Italian meal. Those big family dinners are the basis for some of my fondest memories growing up.

I've had the opportunity to travel to Italy and I am very happy about that. I was doing a movie in Italy, and my sister came over with me on this particular trip. We thought that since our family had not been back to its roots since it originally came to America it was time for me and my sister to go back to Naples to try to discover our heritage. We didn't have much information to go on, and I didn't have as much time as I would have liked to explore because I was working on that movie. We searched through the Naples phone book and there were actually sixty-five pages of Falcos! It's like the Smith of Naples, which I hadn't realized. We walked all through Naples and met many families, but no luck.

After spending a long time walking in various Naples neighborhoods, we found a stone gate outside a house and within the stone someone had carved "Falco." My sister and I stood in front of the "Falco" stone sign and someone took a picture of us. Later, we told everyone that we found the home of our relatives! For a while my sister and I kept to that story, but, eventually, told our family the truth. I'm a little embarrassed, but it was impossible to find our actual roots. So my sister and I said to each other, "This is going to have to do!" It was kind of an innocent thing to do because we didn't want to disappoint our family back in America.

Today, I really enjoy Italian cooking and I would love to delve into it more. I am just trying to find the time. I have a magnificent kitchen where I live now. In truth, it sits there and looks like it's sort of glowing—waiting for me to attack it. I have so many creative interests. My father is a painter and a sculptor, and I definitely inherited that creative gene. I like to sing as well. But, of course, my passion is acting. I am excited about the many ways to be creative, and cooking is definitely on my list. Cooking definitely calls out to me. My character on *The Sopranos*, Carmela, cooks. So I get the best of both worlds on our TV show, because not only do I get to act, but I also get to cook. I love working with Jimmy Gandolfini so much. It is funny when it comes to the food on *The Sopranos*. He has the tendency to eat all the prop food, to the point that the prop guys look at each other and say, "Do you think we have enough of this stuff?" Jimmy is so much fun and a great man to work with. Throughout my acting career, on shows like *The Sopranos* and in movies like *Cop Land*, it has been interesting working with Italian-American actors. From James Gandolfini to Ray Liotta to Sylvester Stallone, it's almost as if you look at each other like you are members of a secret club. You all sort of feel like family members due to your Italian roots. Liotta has lighter-colored eyes and Stallone has darker features, but yet, they all look like variations of my own family members. They all feel like brothers, uncles, cousins, and dads. I love it. On a certain level, it adds a feeling of safety and camaraderie when I am working with them. It is really great. I also admire many Italian-born actresses who paved the way for us. That wonderful Italian actress Giulietta Masina was brilliant in *La Dolce Vita* and *La Strada*. The very last moment of *La Strada*, when the audience makes eye contact with the character of Gelsomina, played by Masina, is extraordinary. Throughout the film, Masina has maintained the fourth wall. All of a sudden, she breaks that wall by looking directly at you, her audience, and it knocks the wind out of you, me, and anyone else watching the movie, I'm sure. Then, the screen goes black. I also admire Sophia Loren, who has done so many varied roles.

Food can offer me comfort when I'm putting in long, long hours acting. Whenever I am performing on Broadway and I do a matinee and evening performance, I eat a plate of pasta in between shows. It is the perfect energy food, and it is also very comforting for me. I always eat at Angus McIndoe on West Forty-Fourth Street, which is sort of an "after the theater" kind of place. They prepare this Italian dish that is basically penne pasta with sausage, and it's often been the only thing that's helped me get through a performance. My cast mates and I would always whisper to each other, "If we can just get through the second act, we can have Angus's pasta dish!" It was so delicious and it would truly get me through the rough days onstage. When I want to cook a meal for myself, I often make my fettuccine alfredo, which I really enjoy. *Mangia!*

EDIE FALCO graduated from the acting program at the State University of New York at Purchase. She made her Broadway acting debut in the Tony Award–winning play *Sideman*. Falco has appeared in many popular motion pictures such as *Cop Land*, starring Sylvester Stallone, Robert DeNiro, and Ray Liotta; and Woody Allen's *Bullets Over Broadway*, starring John Cusack and Chazz Palminteri. Falco has also acted in roles in highly acclaimed television shows such as *Will & Grace, Law & Order, Homicide*, and the HBO dramatic series *Oz*. For her role as Carmela Soprano in *The Sopranos*, Falco became the first actress to ever sweep all three top American television awards by receiving the Emmy Award for Outstanding Lead Actress in a Drama Series, the Golden Globe for Best Performance by an Actress in a Drama Series, and the SAG Award for Outstanding Performance by a Female Actor in a Drama Series. That was in the year 2000 and she's been going strong ever since. In between the time spent on camera for *The Sopranos*, Falco still performs in live theater, recently starring in the hit production of *Frankie and Johnny* on Broadway.

FALCO'S FETTUCCINE ALFREDO

THIS IS THE AUTHENTIC ROMAN FETTUCCINE ALFREDO RECIPE—
SIMPLY BUTTER, CHEESE, AND SALT AND PEPPER. THAT'S IT!

■

6 quarts water

2 tablespoons salt

1 pound fettuccine

1 stick salted butter, clarified

4 tablespoons Pecorino Romano cheese

Salt and pepper to taste

Bring water to a boil and add the 2 tablespoons salt. Cook the fettuccine until tender yet al dente. Drain the pasta. Clarify the butter: Melt the butter in a saucepan on high heat. The milk byproduct of the butter will float to the top of the pan. Skim it off with a spoon and you will be left with clear, clarified butter. In a sauté pan add the clarified butter and bring to high heat. Add the fettuccine, cheese, salt, and pepper and sauté for 2 minutes, stirring quickly.

SERVES 4

PENNE WITH SWEET SAUSAGE

COURTESY OF ANGUS MCINDOE
258 WEST FORTY-FOURTH STREET
NEW YORK, NY 10036
212-221-9222

■

2 tablespoons kosher salt
1 pound penne
3½ cups tomato sauce (recipe follows)
2 tablespoons olive oil
1 pound sweet Italian sausage links, sliced to ¼-inch thick
Freshly grated Parmesan or Pecorino Romano cheese
Salt and pepper to taste
Basil leaves, for garnish (optional)

Bring a large pot of cold water to a boil over high heat, and then add the kosher salt. Add the penne and cook to al dente (tender, but not mushy). Set a colander in the sink and drain the penne.

Meanwhile, prepare the pasta sauce. In a large sauté pan, heat olive oil and cook the sausage over medium-high heat until brown, about 4 minutes. Add tomato sauce and cook until thick and fragrant, about 5 to 7 minutes. Transfer the penne to the sauce and toss. Add Parmesan and basil, and season with salt and pepper. Garnish with basil leaves (optional).

SERVES 6

Basic Tomato Sauce

2 tablespoons extra-virgin olive oil
1 medium onion, diced
4 cloves garlic, chopped
1 fresh thyme sprig
3 leaves fresh basil
½ teaspoon crushed red pepper
1 (28-ounce) can whole, peeled canned tomatoes in puree, chopped
3 plum tomatoes, seeded and chopped (optional)
2 teaspoons kosher salt
Freshly ground black pepper to taste

Heat two tablespoons of olive oil in a medium saucepan over medium-high heat. Add the onion, garlic, fresh thyme, basil and red pepper, and cook, stirring, until lightly browned (about 3 minutes). Add the tomatoes (both canned and fresh) and their juice, and bring to a boil. Adjust the heat to maintain a simmer for a few minutes until the tomatoes are cooked through.

Remove and discard the herb sprigs. Stir in the salt and season with pepper. Use immediately, store in the refrigerator for up to 3 days, or freeze for up to 2 months.

YIELDS ABOUT 3½ CUPS

Cook's Note: For more texture, add seeded, chopped tomatoes at the end.

DANNY AIELLO

AFTER I WAS born on West Sixty-eighth Street in Manhattan, I moved with my family to the Bronx. As a neighborhood, the Bronx was extremely diverse back then, but in my home there was a very strong sense of Italian heritage. That was mainly thanks to my mother. Elements of our family come from Sorrento, but, basically, we are Neapolitan, from Naples. The centerpiece of every Sunday was a big Italian dinner in our home in the Bronx. We generally ate at two or three in the afternoon and

Tony Lip and Danny Aiello making some gravy at Hoboken's best Italian restaurant, Tutta Pasta

we feasted for up to four hours. Holidays were big too. To be honest, every day of the week, my house was permeated with the smell of wonderful Italian food. We often had macaroni, meatballs, pork, and sausage, all with pignoli nuts in the gravy, which I love. Mama made a puree gravy, which was without chunks of tomatoes. I hate tomato chunks. It has to be smooth, almost like ketchup. Like most Italians, we called it gravy, not sauce. Mama would cook the gravy for five and a half hours. I don't like onions. Actually, I pretended to be allergic, just to avoid them. My mother cooked with onions for other relatives, but never for me. She would never put onions in the sauce. Also, wine was not on our table. Isn't that weird for Italians? Anyway, we are not a family of drinkers. I never went around preaching that alcohol was bad, but we just never liked it. I never, ever saw my mother or father with a drink in their hands. Many people think that wine goes hand in hand with being Italian, but as far as our family goes, that was just a cliché.

SHUT UP AND EAT!

Tony Lip, Danny Aiello, and Fortunado Di Natale enjoying some fresh pasta at Tutta Pasta restaurant

Later in life, when our kids were growing up, my wife, Sandy, would cook on Sundays just as my mother did. She picked up the art of Italian cooking from my sister, Gloria, and my mother. When it comes to my turn at cooking, the tomato sauce I make is a reasonable facsimile of my mother's. To be perfectly honest, I don't feel it's that close to what my mother did, but it's not bad either.

I love going back to my Italian roots. I went to Italy and did three movies in Rome. The food is always sensational! There is a restaurant that

I love in Rome called Toscano Ristorante, right off the Via Veneto. When I was in Rome, I would go there as much as I could. Their philosophy was, "Sit down and we'll feed you." At this restaurant, you do not order, but leave your meal up to their excellent judgment. You pay for it, of course, but, man, do they feed you! When I am back in New Jersey, where I live now, my favorite restaurant in Hoboken is Tutta Pasta at Second Street and Washington Street. In Boonton Township, New Jersey, I go to Il Michelangelo. In New York City, I love Gigino's. Gigi is the chef and I just love the food. I actually shot a movie there called *Dinner Rush.* The preparation of the food in that movie was not all of the film, but that was a very central part of it. The things that were happening in that kitchen were almost like a ballet. And that is what the creation of fine food should be regarded as— a true art form.

As far as my pal Tony Lip is concerned, he is a fine actor, but he is also a great chef. He knows more about food than I do. Tony would come over to our house and cook. He used so many damn pans! I have a tremendous dishwasher, but I do not believe in dishwashers. I like to wash the dishes by hand, and then I put them on the rack to dry off. Tony generally leaves the house before my wife comes home. Sandy usually arrives and sees all the dishes drying. However, she doesn't trust them being washed and dried by me in that way. So my wife rewashes all of them. In fact, she ultimately rewashes everything that I originally washed by hand.

For this book, I want to share with you some special recipes. The last is a recipe from Tutta Pasta, which is not only one of my favorite restaurants, but its owner, Fortunado DiNatale, is one of my best friends. But first, I am going to give you my personal recipes for the two soups that I love. I love tortellini in brodo. In plain English, that's simply tortellini in broth. But one sip of this soup, and in your mind's eye you are sitting on the Via Veneto in Rome! Remember, the tortellini must be filled with cheese. With that tasty clear broth, it is wonderful. Also, lentil soup is one of my favorite things, especially from the time when I was growing up. Mama made it with elbow macaroni. The soup was never red and we used tomato puree, which had a reddish-brown look. It was filling, nourishing, and inexpensive, which is important because we were poor. So Mama made this for seven of us children and for herself for a total cost of about thirteen cents. We practically lived on my mother's lentil soup and it was such a healthy meal. That is truly my favorite soup of all time. I'm getting hungry just thinking about it!

BORN DANIEL LOUIS AIELLO, JR. in New York City, actor Danny Aiello has proven his versatility on international motion picture and television screens again and again. Starting with the Academy Award–winning movie, *The Godfather, Part 2*, Aiello has appeared in an impressive array of top box office films. Aiello was nominated for an Oscar for his role of Sal in acclaimed director Spike Lee's *Do the Right Thing*. Later, he brilliantly played the Italian-American mama's boy fiancé of Cher in *Moonstruck*. Aiello has been on both sides of the cinematic law, playing cops and hoods with equal conviction. Movies like *Fort Apache The Bronx, Once upon a Time in America, Ruby, 29th Street, Once Around, The Professional, Hudson Hawk, City Hall, 2 Days in the Valley, Hitman's Journal* (directed by son Danny Aiello III), *The Last Don* (Parts I and II), *Lobster Farm,* and many others have all featured various sides of Aiello's creative on-screen persona. Aiello is capable of reflecting anything he wants to when he's acting, always delivering his performance with style. Danny Aiello showed his versatility once again when he released his first musical vocal album entitled, *I Just Wanted to Hear the Words*. It debuted April 20, 2004, and hit number four on the Billboard traditional jazz chart.

LENTIL SOUP

1 ham or pork bone
1 pound dry lentils
2 to 3 quarts water or chicken stock
Salt and freshly ground pepper to taste
½ teaspoon garlic powder
1 teaspoon thyme
¼ teaspoon nutmeg
1 (8-ounce) can tomato puree
Chopped parsley, crisp croutons, or Italian bread, toasted, for garnish

Put the bone and lentils in a deep pot with the water or stock, and cook over low heat until lentils are very soft, about 1 hour. Put them through a sieve or food mill, or puree in a blender or food processor. Taste the pureed soup for seasoning, and add salt and pepper. Add garlic powder, thyme, nutmeg, tomato puree, and additional water or stock, if necessary, to make a good thick soup. Simmer for 30 minutes. Taste for seasoning again and serve topped with chopped parsley, crisp croutons, or toasted Italian bread.

SERVES 6

TORTELLINI IN BRODO

½ pound escarole
Olive oil, for sautéing
4 cloves garlic, thinly sliced
2 quarts chicken stock
Salt to taste
1 (13-ounce) package fresh cheese-filled tortellini
Pecorino Romano cheese, grated, to taste

Clean escarole well, soaking in cold water and salt to remove any dirt or sand. Drain and rinse with cold water. Heat sauté pan and add enough olive oil to just cover the bottom of the pan. Add garlic and escarole and cook until leaves are translucent. Remove from heat and let cool. When escarole is cool enough to handle, chop it up and set aside.

Bring stock to a boil and add salt to taste. Add tortellini to stock and cook until tender, 5 to 7 minutes. Throw in the escarole and cook for another 2 minutes. Serve with grated cheese.

SERVES 6

FRESH FETTUCCINE WITH FENNEL

COURTESY OF TUTTA PASTA
200 WASHINGTON STREET
HOBOKEN, NJ 07030
201-792-9102

■

2 garlic cloves, chopped
1 small onion, chopped
¼ cup extra-virgin olive oil
2 plum tomatoes, chopped
¼ cup shitake mushrooms, sliced
½ teaspoon salt
½ teaspoon crushed red pepper
1 ounce dry white wine
½ cup chopped fresh fennel
1 pound fettuccine
3 to 4 basil leaves
Grated Parmigiano cheese to taste

Using a large sauté pan, brown garlic and onion in olive oil. Add tomatoes, mushrooms, salt, red pepper, and white wine, and add fennel last. Cook about 5 minutes on low heat.

Cook fettuccine al dente, strain, and pour over sauce in sauté pan. Add 3 to 4 basil leaves and grated cheese.

SERVES 4

FRANK VINCENT

MY FATHER'S SIDE of the family came from Palermo, in Sicily, and my mother's side came from Naples. One of my life dreams is to go back to my roots in Italy. It's one of those things that I have kept putting on the back burner because I have always just gotten too busy to go. However, I plan to visit Italy very soon.

I grew up in Jersey City, New Jersey, in an Irish neighborhood. I went to St. Paul's Grammar School, which was a predominantly Irish Catholic grammar school, so my Italian family was a minority in that neighborhood.

The Italian food I ate growing up would probably be defined as "peasant food." We ate every kind of pasta imaginable. From *cannelloni* (large pipes) to the wire-thin *capellini d'angelo* (angel hair) to *spaghettini* to *vermicelli* to *ziti*, we ate it all. My mother would often combine the pasta with lentils and other hearty beans. It was a big day if my mother made her veal cutlets, which melted in your mouth. Of course, on Sunday, we ate macaroni with meatballs and the other traditional Italian foods. Overall, food was a significant part of my childhood. I have two brothers and my mother had four siblings of her own. They also had families. One of my mom's siblings even lived in the same house as us when I was growing up. During the week, my family ate together every single night. On the weekends and on holidays, we would have more members of our family come over to join us, as well as close friends, to eat a big meal. Eating Italian food has always been a bonding experience that has continually brought my big family together.

As far as food scenes in my acting career, I have a film that is soon to be released entitled *A Tale of Two Pizzas*, which is centered around Italian food. Vinny Pastore and I are in the film together, and we play two competing pizza-parlor owners in Yonkers. Vinny's pizza is considered by the locals in the neighborhood to have the best sauce. My pizza is considered to have the best crust. Vinny's character has a daughter and my character has a son. His daughter comes back from the fashion school FIT in New York City, and revamps his pizzeria—new uniforms and two-for-one specials. With that, a pizza war starts! My character sends his son over to Vinny's house to try and date his daughter. The motive is to try to find out the secret to the sauce and what makes it taste so good. It is a cute comedy all about Italian food. In the movie, Vinny and I even have a fight with our pizza paddles! A great Italian-American actor is in the film, Louis Guss, who plays the "pizza mentor" of the neighborhood, who started both Vinny and me in the pizza business. I got the chance to learn how to make pizza right on the set. The story really attracted me because it was totally different for me not to have to play a "tough guy." Don't get me wrong, I love playing "tough guys," but this was a nice change of pace.

I think that mob movies are very popular because the audience gets to escape their middle-of-the-road kind of life. You see, the gangster characters in the movies usually have a lot of money, designer clothing, and beautiful women. They can do what they want to do and there are no rules. It seems like a glamorous way of life and people are attracted to it because it reflects something that they usually don't have. I am happy to have appeared in classic mob movies like *Goodfellas*, where I played Billy Batts, a part fans remember and constantly mention to me. I'm equally happy that I have had the opportunity to play comedic roles like my part in the aforementioned film, *A Tale of Two Pizzas*.

When my wife, Kathy, and I go out to eat, one of our favorite restaurants is, coincidentally, named Goodfellas, located in Garfield, New Jersey. The atmosphere is wonderful and the chef, Vincent, is one of the most consistent chefs around. He never misses the boat on any meal he cooks. The food is traditional Italian cuisine, nothing too fancy, and they make it tasty and wonderful. In Los Angeles, I like to dine at Ago's on Melrose Avenue. The food there is very special.

In truth, Kathy and I really enjoy a nice home-cooked meal as well. However, the best part about cooking for me is eating. As far as favorites at home, we enjoy having striped bass. I like to put garlic and a lemon sauce on that dish for added flavor. It is great to have it with a nice glass of white wine. I suggest a Pinot Grigio. My wife and I like wine, but we are not big wine drinkers and we usually enjoy a martini before dinner. We often make a great fish called tilapia and have it with a side of broccoli rabe. You start with a fresh mixed green salad, and it becomes a very healthy, light meal. After dinner, I enjoy a nice light blend of a Churchill cigar. Also, let me tell you that cooking can be very romantic. Take my advice. You wear something loose and you have your lady put on something tighter. Then have some wine and get in the kitchen together and start shaking and baking! Cooking can be a lot of fun when you make one of the ingredients romance.

AS AN ACTOR, Frank Vincent may physically look the real "mob guy" part, but one only has to see him at work in classic movies like *Raging Bull*, *Do the Right Thing*, and *Jungle Fever* to be convinced of his acting depth. Vincent is an actor, musician, writer, and producer. His passion for music and playing the drums led to a successful career as a recording drummer for such prominent names as arranger Don Costa, as well as singers Paul Anka and Trini Lopez.

As an actor, Vincent debuted in 1975 in Ralph De Vito's *Death Collector*, where he impressed director Martin Scorsese with his on-screen work. Scorsese cast him in the Academy Award–winning film *Raging Bull*, and the rest is cinematic history. Vincent has gone on to appear in over fifty feature films. He has worked for some of the greatest directors of our time, in addition to Scorsese. Brian DePalma, Spike Lee, and Sidney Lumet are among the esteemed. He plays the parts that audiences remember long after they walk out of the theater. In fact, who could forget him as the infamous Billy Batts in *Goodfellas*, where he tells Joe Pesci's character to "go home and get your shine box!"

Most recently, you can see Vincent in the reoccurring role of Phil Leotardo on *The Sopranos*. He's also proud that his voice is featured in the multimillion dollar PlayStation game *Grand Theft Auto III*, as the character Don Salvatore Leone. In 2002, he received the Italian American Entertainer of the Year Award, presented by the *Italian Tribune*. That same year he was also the recipient of the Back East Picture Show Lifetime Achievement Award. His first book, *A Guy's Guide to Being a Man's Man,* will be published by The Berkley Publishing Group in spring 2006. Check out his fantastic Web site at www.frankvincent.com.

STRIPED BASS WITH GARLIC
AND BUTTERED LEMON SAUCE

½ cup all-purpose flour

1 teaspoon baking powder

Salt and pepper to taste

4 filets striped bass

4 tablespoons unsalted butter

¼ cup olive oil

3 cloves garlic, minced

½ lemon

3 ounces white wine

½ cup clam juice

3 sprigs Italian parsley, chopped, for garnish

Mix the flour with the baking powder, add the salt and pepper, and dredge the striped bass on both sides. Add the butter and olive oil to a large sauté pan on high heat. Place the striped bass into the pan slowly, and do not shake pan. Fry bass for 3 minutes and turn over on the other side for 3 more minutes. Add garlic and sauté for 1 minute. Pull the pan away from the heat and squeeze the lemon in the pan. Cook for 2 minutes. Take the pan away from the heat again, and add the wine. Cook down for 1 minute and add the clam juice. Cook for another 3 minutes on high heat until you have a nice thick sauce. Remove bass from pan, and place one filet on each plate. Pour a little sauce over each of the filets, garnish with parsley, and serve.

SERVES 4

SHUT UP AND EAT!

TILAPIA VINCENZO

COURTESY OF GOODFELLAS RISTORANTE
661 MIDLAND AVENUE
GARFIELD, NJ 07026
973-478-4000

■

2 (8-ounce) pieces tilapia
1 teaspoon salt
½ teaspoon pepper
¼ cup fresh basil, chopped
¼ cup fresh parsley, chopped
¼ cup dry white wine
¼ cup clam broth
1 tablespoon salted butter
¾ cup Italian seasoned bread crumbs
¾ cup shredded Parmigiano-Reggiano cheese
⅛ cup olive oil, plus ¼ cup
2 cloves garlic, minced
1 head escarole, washed and chopped into large pieces
1 tomato, diced
1 (9-ounce) can cannellini beans, drained

Place tilapia in a baking dish and season with salt, pepper, basil, and parsley. Pour wine and clam broth over fish. Put ½ tablespoon of butter on top of each piece of fish. Broil 4 to 5 minutes. Remove from heat.

In a small bowl, mix bread crumbs, Parmigiano-Reggiano, and ⅛ cup olive oil. Place bread-crumb mixture on top of fish, lightly pushing it down.

In sauté pan heat ¼ cup olive oil, add garlic and sauté until browned. Add escarole and tomato. Cook 2 minutes and add beans. Cook until moisture is absorbed.

Place tilapia under broiler, and cook until brown on top. Spoon escarole and beans onto plate. Top with tilapia. Serve immediately.

SERVES 2

SHUT UP AND EAT!

VEAL CAPRESE

COURTESY OF GOODFELLAS RISTORANTE
661 MIDLAND AVENUE
GARFIELD, NJ 07026
973-478-4000

■

8 ounces veal top round
½ cup flour, plus 1 tablespoon
3 tablespoons olive oil
6 slices tomatoes
6 slices roasted red bell peppers
6 slices fresh mozzarella
1 tablespoon melted butter, plus 2 tablespoons
¼ cup dry vermouth
½ cup Knorr's Select beef stock
2 basil leaves, chopped
2 cloves garlic, minced

Preheat oven to 350 degrees. Cut veal into 6 pieces and pound until thin. Dredge lightly in ½ cup flour. In frying pan heat 2 tablespoons olive oil over low heat until hot. Place veal in pan, and cook both sides until browned. Place veal on baking sheet. Top each piece with a slice of tomato, roasted pepper, and mozzarella. Place baking sheet in oven until cheese melts. Remove veal from pan and set aside. Place pan on top of stove on medium heat. Add vermouth and beef stock, scraping any brown bits off the bottom of the pan.

Make a paste of 1 tablespoon butter, basil, and garlic, and add to the pan. Simmer and stir until sauce thickens, about 3 to 4 minutes. Place veal on plates. Spoon sauce over veal. Serve immediately.

SERVES 2

Michael Badalucco

WHEN YOU ARE Italian, food is as much a part of you as your blood. It is the life force that is within you. Growing up Italian American, as with many Americans who have strong immigrant roots, I learned that the dinner table was the place where you would find out about what happened during every family member's day. You'd also laugh and cry, but one thing's for sure, even if your mom made something as simple as a fritatta and some escarole, your taste buds would always be astonished.

To me, the dinner table is one of the most important parts of any family, and the family is one of the most important parts of being Italian. They truly go hand in hand. Sitting and conversing at the kitchen table was the major part of my growing up. Nowadays, I have lots of nieces and nephews who live close to me, and I notice that they are always running somewhere else. They grab a meal and eat it on the run as they go off to the soccer field or the baseball field. The important element of sitting down at the table and being a family unit is missing. However, we still try very hard to keep it alive whenever we can and attempt to instill it in others in our family.

I grew up in a modest house in the Midwood section of Brooklyn. One of the most important parts of living in that house was the backyard. We had a big peach tree growing out there, and my father had so much pride in it. In the summertime, it would yield about a hundred pounds of peaches every year. My father would go around to all the neighbors and give them bags of peaches. Every Saturday and Sunday in the summer we would have barbecues with tons of food, including skinny Italian sausage, fresh vegetables, and eggplant parmigiana. All of our relatives and friends would come over and we would talk, talk, talk and eat, eat, eat! It was a vital part of living and I can't believe how much I learned from those days. Holidays were so much fun as well. When it was holiday time we would all sit in our finished basement and everybody would come over—grandparents, aunts, uncles, cousins. It was just like camping out, from the day before Christmas Eve to the day after Christmas, and cooking was constantly going on. I remember there was such a wonderful aroma in the air. As I look back now on those days, they were truly incomparable. It was all centered around the food and what we were eating. The eating seemed like it would never end! So you not only had the anticipation of Christmas and all of the gifts, but you couldn't wait for the delicious food, too. In a sense, the wonderful food was a gift as well.

Many people ask me at what point in my life I first started acting. I honestly tell them that it was in the basement of my parents' house at Christmas. You see, we used to perform skits for the family. For example, we mimed songs such as "Stop! In the Name of Love" by the Supremes, and we dressed up like women. It was hilarious! Those were great times that I'll never forget.

SHUT UP AND EAT!

You can often learn life lessons from food when you're young. I remember when I was a kid, my father loved eating clams. He would often bring me to his favorite clam bar, called Lundy's, in Sheepshead Bay, Brooklyn. My father would order a dozen clams, but I didn't eat the clams. I would eat the oysterettes, which are the little crackers they serve alongside. A couple of years went by and during our many trips to that restaurant, my father never once said to me, "Do you want to try a clam?" Never. When you're a kid and you see the half shell of a clam, it looks kinda slimy and unappetizing. My father never forced it on me. I remember very vividly that one day I said to my father, "Daddy, can I have one of those clams?" He replied, "Sure. Do you want a little lemon on it?" I said, "Yes." After he put some lemon on it, I tasted it and thought the clam was delicious. I haven't stopped eating clams since. The life lesson I learned from my father was that you can lead by example, and you don't have to shove something down a kid's throat. That doesn't just apply to eating clams; it could also be an example of how to lead your life and how to treat other people. He taught me that if you "do" in a positive way, then others will follow. My father "did" in a nice way and I followed by eventually wanting to try a clam. Anyway, I've been eating clams by the dozen ever since.

My father is a great man and I love him dearly. My father was born in Sicily just like my mother's parents. My mother was a first-generation American from Brooklyn. She had four siblings in her family, and she would cook and watch her brothers and sisters when her parents went off to work. My mother never finished her education beyond grammar school, but she really knew how to cook!

I had always dreamed of going to visit Italy, so I saved my money and the first time I went to Italy was when I was a senior in college. The first place I wanted to go was to my father's hometown of Paceco, Sicily. We had cousins who had taken care of my grandmother in another town right nearby. So I got off the plane in Italy and was met by my cousin Giovanni. I wanted to see the house where my father was born and it was very emotional when I finally did see it. When I was in Italy, it almost felt like I had been there before. Of course, I was never there. I was born and raised in

Brooklyn, U.S.A. But I had this genuine feeling that I had been there already. My extended family in Italy was very gracious and happy to meet me. I loved my vacation so much that the next year I saved all my money and went back for a three-week trip. If you appreciate fresh Italian food, then you'll fall in love with Italy!

I married a wonderful woman named Brenda Heyob, who really loves to cook Italian. Hey, I love to eat Italian, so it's a perfect match. After we got married, we went on our honeymoon to Italy. While we were there, we went to a restaurant in Rome called Pommidoro on the Piazza Sanniti, 44. A woman named Anna serves your food there. I spoke some broken Italian with her, and my wife and I had a wonderful time. Whenever I hear anyone is going to Rome, I tell them to go to Pommidoro and to tell Anna that Michael Badalucco sent you. On another trip I discovered that there's a small town in the northern part of Italy called Badalucco. I visited there and made lifelong friends. As far as I'm concerned, Italy is a magical place.

As you can tell, food has always been a part of my life, ever since I was a young boy. I've even made it a part of my work. When I was on *The Practice*, I became good friends with Arthur Africano, who was the camera assistant on the show. During the first season of *The Practice*, Arthur said to me, "It's Christmastime and I want to order some special cheese and salami from Mike's Deli in the Bronx so that people connected with our show can bring it home to their families for gifts. Can we use your dressing room to store the food? Because some people don't especially like the smell of cheese, salami, and sausages." I replied, "That's the smell that reminds me that I'm alive! Sure, you can store it in my dressing room." So we then proceeded to take orders from everybody—a pound of this and a pound of that, etc. There were so many people that wanted this special Italian food that when we phoned cross-country to David Greco, the owner of Mike's Deli, he told us that he had a great idea. With this kind of weight being shipped to LA, it would be cheaper for us to buy a ticket for Arthur's sister and her boyfriend and have them bring the food directly. So that's exactly what we did. They packed their bags with wheels of Parmigiana cheese, wheels of Romano cheese, sausages, and so on. They got on the plane, landed in Los Angeles, and

Mike's Deli

Owners of Mike's Deli (left to right), David Greco and Michele Greco, with actor and Italian food lover Michael Badalucco

brought it straight to my dressing room. Then they proceeded to cut the appropriate portions for everybody who originally placed an order. My dressing room turned into an Italian deli and the crew loved it. This little event was so popular that we decided to throw a party every couple of months, with the catering provided by Mike's Deli in the Bronx. These native California grips and teamsters were tasting genuine New York City Italian cuisine for the first time. It was as if they were being blessed! They told

Arthur Avenue Café

me they had never tasted anything that good in their lives. We worked fourteen long hours a day, and this was a nice way to relax for everyone, cast and crew alike. E! Entertainment Network did a whole segment on me, and the parties that I threw, for their show called *Celebrity Dish*. David flew out to LA and cooked on the set for the show. He actually shipped a thousand pounds of food from Mike's Deli in the Bronx to the set of *The Practice* in LA. David and his crew made lasagna, baked clams, risotto, chicken, veal, meatballs — you name it! They turned the hallway of *The Practice* into a San Gennaro Feast. His brother, Marco Greco, came and actually made fresh mozzarella. We had live Italian music playing just like in Little Italy, New York. The party was unbelievable!

Now that *The Practice* has ended, I'm spending more time in New York City. It's been great to come back home to the many restaurants I love. In fact, I'm going to tell you about a few of those places and give you a couple of their personal recipes. The first is Gargiulo's, located in Coney Island, New York. It's owned by the Russo brothers and they are so personable to their customers that it feels like they're your real cousins. Gargiulo's has been around for seventy-five years, and if you want to have a wedding, retirement party, birthday party, or any other meaningful family function, it's a great place to do it. They have photos all over the walls of people who celebrated their first communions, weddings, birthdays, and other special events there. In fact, my friend Ray celebrated his communion there, and later in life, his own children celebrated their communions there. His brother, Jamie, had his children's baptism party there, so it's a place for a real family celebration. Then, if you want a great dessert, you have to get a cheesecake from the Arthur Avenue Café in the Bronx. I also love Joe's of Avenue U in Brooklyn, New York. I've been going there since I was a kid, and they make genuine Sicilian specialties like vastedda and arancine (rice balls). I also love La Focacceria in the East Village in Manhattan. It was established in 1914 and has been going strong ever since. You can go there and then head up three blocks to De Robertis for your dessert. Their sfogliatelle is outstanding! Here are two recipes from some of those favorite New York–based Italian places of mine and one of my favorite family recipes. I am proud that Italian food has always been a part of my heritage. I wouldn't trade it for anything. My parents took the time and care to instill their Italian heritage in me, and I hope to do the same for other people. *Mangia bevi e divertiti!*

BORN AND raised in Brooklyn, New York, Michael Badalucco is extremely proud of his Italian roots. After attending the State University of New York at New Paltz, Badalucco set his sights on working in the film industry. For close to twenty years he was a propman in New York, working on such popular films as *Superman, Manhattan, The Godfather, Part III*, and *Sleepless in Seattle*. Badalucco often got bit parts in the motion pictures and started being noticed by more and more well-known movie directors. Badalucco has appeared in such popular films as *Jungle Fever, The Professional, One Fine Day, The Man Who Wasn't There*, and *O Brother, Where Art Thou?* He's acted in major motion pictures for such acclaimed directors as Nora Ephron, Woody Allen, Spike Lee, and the Coen Brothers. Badalucco eventually caught the eye of executive producer/writer David E. Kelley, who was putting together a show called *The Practice*. He was cast by Kelley as Jimmy Berluti, one of the main characters in this highly popular network series. He went on to win an Emmy and remained on the show for eight seasons. Michael Badalucco is also involved with various charities including HeartShare Human Services of New York and the Little Sisters of the Poor.

ARANCINE
(Rice Balls)

COURTESY OF MIKE'S DELI
2344 ARTHUR AVENUE
BRONX, NY 10458
718-295-5033

■

4 cups Arborio rice

1 packet saffron (.5 grams or .04 ounces)

1 tablespoon salt

¼ tablespoon pepper

1 cup grated Pecorino Romano cheese

1 pound plus 1 tablespoon grated dry mozzarella

10 large eggs

1 quart vegetable oil, for deep-frying

1 tablespoon olive oil

1 medium onion, diced

1 garlic clove, diced

½ pound chopped meat

2 cups tomato sauce

1 cup frozen peas

2 cups bread crumbs

Cook the rice in 8 cups of water with the saffron and salt to al dente, about 15 to 20 minutes. Spoon rice into a large bowl or spread onto a sheet pan to cool. When the rice has cooled, transfer to a bowl and mix in the pepper, Pecorino Romano, and 1 pound of the mozzarella. Stir in 2 whisked eggs.

Heat the oil for deep-frying, to about 360 degrees. There should be enough oil in the pot to cover the rice balls.

To make the center stuffing, heat the olive oil in a sauté pan over medium-high heat, and sauté the onion and garlic until golden brown. Add the chopped meat and sauté until cooked all the way through, about 3 or 4 minutes. Add tomato sauce and peas and heat through. Let the mixture cool completely, and then stir in the remaining 1 tablespoon of mozzarella.

Fill a wide, shallow bowl with water and dip the palms of your hands. Grab a handful of rice and form into a ball about 3 inches in diameter. While holding the ball of rice in the palm of one hand, gently push the thumb of your other hand three-quarters of the way into the rice ball, making a large, round indentation, and then stuff the ball with a couple of tablespoons of the chopped meat mixture. Seal the meat inside the ball with more rice, and using your palms, roll the ball gently to reshape. Continue with the rest of the rice and meat mixture. Whisk the remaining 8 eggs in a bowl. Coat the rice balls in egg and then in the bread crumbs, coating completely; repeat this 3 times. Fry until deep golden, about 4 to 6 minutes, and set on paper towels to drain. Serve warm or at room temperature.

SERVES 12

MAMA GRECO'S ITALIAN CHEESECAKE

COURTESY OF ARTHUR AVENUE CAFÉ
2329 ARTHUR AVENUE
BRONX, NY 10458
718-562-0129

■

3 pounds fresh ricotta cheese, drained in a colander
lined with cheesecloth or a coffee filter
2 cups sugar
8 eggs, separated
½ cup sifted all-purpose flour
Grated rind of 1 lemon
1 teaspoon vanilla
½ cup cream cheese, softened
Butter, to grease bottom of pan
½ cup graham cracker crumbs

Preheat oven to 425 degrees. In a large bowl, beat drained ricotta cheese until smooth. Gradually add 1½ cups of sugar and egg yolks, one at a time, beating after each addition. Beat in flour, lemon rind, and vanilla. In a separate bowl, beat egg whites with remaining sugar until stiff. Add cream cheese and mix. Fold into ricotta mixture.

Line the bottom of a 12-inch springform pan with waxed paper, parchment, or tin foil. Grease the pan liner with butter and sprinkle with graham cracker crumbs. Pour the batter into the prepared pan.

Bake 10 minutes at 425 degrees, then lower temperature to 350 degrees, and bake for 1 hour more. Turn off the oven and allow to cool in oven with the door closed.

SERVES 8

NANA TILLIE'S SPIEDINI

3 large onions

3 tablespoons olive oil

1 (8-ounce) can tomato sauce

Salt to taste

1½ cups bread crumbs

1 cup grated Italian cheese

¼ cup minced garlic

1 cup chopped parsley

Black pepper to taste

½ cup bay leaves

3 pounds pork or veal cutlets, pounded very thin
and cut into 2-inch-by-2-inch strips

12-inch wooden skewers

Slice 2 onions very thin, and sauté in a 10-inch frying pan with olive oil. When onions are soft, add tomato sauce and salt, and let cook slowly, approximately 30 minutes. Mix bread crumbs, grated cheese, garlic, parsley, and black pepper, and add to pan. Stir together. Next, soak bay leaves in water for 30 minutes. Cut third onion into 2-inch strips, and soak in olive oil for 30 minutes. When 30 minutes has elapsed, dab each meat slice with olive oil (from onions), and add a small amount of bread crumb mix onto meat. Roll and insert onto 12-inch wood skewers. Alternate bay leaf, rolled meat, and onion slice until full. Broil or barbecue until browned on each side.

SERVES 6

LORRAINE BRACCO

MY MOTHER IS English and I was brought up in a predominantly Norwegian neighborhood in Brooklyn. My father is Italian and comes from Palermo. Since my mother is English, things foodwise got a little confusing growing up. However, I do love Italian food. In fact, I love all food, period. I think that celebrating with good, wholesome food is beautifully instilled in many cultures, not just the Italian culture. For instance, the Irish Catholics, Muslims, and Jews all celebrate their holidays with unique foods. However, I think it comes down to the fact that maybe, in general, Italian food is just a little bit tastier to a broader number of Americans.

Italian-American traditions are very strong and important in my own family. There are certain Italian things that my kids want to eat every holiday, because we have been eating those things every year since they were very young. I guess it would not be considered the holidays if we did not serve and eat those particular foods every year. For example, every Thanksgiving and Christmas, my father makes delicious roasted chestnuts. Without those traditional chestnuts, it just isn't the holidays for us. We love to have Italian pastries on holidays as well. My children are learning now to make those things so that they can someday prepare those foods themselves and keep our family food traditions alive.

My kids and I have been to Rome and to the Isle of Capri in the Bay of Naples and we loved it all. I adored the food when I went to Italy. One trip I made was to the Almafi Coast and I really enjoyed going to the beach. There was a restaurant outside right on the beach that I would eat at every day. The scenery near that restaurant was beautiful, very picturesque. In fact, all of Italy is stunning. I would like to go back to Italy again; I'm not finished traveling there, by any means. There are a lot of places in Italy that I'd like to explore. I love Paris as well. One of my favorite Italian restaurants is in Paris and is called Stressa. It is near the Avenue Montaigne. The food is fabulous—I love their figs and prosciutto and really fresh mozzarella! I go back every time I am in Paris.

Silvano Marchetto, owner of Da Silvano

When I am home in New York, I love to eat at a few different Italian restaurants in the city. I love to dine downtown at Da Silvano on Sixth Avenue between Bleecker and Houston, and at Il Mulino on Third Street

Da Silvano restaurant

between Sullivan and Thompson. When I'm uptown, I eat at Campagnola on First Avenue between Seventy-Third and Seventy-Fourth Streets. I usually go for the specials when I eat at each of those fantastic restaurants.

Since I work a lot, I'm especially happy that we have such a great chef on *The Sopranos* set. His name is Michael Hernandez and he is a caring and wonderful chef. The truth of the matter is that he will make me anything I want. I can't ever complain about that! Luckily, I have had the opportunity to act in various movies where Italian food is really celebrated. For instance, there were some great food scenes in *Goodfellas*.

When I am not working, and I have the opportunity to cook, I enjoy making a few dishes. My favorite food in the whole world is artichokes. When I was in Italy, I would ask the waiters for *carciofo*, which is artichoke in Italian. I like them prepared any way. I also love nonbreaded veal cutlets with mushrooms and capers. I enjoy fresh Parmesan cheese with my meals. I'm a big caper, artichoke, and garlic girl. I hope that everyone enjoys my recipes!

NEW YORK–BORN Lorraine Bracco made her screen debut in a French-made film while working as an on-air disc jockey for Radio Luxembourg in Europe. That was followed by work with the esteemed Italian film director Lina Wertmuller in the mob movie *Camorra: The Naples Connection*. Bracco returned to New York City and studied at Stella Adler and the Actors Studio. She made her American feature film debut in the 1987 Ridley Scott–directed thriller, *Someone to Watch Over Me*. Bracco's brilliant portrayal of Mafia wife "Karen Hill" in the Martin Scorsese–directed *Good-fellas* earned her an Oscar nomination for Best Supporting Actress. She took her New York persona to new heights as psychiatrist Dr. Jennifer Melfi, who treats Mafia boss Tony Soprano in *The Sopranos*. Bracco's concise, understated portrayal has earned her multiple Golden Globe, Emmy, and Screen Actors Guild nominations for Best Actress in a TV Drama. Her first book, *On the Couch*, will be released spring 2006 by G. P. Putnam's Sons.

STUFFED ARTICHOKES

4 artichokes
1½ cups bread crumbs
¾ cup grated Parmesan cheese
½ cup Italian parsley, chopped
½ cup chopped chives
1 tablespoon grated onion
2 cloves garlic, finely chopped
¼ pound softened butter
¼ cup chicken broth or water
1 tablespoon olive oil

Preheat the oven to 350 degrees. Remove artichoke stems. Cut about 1 inch from top of artichoke, and spread the leaves open with your fingers. Set aside. For the stuffing, combine the bread cumbs, Parmesan, parsley, chives, onion, garlic, and butter. Press the stuffing down among the leaves of the artichokes and across the top. Place artichokes in an earthenware casserole with the broth, and dribble the olive oil over the tops. Cover with foil and bake in oven for 1 to 1½ hours.

SERVES 4

LAMB CHOPS EMPOLESE

COURTESY OF DA SILVANO
260 SIXTH AVENUE
NEW YORK, NY 10014
212-982-2343

■

8 baby artichokes
Juice of 2 lemons (about ¼ cup)
1 cup extra-virgin olive oil
12 lamb chops
½ cup flour
2 egg yolks, beaten
½ cup bread crumbs
Salt and pepper to taste

Remove outer leaves of artichokes. Cut each in half lengthwise and then thinly slice. Cover artichokes with the lemon juice and ½ cup of the olive oil so they don't become black. Put them aside for later.

Heat the remaining olive oil in a pan. Lightly pound the lamb chops, then dredge them in the flour, egg yolks, and bread crumbs, and sauté them until golden brown.

Arrange the chops on a large tray like the rays of the sun, with the bones facing out. Cover the center with the seasoned slices of artichokes, and sprinkle with salt and pepper.

SERVES 4

COZZE E CANNELLINI

COURTESY OF DA SILVANO
260 SIXTH AVENUE
NEW YORK, NY 10014
212-982-2343

■

½ cup extra-virgin olive oil
2 cloves garlic
2 pounds Prince Edward Island mussels, cleaned
3 sage leaves
1 cup plum tomatoes, lightly crushed
½ pound cooked cannellini beans
Salt and pepper to taste
1 pinch crushed red pepper

First, coat the bottom of a pan with ¼ cup of the olive oil. Add 1 garlic clove, and sauté until brown. Add the mussels, and in a few minutes, they will open up. Remove from the heat and, when lukewarm, take them out of the shells.

Brown the other garlic clove and sage in the rest of the olive oil. Add the tomatoes. Cook for about 1 minute. Add the beans and cook for another 5 minutes. Add the mussels and stir with the beans for 3 minutes. Season with salt and pepper to taste. Serve in a bowl, dust with the crushed red pepper, and you are ready to go!

SERVES 4

ROBERT LOGGIA

JUST AFTER MY birth in 1930, my mother, father, sister, and I moved from Staten Island to Madison Street on the Lower East Side of Manhattan. Madison Street was totally Italian in those days. I went to P.S. 1, which has the distinction of being the first public school in New York City. The school had its hundred-year anniversary a few years ago, and it was given a proclamation as the first and oldest public school in New York City by Mayor Rudolph Giuliani. He acknowledged that I as well as Jimmy

Durante went there. The neighborhood back then was a mixture of Chinese, Jewish, and Italian, which was pretty much the same mix at P.S. 1. When I was a kid, ethnic slurs against Italians were very common at school. I remember telling an Italian-American buddy of mine when we were ten years old, "If anybody calls you a 'wop,' let me know." One day, my school pal told me someone called him a wop, and there I was later in the schoolyard, slugging it out with some kid. Luckily, I beat him up. Any ethnic slur cuts very deeply, especially to me because of my deep respect for my Italian background.

My father, Giagio, was born in a small place called Palma di Montechiaro, Italy, and my mother, Elena, was from Victoria, Italy. Both are towns in Sicily and the largest cities nearby are Messina, Catania, and Taormina. I recently pulled up all the records on the computer at Ellis Island and found out what boat my parents came here on, when they arrived in the United States, and how old they were at the time. My father was a shoe designer, a real artisan. When he came over to America after World War 1, which he fought in, he had great praise for this country. My father told me that he emigrated here for one reason and one reason only—to give his children an opportunity. That was instilled in me and it is something I have tried to live up to. My mother came over from Italy when she was three years old. She had no accent, but my father had a very strong Italian accent, which I loved. He pronounced Sunday as "Soonday." Sometimes he would say things like, "behava you self." When my father came home, I always kissed him on both cheeks and said in Italian, "Bless you, Papa." It was a ritual that I look back on with great fondness now. My father met my mother when she was very young. My grandfather never forgave my father because he eloped with her when she was seventeen and my father was ten years older. My mother was a pianist and played beautifully. She was being groomed to be a concert pianist. Growing up, I used to love to sing with her at the piano. Today, I have her picture on my piano in my dressing room, and I sing to her every day. She smiles down at me and I smile up at her.

My mother was one of six sisters. My grandmother, grandfather, and three of her sisters lived on Staten Island, so it was a very extended family for me as I grew up. Due to the Depression years, we always pulled together to survive. We would eat at my grandpa and grandma's house often. My grandfather did not speak a word of English, but that did not inhibit our communication. I remember sitting on his lap and he would give me a small sip of wine. Grandpa would smoke his pipe as we played checkers together. I adored him. It was a very connected, loving, extended family experience. That was typical in the America of yesteryear. Families today do not bond together in the way that they used to.

Unfortunately, I was pretty much kept in the house on the Lower East Side because there were no green fields to play in. So, when we would go to Staten Island to visit my grandparents, it was like being let out of a cage. I always yearned to be there. Then, in 1940, my dream came true when we moved from the Lower East Side back to Staten Island. When we got back there, I soon realized that I was a jock. I played football, baseball, and basketball in high school. Then, I got a scholarship to play football at Wagner College. Eventually, I transferred to the University of Missouri and got my degree in journalism. But, like a lot of Italian-American boys, I was a "mama's boy," and came home to visit often. Even though they are jocks and tough as nails, they still tend to be mama's boys. It happens with African-American jocks too, because they are so connected to their mothers. I am always amused when I see some big three-hundred-pound tackle on the football field waving to the television camera and saying, "Hi, Mom!" It's almost never "Hi, Pop!"

I was very close to my mother, who was a great cook, and I often helped her cook her delicious Italian meals. She made me a homemade apple pie every day, which I loved. I used to drink two quarts of milk with it. I guess that is why I have very strong bones.

My parents thought it was important to instill their Italian heritage in me. However, when I did my first TV show, *Tales of the City*, with Hume Cronyn, my father said to me, "You are never going to get anywhere with a name like Loggia." I responded to my papa, "What last name do you want me to use?" He answered, "Logan." I looked very Italian with my dark curly hair and prominent facial features. Later, Hume Cronyn kept looking at me and said, "My boy, I think you have talent, but is Logan your real last name?" I replied, "No, my real name is Loggia, but my father said I would get nowhere with an Italian name like that." Cronyn then said, "You change it right back." So I realized that I should stay true to my own Italian identity, and I have to thank Hume for that. I am very glad that I changed it back.

Fortunately, I've traveled back to Italy to visit my roots. Once, we were staying at Sicily's Drake Hotel in Taormina, which was one of Sir Winston Churchill's favorite resorts. It turned out to be very snobby and the head honcho there was actually wearing tails—very formal clothing. He asked us what we planned to do on our trip. I said that we were going to visit my father's hometown of Palma di Montechiaro. He looked shocked and replied, "Why would you want to go there?"

My wife, Audrey, who is of Irish descent, and I visited the town anyway, but the guy was right. The place was so run-down, it looked like the town from the movie *Bad Day at Black Rock*. My wife turned to me and said, "I'm scared. Let's get out of here." So we took off and traveled all over Italy and had a wonderful time.

I enjoy cooking. In fact, I do virtually all of the cooking at our house. My favorite dish to make is affectionately called Fried Chicken alla Mama Loggia. It is something my mother taught me as a child. I loved helping my beautiful mama prepare this dish, which is actually a variation on veal milanese. My mother used chicken instead of veal, I guess, because it was cheaper, and, of course, it is healthier. I used to take a slice of chicken to school almost every day for lunch. The Irish kids used to tease me about the grease spots on my lunch bag. I loved this dish as a child and have made it for friends of mine over the years. I cooked it for Henry Mancini. My pal Pete Rugolo helped me prepare it that time. Rugolo, who could write jazz or do entire soundtracks for movies, was one of the greatest composers and musicians of our time. He was born in Sicily, and was also a great cook. I can honestly say that Mancini enjoyed the meal. I like to serve sliced lemon on the side of the chicken. You should start with a nice plain arugula salad with shaved Parmesan and olive oil as a first course, and then enjoy the chicken with a nice Corvo wine, and you will have the perfect meal.

ROBERT LOGGIA'S illustrious acting career has spanned almost fifty years. A graduate of the Actors Studio, Loggia made his film debut in 1956 when he appeared in the movie *Somebody Up There Likes Me*. Early in his career, Loggia became successful through television roles, starring in such popular network shows as *The Nine Lives of Elfego Baca* in 1958, and then receiving top billing as the good-guy burglar in *T.H.E. Cat* in 1967. He went on to feature roles in major movies such as *An Officer and a Gentleman, Curse of the Pink Panther, Scarface,* and *Prizzi's Honor.* He was nominated for an Oscar in 1985 for his role in *Jagged Edge.* However, who could forget Loggia's classic scene in *Big,* where he and Tom Hanks danced on the gigantic keyboard at the world-famous FAO Schwartz toy store in New York City? Loggia has continued to score major roles, appearing in such popular films as *Necessary Roughness, Innocent Blood,* and *The Crew,* and in a prominent role on *The Sopranos.*

FRIED CHICKEN ALLA MAMA LOGGIA

8 boneless, skinless chicken breast halves

3 cups bread crumbs

1 cup Parmesan cheese, grated

1 cup basil leaves, chopped

2 tablespoons oregano

4 eggs, beaten

2 cups olive oil

Pound the chicken breasts to thin pieces. Mix bread crumbs, Parmesan, basil, and oregano on a platter. Dip each breast, one at a time, into the egg and then into the bread crumbs to coat. Heat oil in a large frying pan on high heat. Place 4 chicken breasts at a time into the frying pan to brown quickly. Turn over once only to brown the second side quickly. (Cook about 3 minutes on each side.) Remove chicken breasts to a platter and repeat the same procedure with the other batch of chicken breasts.

SERVES 8

FRANK PELLEGRINO

NEW YORK CITY has changed so much since the days when I grew up in East Harlem on 114th Street. Back then, it was an Italian neighborhood. Rao's, our family restaurant on that street, opened in 1896, and I've been working there for over thirty years. My aunt, Anna Pellegrino Rao, and my uncle, Vincent Rao, really kept it going. They both passed away in 1994, and a cousin of mine, Ron, now owns the place with me. I didn't actually eat there as a child because it was totally an adult hangout back then. The majority of my eating was done at home, and my mother would cook Italian food every night. I loved the dinners on the nights she prepared her eggplant parmigiana or chicken cacciatore. Of course, pasta was always on our "menu" at home. On Sunday, we would have the meat gravy with the braciole, sausage, and meatballs. That was the good stuff.

When I was growing up, most of my friends were Italian, and out of all my friends' mothers, mine was in the running for being the best cook. I want to point out that all the mothers of my friends were very good cooks back then. You could eat at any of my friends' houses at that time and not be disappointed.

I started out my performing-arts career as a professional singer. I was singing pop tunes in places like nightclubs and cruise ships. Then I got into the restaurant business because I had a wife and two kids to provide for and I had to make a real living. I started working at Rao's when I was about twenty-nine years old, beginning first as a bartender before I took over the floor as a manager. The restaurant was nicknamed The Hole because you had to walk down four steps to enter the place. When my aunt starting cooking in the restaurant, word started spreading about how great it was, and the clientele began to change. It wasn't just neighborhood people anymore. When the critic Mimi Sheraton gave us three stars in the *New York Times*, things really picked up and the clientele became "upscale." My aunt was an elegant person, a terrific cook, and an important force in making it all happen for Rao's. She believed in simplicity, which is really the key to good Italian cooking.

I have been acting in movies for over twenty-five years. The first acting role that I had—the one that really got me started—was in Woody Allen's film *Broadway Danny Rose*. The character that Mia Farrow played, Tina, was actually modeled after my own aunt. So that was how I got involved with acting. Then I fell in love with the whole process of the film business. Having been a professional singer prior to that, I found that acting was just another creative facet of the business. It was kind of easy to make the transition and I've never stopped acting. Things in my acting career got better and better, thank God. In fact, they have been really good for the last fifteen years. I loved doing the television movie *Gotti* with Armand Assante, and I loved working with James Caan and Hugh Grant on the film *Mickey Blue Eyes*. Jimmy Caan and I did nothing but laugh and have a really great time together off camera. We had a funny eating scene in that film where Hugh Grant is trying to pretend he's a mobster and it is hilarious. I've also done a lot of acting in television series where I've been involved in food scenes as well. I like to eat in these kinds of scenes because it feels very natural.

I can't begin to list all of the movie food scenes I've acted in. However, I thoroughly enjoyed the scene in *Goodfellas* where we were cooking while we were in prison and I was frying steaks in a pan. In the scene, I asked the character of Vinnie how he would like his steak cooked. He replied, "Medium rare." Then I commented, "Hmm, an aristocrat." The origin of that line is interesting. My father used to love his meat well done. When anyone wanted his meat prepared rare or medium rare, my father would say, "Hmm, an aristocrat." So that was my father's line and it just came to me. If you listen closely to the scene, it is all ad-libbed—all improvisation. It was just perfect. Working with director Martin Scorsese and all the fine actors and actresses in that film was an unforgettable experience.

I also enjoy my role as the FBI agent on *The Sopranos*. That's been marvelous for me and not just because the show has excellent writing and directing, which it obviously has. A key part of the fun is that many of my longtime real-life buddies are on the show—actors like Tony Lip, Vincent Pastore, and Tony Sirico. They are great guys and we always have a lot of good times together. I have known most of the guys on the show for a long, long time. In fact, many of these fine people have been struggling actors over the last twenty-five years. I was happy to see that many of these talented actors that I've known for so many years have had such a great success on the very same show, *The Sopranos*. They all got their careers really moving with that show, and that's made me extremely happy. To me, that's the best part of working on that show.

So I've been in show business for over forty years. There is that creative side of me that loves the challenge of acting—bringing a character to life. The restaurant business is great fun too. I love them both and enjoy them both equally. Rao's has been a major part of my life and my family's life. The restaurant has been open for over one hundred years and I wouldn't change a thing about it. It is this little jewel that is a part of history. Rao's is not about money. It's about southern Italian hospitality and southern Italian food. It's also about culture, tradition, and warmth.

The other wonderful thing about Rao's is that it's given me the opportunity to meet so many incredible people that I may not otherwise have had the chance to meet. Because of Rao's I've been able to develop relationships and friendships that I value very much. It is one of the most rewarding facets of the restaurant business. My son, Frank Jr., is in the restaurant business and has a restaurant on West Forty-Ninth Street called Baldoria. He worked with me in my restaurant for fifteen years. My son went to the School of Visual Arts and is a graphic design artist, but I think he realizes that the restaurant business can be incredibly rewarding and can involve many creative things, if you do it right.

I love to go into the kitchen of Rao's and cook. I like to make anything—traditional dishes like pasta fagiole or a tomato sauce with mushrooms and sausage. I first learned how to cook from my mother when I was seventeen years old. Then, later, I learned from my aunt and uncle. I apply that knowledge in my private life and I also do my fair share of cooking at home. Recently I had some guys over and I made them peppers and eggs. A cousin of mine stopped by the other day and wanted some risotto. So I made some. As I write this my wife is in the kitchen preparing steak, mushrooms, corn, and baked potatoes, and we're going to have that with a nice salad. It's wonderful that we both love to cook. I also enjoy making traditional tomato sauce.

Holidays are still a big deal in my family. However, when my father and mother were alive, holidays were just incredible! Since they have been gone, the holidays have been good, even great, but just not the same. Deep down, I think it's very important to keep our Italian heritage alive. A key to happiness is keeping your home filled with people who are cooking and enjoying each other's company. Out of all of the things I have done in my life, the very best times were at my mother's house with all my family there. We would eat a great big Italian meal and, afterwards, play cards. It was just wonderful, nothing but fun! The beauty of food is that it brings you memories of being some place special with special people and eating together. That's the amazing part of a great meal, and you really must feel compelled to maintain that culture of cooking Italian food together with family and friends.

FRANK PELLEGRINO is on a first-name basis with some of the most famous actors, actresses, and citizens of the financial and political world. First, he's an Italian restaurant owner of renown (he co-owns the popular Rao's in New York City), and, second, he is an actor with more than forty motion pictures and television shows to his credit. When he is not holding court at Rao's, welcoming international guests and overseeing the Italian cuisine at his always packed restaurant on Pleasant Avenue and 114th Street in Manhattan, Pellegrino is emoting in front of movie and TV cameras for some of the most well-known directors and producers of our time. He got one of his first parts in Woody Allen's *Broadway Danny Rose* and the momentum grew. Pellegrino has distinguished himself in mob-oriented films, such as Martin Scorsese's *Goodfellas*; *Gotti,* starring Armand Assante in the title role; *Cop Land; Hitman's Journal; Mickey Blue Eyes;* and *Knockaround Guys*. Rao's Italian sauces and pastas are available in supermarkets everywhere.

STEAK PIZZAIOLA ALLA RAO'S

COURTESY OF RAO'S
455 EAST 114TH STREET
NEW YORK, NY 10025
212-722-6709

■

½ cup vegetable oil
4 (16-ounce) rib eye steaks, trimmed of all fat
2 bell peppers, cored, seeded, and cut lengthwise into ½-inch slices
2 large white onions, sliced
3 cups sliced white mushrooms
1 tablespoon minced garlic
1 cup white wine
1 (16-ounce) can crushed tomatoes
2 pinches dried oregano
2 pinches crushed black pepper
Salt to taste

Using two large sauté pans, heat ¼ cup of oil in each over medium-high heat. Add two steaks to each pan, and fry on one side for 4 minutes or until very brown. Turn and add half the peppers, onions, mushrooms, and garlic to each pan. Fry for an additional 4 minutes.

Drain off excess oil and remove steaks from the pans, leaving the vegetables. Return pans to medium-high heat.

Add ½ cup of wine to each pan and bring to a boil. Into each pan, stir half the tomatoes, a pinch of oregano and black pepper, and salt. Return to a boil. Lower heat and allow sauce to cook for about 5 minutes, or until slightly thickened. (If sauce is too thick, thin with a bit of chicken broth or water, using no more than ¼ cup.) Return steaks to sauce and allow to cook for 4 minutes. Remove from heat. Cut meat from around the bone and slice steak on the slight diagonal, discarding the bone. Place on a serving platter, pour sauce over the top, and serve.

SERVES 4

SHUT UP AND EAT!

ROBERT DAVI

EVERY RELATIVE IN our family came to our house to eat on holidays because they knew we would have the best food and wine. Italian food was very important to my family. My grandparents lived with us in Dix Hills, New York, which was great because my grandmother made delicious food and my grandfather made incredible homemade wine. I used to help him make wine when I was a kid. We'd travel to Manhattan, pick out crates of grapes at the market, and bring them back to Long Island. Then

I would help my grandfather with the process of making the wine—separating the stems from the grapes, crushing the grapes, and so on. I was about six years old when I had my first taste of wine. My parents and grandparents used to put some wine in my cream soda. Unfortunately, it was mostly cream soda! My grandfather had many barrels and used to make gallons and gallons of wine. Also, it wasn't just my immediate family who enjoyed my grandfather's wine. All of our neighbors and even shop owners in our town raved about it. I remember going with my grandfather to the different shops, the markets, and even the local barber. Wherever he brought his wine, the people loved it.

My love of Italian wine grew during my visits to Italy. I love the Sicilian reds and also the red wine from the Tuscany region. Italians have a deep appreciation and pride in serving quality wine. My mother's parents are from the town of Nusco in the province of Avellino near Naples. I own a Neapolitan mastiff, one of the oldest K-9 breeds of dog, which actually came from the hometown of my mother's father in Avellino. My father's parents are from just outside of Palermo, Sicily.

After I moved to California to pursue my acting career, I missed those close family gatherings. Sure, I get together with friends and family today, but I will never forget those close Italian family dinners when I was young. I've been lucky to have had wonderful food experiences on sets during the shooting of a few of the movies I've appeared in. When I acted in *Son of the Pink Panther* with the great Italian actor-filmmaker Roberto Benigni, we shot the movie in the south of France. The film was directed by Blake Edwards and the production was first class. We had lunch outside often on the Cote d'Azur, the beautiful French coast on the Mediterranean, and the chef would make anything you wanted. There was a bottle of red wine on each and every table, making that movie a lot of fun.

When I worked on *Raw Deal* in North Carolina at Dino De Laurentiis Studios, the great Italian producer lived up to his reputation and spared no expense on good food for his cast and crew. Dino had the chef, Giuliano, who now owns a very good Italian restaurant in Beverly Hills called

Trilussa, do all of the catering. Giuliano used to be the exclusive caterer at the De Laurentiis Studios, and he would ask you, "What do you want to eat today?" Working with Dino was fantastic. He's a great producer.

Another fantastic producer that I worked with was the late James Bond producer Albert "Cubby" Broccoli. I played the villain in the 007 film *License to Kill*. Cubby would have great feasts at his house in Beverly Hills. Frank Sinatra, the star of one of my earliest movies, *Contract on Cherry Street*, would be there often. Cubby grew up on Long Island too. In fact, he was born in Astoria, where I was born. So it was an amazing connection, and I really felt very close to him. One night, the Bond writer Richard Maibaum was watching me on television in a movie I did called *Terrorist on Trial*, which was produced by George Englund. Maibaum phoned Cubby and told him to turn on his TV and pointed me out. Maibaum said, "That guy is our new Bond villain." Cubby replied, "I think so too." They called me in the next day to meet with them. However, as the familiar Hollywood story goes, all the big name agencies in town were pushing the "usual suspects" for the bad-guy part. They tried to push Cubby in another direction. Cubby was firm and said, "No, I want to go with the Italian kid." Cubby was amazing and I'll never forget him for sticking with me and giving me that opportunity. That Bond film was one of Cubby's last movies, and I am honored to say that I worked for him. Cubby was a great man.

I like to cook, but I'm also crazy about going out to eat at good Italian restaurants. Near my house, I love to go to the San Carlo Deli. It's a real old-style, old-world Italian deli where they make everything homemade, even the Italian bread. Bread is at the top of my list when it comes to a good meal. What's the first thing they bring out at a restaurant? Right, bread. If the bread is bad, then I'm out of there. I believe that the bread sets the standard for the rest of the dinner. Even with the current low-carb fad, I still have to test the bread because I love eating it. I also enjoy all of Celestino Drago's restaurants and frequent the Enoteca Drago branch in Beverly Hills quite often. When I cook, I love to make eggplant rollatini with a side of broccoli rabe. I hope you enjoy my recipes. God bless!

DIVERSITY IS the cornerstone of Robert Davi's career. Perfecting his acting skills with his mentor, Stella Adler, and later at the Actors Studio, Davi has become one of Hollywood's most recognizable motion picture and television actors. A constantly "in-demand" actor, Davi's big break came opposite Frank Sinatra in the television movie *Contract on Cherry Street* in 1977. Since then, he's gone on to work in film projects with Marlon Brando, Danny Glover, Clint Eastwood, Arnold Schwarzenegger, Bruce Willis, and Roberto Benigni, to name just a few. Whether Davi portrayed one of the notorious Fratelli Brothers in the hit film *The Goonies* or James Bond's Central American druglord nemesis Sanchez in *License to Kill,* Davi's tough-guy persona emerged. Known for bringing reality and depth to his roles, Davi's first good-guy role was as FBI agent Bailey Malone in the NBC-TV show *Profiler.* He is the national spokesperson for i-SAFE America, the most extensive Internet safety program in all fifty states, which is funded by Congress. He is proudly involved with numerous charities like the Exceptional Children's Foundation, the Italian-American organization Unico, and the Heart of a Child Foundation and is on the steering committee of George Washington University's Policy Institute. In 2004, Robert Davi was awarded the Royal Court of the Golden Lion by the Sons of Italy, Western Conference Division. Later that year, he was the keynote speaker and recipient of the Science Education Technology Conference Award, chaired by Congressman Ken Calvert. In June 2004, Robert Davi was also honored with the Los Angeles–based KNX Radio Citizen of the Week Award, for saving a young girl from a fire at her home.

SAN CARLO STUFFED PEPPERS

COURTESY OF SAN CARLO ITALIAN DELI
10178 MASON AVENUE
CHATSWORTH, CA 91311
818-727-0890

■

6 green peppers
1 cup rice
1½ pounds ground beef
3 eggs
1 cup bread crumbs
½ cup grated Romano cheese
Salt and pepper to taste
1 quart marinara sauce
8 ounces mozzarella, grated

Preheat the oven to 350 degrees. Cut peppers in half and take seeds out. Lay in tray. Boil rice for 10 minutes and rinse with cold water when finished cooking. In a separate bowl, mix the meat, eggs, bread crumbs, grated Romano cheese, and rice. Add salt and pepper. Then proceed to stuff the peppers. When finished stuffing, pour the marinara sauce over all peppers. Place grated mozzarella cheese on top of each pepper. Cover whole tray with aluminum foil and bake for 40 minutes. Bake uncovered for the last 5 to 10 minutes.

SERVES 6

EGGPLANT ROLLATINI
WITH A SIDE OF BROCCOLI RABE

2 large eggplants
5 eggs
Salt and freshly ground black pepper to taste
3 cups all-purpose flour
4 cups vegetable oil
2 pounds fresh spinach
1½ pounds part-skim ricotta
3 garlic cloves, finely chopped
¾ cup grated Pecorino Romano cheese
1 (16-ounce) can plum tomatoes with basil
¾ pound shredded mozzarella

Wash the eggplants and cut the tops off. Put the flat end down onto the cutting board and slice the eggplants lengthwise into ¼-inch-thick slices, to make about 16 slices or more. Beat 4 eggs; add salt and pepper to season. Coat each eggplant slice with flour, dip into the beaten eggs, and dredge through the flour again. Heat oil in a large skillet, and fry the eggplant in batches. Put no more than 3 slices of eggplant in the pan at a time, and make sure you don't burn them! You want the eggplant to be a golden brown on both sides; a fork should go through easily (cook about 3 minutes on each side). Remove eggplant from pan and let drain on paper towels. Allow to cool.

Meanwhile, wash the spinach thoroughly, rinsing with cold water 3 times. Bring a large pot of water to boil. Add spinach and cook for only a few minutes, until spinach is bright green. Strain and squeeze out all excess water. Allow to cool. Then combine spinach, ricotta, remaining egg, garlic, and ⅓ cup of the grated cheese in a bowl. Mix well. Add salt and pepper.

Open a can of tomatoes and mash with a masher or your hands. In a baking casserole, place 1 cup of the tomatoes onto the bottom. Spoon 1 to 2 tablespoons of the ricotta mixture onto the wide end of each piece of eggplant. Then roll up each piece and place in the baking dish. Top with remaining tomatoes, shredded mozzarella, and remaining grated cheese. Cover with foil and bake for 45 minutes, until the tomato sauce is bubbling and the filling is hot. Let rest for 15 minutes before serving.

SERVES 8

BROCCOLI RABE

1 bunch broccoli rabe
5 tablespoons olive oil
5 cloves garlic, chopped
1 teaspoon salt
1 teaspoon crushed red pepper
1 cup water

Wash broccoli rabe 3 times under cold water to get the sand and bugs off the vegetable. Peel off outer skin from the bottom up to the leaves, without destroying the top part of the rabe. This will allow the broccoli to cook faster than if you left the skin on. (It's okay to leave the skin on, but cut at least 2 inches off the bottom.) In a sauté pan, bring olive oil to high heat. Add the chopped garlic, salt, and red pepper. Add the broccoli rabe, and sauté on high heat until the rabe turns a dark green. Add the water and when the mixture reaches a boil, lower heat and simmer for 15 minutes, or until fork tender.

SERVES 8

FARFALLE AL SALMONE AFFUMICATO
(Pasta with Smoked Salmon Sauce)

COURTESY OF ENOTECA DRAGO
410 NORTH CANON DRIVE
BEVERLY HILLS, CA 90210
310-786-9236

■

1 pound farfalle pasta

¼ cup brandy

2 cups whipping cream, plus 4 tablespoons

2 tablespoons butter

½ tablespoon chopped shallots

4 ounces smoked salmon

White pepper to taste

3 egg yolks

4 tablespoons salmon caviar

1 tablespoon chopped parsley or chives

Cook the farfalle pasta for 8 to 10 minutes (al dente) in salted boiling water. While pasta is cooking, add brandy to a sauté pan and cook for 2 to 3 minutes on high heat; let the alcohol evaporate. Add 2 cups whipping cream and let it reduce for 5 minutes on a low heat. Put the butter in a saucepan over low heat. Add the shallots and sweat until soft. Then add the white pepper. Sauté for a couple more minutes.

In a bowl, whip the egg yolks with 4 tablespoons whipping cream. Set aside.

When the pasta is finished cooking, drain and toss it into the sauté pan. Add the smoked salmon, sauté for 1 more minute, and then remove from the heat. Add the egg yolks and mix well. Garnish with salmon caviar and fresh parsley or chives.

SERVES 4

SHUT UP AND EAT!

RAY ABRUZZO

IT'S A LONG way from Sicily to New York, but that's where all four of my grandparents emigrated from. My father's parents, Joseph and Josephine Abruzzo, went to the Williamsburg section of Brooklyn, where my grandfather (and, later, my father) sold fish from a horse-drawn wagon. My mother's parents, Antonio and Rose DiFalco, first settled on the Lower East Side of Manhattan, where my grandfather had a liquor store on East Eleventh Street, right next door to the famous Veniero's bakery. I was born in Astoria and grew up in the Rego Park section of Queens, a neighborhood that was ethnically mixed. I lived in an apartment building where my friends were Italian, Irish and Jewish. My father worked two jobs, and even though my mother, Margherita, worked a full-time job, she managed to do all the cooking. And, as an added bonus, my mother's parents lived in the same building. My grandmother Rose, "Nonni," was always preparing Italian dishes that smelled as good as they tasted.

What do I remember most from my childhood? The holiday feasts! The whole family would get together and eat a huge Italian meal that went on for hours. Christmas was always a phenomenal experience, a two-day affair. On Christmas Eve at my house, everybody, and I mean everybody, would show up. Naturally, there would be tons of family members, but even some of the people who lived in our building would come and join the festivities. One of the delicious dishes that we as kids would fight over was my aunt Frances's spiedini (we would literally wrestle for the last piece!). Spiedini is an extremely tasty meat appetizer that just melts in your mouth, and it's well worth the time and care it takes to prepare. The meat would be specially ordered from the butcher, who would slice it paper thin. Then, it was brought home and proudly placed on the kitchen table. Finally, the ritual would begin: Each slice would receive a tablespoon of the family stuffing, ladled on lovingly by my aunt Frances herself; then her husband, Sam Garufi, would perform the tedious task of rolling each tiny piece and skewering it with a toothpick. They actually had to make several trays of these mouthwatering delights to make sure us kids didn't kill each other over not having enough. For us, it was like eating some kind of meat candy! Before my aunt Frances passed away, I was lucky enough to videotape her at the kitchen table describing how she made the spiedini in perfect detail.

On Christmas day, when I was young, we would go to mass and then head into Manhattan for dinner at Jimmy's restaurant in the East Village. The meal was hosted by my mother's brother and my godfather, the Honorable S. Samuel DiFalco, surrogate court judge and founder of New York's famed Columbus Club. Needless to say, there was no fighting over food at this event; my brother, Paul, my sister, Claudette, and I were always on our best behavior.

The times I cherish the most are when I can get together with good friends, relax, and have a good meal. Recently, I was treated to a great evening at Rao's restaurant in Harlem by Frankie Valli, the legendary lead singer of the Four Seasons. (He also plays my consigliere, Rusty, on *The Sopranos*.) Delicious Italian food was brought to our table nonstop. Eating at Rao's is something everyone should experience, *if* you can get in.

During my years on *The Practice*, I had the privilege of acting alongside Michael Badalucco. Michael lives for Italian food and would often do a unique and generous thing for the cast and crew of the show: with the help of the camera assistant, Arthur Africano, Michael would have Italian food shipped from Mike's Deli, located in the famous Arthur Avenue section of the Bronx, right to our set in Los Angeles. It became such a tradition that the owner of Mike's Deli actually came out to the set of *The Practice* and personally prepared what felt like every Italian dish possible. There was an accordion player and even a guy singing Neapolitan songs. With the sounds, the tastes, and the smells, you could swear that you were on Mulberry Street! Thanks, Michael.

To this day, my relatives and I get together on the holidays for a big Italian meal; now it is hosted by my sister Claudette at her home in Santa Barbara, California. In fact, my sister has taken over the helm as the "family chef" and she re-creates the dishes that were passed down for generations. Another one of these traditional holiday favorites is Grandmother Rose's risotto. Now, this is not an ordinary risotto, like the ones I've seen in restaurants; this is a special dish more like lasagna, but made with rice instead of flat pasta. My sister invites the whole family over, and there's still the open-door policy for friends and neighbors. There are always new faces. However, those new faces eventually become familiar faces because the food is so good that they come back year after year! That's the way it was when I was a boy in Queens. Thankfully, my sister and mother have kept the tradition of the family feasts a joy to this day.

Unfortunately, I never made it to Italy until late in my life, a major regret.

That being said, it is now a mission of mine to go back whenever possible and make up for lost time. Traveling in that beautiful country, while sampling foods and meeting people from different regions, is indeed a dream come true—a dream I will continue to pursue.

When I am home in California, there's one particular restaurant in Malibu that keeps me going. Tra di Noi (which in Italian means "between us") is owned by Tarcisio Masconi. His mother, Rosa, comes in once a year from Italy to check on the restaurant and do some special cooking. That's a treat! The restaurant is small, with approximately twelve tables. The owners are from Italy and it's a pleasure to hear this beautiful language spoken in the restaurant when you're dining. Honestly, it helps you to appreciate the food even more. I'm going to give you a very special pumpkin tortellini recipe from Tra di Noi. I am also going to give you my family's secret recipes for spiedini and risotto. As I said before, these recipes have been passed down to my sister from my mother from my grandmother . . . and who knows how many generations before that! Never before have these recipes actually been written down, so let's keep this *Tra di noi.*

Remember, family, friends, and food are the very best things in life!

RAY ABRUZZO is a proud Italian-American actor who has played many varied parts on the stage and the small screen during his long acting career. Some of you might remember Ray as Sergeant Zorelli on *Dynasty*, or Markie Post's lover/husband on *Night Court*. For six years he played Detective Michael McGuire on the popular ABC-TV television show *The Practice*. He is also well-known for his role as Little Carmine Lupertazzi on *The Sopranos*. Ray has guest-starred, or recurred, on many popular television shows like *Murder, She Wrote*, *LA Law*, *NYPD Blue*, and *Law & Order*.

SPIEDINI ALLA NONA DIFALCO

1 (14-ounce) can chicken broth

1 carrot, diced

1 stalk celery, diced

1 cup Italian-flavored bread crumbs

1 cup grated Pecorino Romano cheese

3 tablespoons butter, with extra for broiling

3 garlic cloves, diced

1 large onion, diced

2 tablespoons white wine

1 (16-ounce) can tomato sauce

16 slices spiedini meat from one filet mignon (see note)

16 bay leaves

In saucepan, combine chicken broth, carrot and celery. Bring to a boil and then simmer until all veggies are cooked, about 15 minutes. In a bowl, mix bread crumbs and grated cheese. In a sauté pan, melt butter and sauté garlic and onion until onion is clear. Add cooked carrots and celery from the broth, wine, and tomato sauce, and simmer while using fork prongs to "smush" all the veggies until a thick paste is formed. Add chicken broth and veggie mixture to bread crumbs and cheese mixture, and mix with hands until all ingredients are very moist and stick together. You may add extra chicken broth and tomato sauce if the mixture is too dry.

Lay a dollop of stuffing paste onto each slice of meat and roll. Skewer the rolls onto rounded wooden toothpicks: 3 to each toothpick with a bay leaf between each roll. It's a tedious and time-consuming procedure, but worth it! Lay the spiedini in a single layer broiler pan (do NOT put one on top of the other) with a dab of butter on each roll. Place under the broiler. Since fillet mignon is so tender and paper thin, you broil for only 3 to 5 minutes. Turn over and broil another 2 minutes or so. DO NOT

OVERCOOK! Remove the rolls from the broiler, serve, and stand back and watch the feeding frenzy.

SERVES 8

Cook's Note: Special order the meat from your butcher. Have your butcher slice a *frozen filet mignon roast* into 16 *very* thin slices and then lay the slices between sheets of waxed paper. (The only way for it to be sliced thin enough is to slice the filet frozen.) When you get home, pound the now-defrosted slices until they become paper thin.

The stuffing can also be used to stuff mushrooms.

RISOTTO CON CARNE ALLA GRANDMOTHER ROSE DIFALCO

1 cup olive oil

1 large onion, chopped

15 cloves garlic, chopped

4 slices bacon, chopped into ½-inch pieces

1 pound sweet or hot Italian sausage

1 whole rack of pork ribs, cut into 3-inch-wide pieces

1 pound ground veal

1 pound ground sirloin

1 pound ground pork

1 cup Italian-seasoned bread crumbs

1 teaspoon salt

¼ teaspoon black pepper

3 eggs

½ pound grated Parmigiano cheese

6 (16-ounce) cans Progresso Italian plum tomatoes with basil

9 leaves fresh basil

1½ pounds rice

2 (16-ounce) Polly-O whole-milk mozzarella

1 (3-pound) container of Polly-O whole-milk ricotta

In a very large skillet, add ½ cup of olive oil and sauté the onions, garlic, and bacon. Remove from pan and put the onions and garlic into a small dish. Save for later to add to the sauce. In the same large pan, sauté sausage and ribs on high until well browned. Remove from pan and set aside.

In a large bowl, add the veal, sirloin and pork, and mix together with your hands or a large fork. When the mixture is thoroughly combined, add bread crumbs, salt, pepper, eggs, and grated cheese, and mix well. Form the round meatballs with your hands using a tablespoon to measure. In the same pan that you sautéd the meats in, fry the meatballs until golden

SHUT UP AND EAT!

brown. If it's needed, add the other ½ cup olive oil. Remove all the meatballs and place in a dish.

Place the tomatoes into a large pot and bring the heat to high. Add the onions, sausage, ribs, and basil, and bring to a boil. Lower heat and simmer for 1½ hours. Add meatballs and simmer for 30 more minutes.

Cook rice according to directions on box. While the rice is cooking, cube the mozzarella and take the meatballs out of the sauce. Using a fork, break up the meatballs into small pieces and set aside.

Take the sausage and ribs out of the sauce and place on a serving dish. When rice is cooked, drain and add about 3 ladles of tomato sauce. Mix until all the rice is covered with sauce. If you need more sauce, add another ladle. Add in the ricotta and ½ cup grated cheese, and mix well.

Preheat the oven to 350 degrees. Cover the bottom of a large baking pan with a layer of sauce. Make a layer of rice, a layer of chopped meatballs, mozzarella, and a sprinkle of grated cheese. Cover with a couple more ladles of sauce. Make as many layers as you can until you get to the top of the pan. Add the rest of the grated cheese, cubed mozzarella, and a couple of ladles of tomato sauce. Place baking dish into the oven and cook until mozzarella is bubbly and rice seems warmed all the way through, about 45 minutes. Take out of the oven and let stand for 15 minutes.

SERVES 16

TORTELLONI DI ZUCCA BURRO E SALVIA
(Pumpkin Tortellini in a Crispy Butter Sage Sauce)

COURTESY OF TRA DI NOI
3835 CROSS CREEK ROAD
MALIBU, CA 90265
310-456-0169

■

FOR THE FILLING

2 pounds butternut squash, skin and seeds removed

¼ cup raisins

¼ cup toasted pine nuts

1 cup Prosecco wine

½ pound fresh ricotta cheese

½ cup freshly grated Parmesan cheese

½ pound Amaretto di Saronno cookies, crushed

3 tablespoons bread crumbs

2 small eggs

Pinch nutmeg

Pinch salt and white pepper

FOR THE PASTA DOUGH

3 cups all-purpose flour, plus flour for dusting

3 large eggs, plus 1 beaten egg, optional

Pinch salt

3 large egg yolks

1 tablespoons extra-virgin olive oil

1½ tablespoons milk

FOR THE SAUCE

¼ pound unsalted butter

20 fresh sage leaves, stems removed

¼ cup grated Parmesan cheese

2 ounces Amaretto di Saronno cookies, crushed

SHUT UP AND EAT!

To prepare the filling:

Preheat oven to 375 degrees. Cut squash into 1-inch cubes. Mix squash, raisins, pine nuts, and Prosecco wine in a lightly greased baking pan. Cover with aluminium foil and bake until tender. (This may take anywhere from 25 to 45 minutes.) Remove aluminium foil and let cool. Place cooled ingredients in a food processor and puree until homogenous. Add the ricotta, Parmesan, cookies, bread crumbs, eggs, nutmeg, salt, and white pepper, and blend together.

To prepare the pasta dough:

Pour the flour in a mound in a large mixing bowl or on a wooden or marble surface, and make a well in the center. Sprinkle with a pinch of salt. Break 3 eggs into the center of the well, add the egg yolks and olive oil, and lightly beat with a fork. Use one hand to gradually fold the flour into the egg mixture. When about half the flour has been incorporated, add the milk and continue folding the mixture.

Use both hands to work the remaining flour into the dough. Continue incorporating the flour until the dough just barely stops sticking to your fingers if you press them deeply into the dough. Dust your work surface lightly with flour, and knead the dough by pushing it away from you with the heel of your hands, then gathering it up with your fingers, folding it in half, and turning the dough slightly. Continue kneading until the dough becomes smooth and elastic (6 to 8 minutes), adding the additional flour in small increments if the dough is sticking to your hands.

Roll out dough until it is about ⅛-inch thick. Using a straight-edged pizza cutter, cut dough into 3-inch-wide strips, then cut strips into 3-inch-squares. Place 1 tablespoon of filling in the center of each square. Brush the edges of the square with water or beaten egg, then gently fold the square in half at the corners to make a triangle, and gently press out any air with your fingers. Place the tortellini's folded edge toward you and take the two bottom ends of the triangle and join them together below the pillow of the filling. A drop of water or beaten egg on the tips of the joined ends of the triangle will help them stick together. Cook pasta in boiling water for about 5 minutes or until al dente. Drain and put in a serving dish.

To prepare the sauce:

Melt the butter in a sauté pan, and add sage. Cook until butter turns brown and the sage is crispy. Sprinkle the tortellini with Parmesan, pour the butter-sage sauce over the dish, and then sprinkle with cookie crumbs and serve.

SERVES 6

DREA DE MATTEO

ALTHOUGH I WAS born in Whitestone, Queens, in New York City, which was very Italian back then, we were certainly not your typical Italian-American family of that era. While most Italian-American moms were homemakers in our Whitestone neighborhood, my mother was always working. My mom was a teacher and a playwright, and my father owned a successful furniture company. Eventually, when I was seven years old, my family moved to Manhattan's Upper East Side. I attended private

Drea and her mother, Donna

school and it was very different from our previous neighborhood in Queens.

Both sides of my family are from Naples. My father's family was right off the boat from Italy, but my mother's family has been in America for a long time. In fact, they were "Harlem Italians," because they immigrated to that section of Manhattan first, when they got here from Italy. My mother's side of the family was super Italian American, very "Sopranoesque," which is the only way to describe it. Every Sunday, we had a big Italian dinner with the whole family. Unfortunately, that ritual has dissipated over time. But my grandmother Rae still cooks everything. Her great dishes include sausage and peppers, lasagna, and her very special Genoese sauce, which is insanely good!

As a kid, I had always wondered what the food was like in Italy. Then, when I was seventeen and had just graduated high school, my parents took the whole family to Italy. The quality of the food was very different there. I felt that their food is more like the gourmet Italian restaurants here in America. To be honest, the food in Italy is the kind of Italian food that I prefer. Often, when you speak to New York City Italian Americans, they say that you don't know real Italian food until you've eaten in Little Italy on Mulberry Street in a real mom-and-pop Italian restaurant. That's fine, but it still doesn't compare to the Italian food I experienced in Italy. For one thing, there were lighter sauces used on the dishes. Also, the pizza was very thin. Plus, they didn't serve enormous plates of spaghetti and meatballs or chicken parmigiana. It was a different kind of Italian cuisine, definitely lighter.

My character, Adrianna, on *The Sopranos* truly loved Christopher; I think she proved to be the only character on the show whose love was pure. She didn't know how to take care of herself; she only knew how to take care of Christopher. Adrianna tried to cook for him, but she probably didn't know the first thing about making a good dish of pasta. I remember one particular episode where Adrianna said to Christopher, "I made you cheese dogs." Cheese dogs! So I don't know what the hell she was cooking.

In my own life, I cook and I make good pasta dishes. The only problem is that I don't like to wash dishes, so that stops me from cooking more often. I have a few guilty pleasures when it comes to Italian food. For instance, I could eat dried hot sausage with fresh mozzarella all day long. I enjoy vodka sauce on pasta dishes, and I love melted mozzarella on everything and anything. I also love Italian cheesecake. I like Italian pastries like zeppole, pignoli cookies, sfogliatelle, and the list goes on. But the key to a good meal is often the company you are with. If I could have a fantasy Italian dinner with a couple of Italian actresses, I would love to sit and eat with Sophia Loren and the late Anna Magnani. They are wonderful, legendary actresses. I also really admire actress Isabella Rosselini.

As far as eating out in my hometown of New York City, I love Il Mulino, which is in Greenwich Village. The appetizers are fantastic there. I am also a huge fan of Rao's and go there whenever I can. It is almost impossible to get a reservation. The owner of Rao's, Frank Pellegrino, is known as Frankie No, because he rejects so many people who want a table. Luckily, that doesn't happen to me. You see, Frank is also a fine actor and his character of the FBI agent on *The Sopranos* always made my character Adrianna cry when they were interrogating her, so Frank owes me for making me cry! I also love the restaurant Il Cortile in Little Italy. However, when it comes to pizza, Lombardi's has the best pizza in the whole world. I love it! Lombardi's is located at 32 Spring Street, between Mott and Mulberry Streets in New York City. Their pizza is probably one of my favorite things to eat anywhere in the world.

My family does not have the big Sunday dinners anymore like we used to. Of course, we still have a big meal on Christmas Eve and Christmas Day. My grandmother, Rae, is ninety years old and still cooking all of these meals. Every Christmas Eve, she makes eight or nine courses for thirty people. It is truly unbelievable. My grandmother's something else, and I love her so much. My favorite is her Genoese sauce, which I mentioned earlier. It is comprised of this brisket kind of beef, which is sautéed in onions for hours and hours until the sauce is the tastiest. Then, you put the sauce on top of a nice plate of al dente ziti or penne pasta. I am going to share her secret recipe with you. Also, I would like to give you the recipes for my two favorite pizza pies at Lombardi's. First, there's the pepperoni and onion pie recipe, which is absolutely unbelievable. Second is the recipe for white pizza, which is delicious too! The crust on Lombardi's pizza is so good that after you eat the cheesy part of the slice, you take the bottom crust and dip it in a bowl, filled with olive oil, hot pepper, salt, and garlic. The taste is insane! I love their pizza, and trust me, you're gonna love it too.

BORN IN New York, Drea has always been extremely proud of her Italian roots. A graduate of New York University's Tisch School of the Arts, de Matteo originally intended to be a director, but it was her acting talents that shined through. Movies and television beckoned and de Matteo found herself in front of the cameras. In addition to her featured role on *The Sopranos*, Drea has appeared in motion pictures like *Made*, *Deuces Wild*, *Prey for Rock & Roll*, *Love Rome*, and *Beacon Hill*, before being cast to costar as Gina Tribbiani in the television series *Joey* (the spin-off of the hit show *Friends*). A true entreprenuer, de Matteo also owns Filth Mart, a vintage clothing store in the East Village neighborhood where she lives in New York City. Drea de Matteo won an Emmy Award for her performance in the final season on *The Sopranos*.

Lombardi's Restaurant

SHUT UP AND EAT!

GENOESE SAUCE ALLA RAE

Olive oil, for searing
2½ pounds beef chuck, cut into 2-inch cubes
1 teaspoon salt
1 teaspoon black pepper
2 tablespoons unsalted butter
5 pounds onions, sliced thin
5 garlic cloves, chopped
2 (10-ounce) boxes frozen peas
1 pound pasta

Heat a large Dutch oven with a tight-fitting lid over medium-high heat. Pour in enough oil to fill the pan about ¼-inch deep. Season the beef generously with salt and pepper, and add to the pot. Sauté the meat, uncovered, stirring occasionally, until well browned, about 9 minutes. Add the butter, sliced onions, and garlic, and stir for about 5 minutes. Add the peas and bring to high heat for 3 minutes. Cover pot, lower heat and let simmer for 1½ hours, stirring occasionally. Meanwhile cook your pasta—I like ziti or penne with this dish—and serve with sauce.

SERVES 6

LOMBARDI'S PEPPERONI AND ONION PIZZA

COURTESY OF LOMBARDI'S
32 SPRING STREET
NEW YORK, NY 10012
212-941-7994

■

FOR BASIC PIZZA DOUGH

1 package active dry yeast

1 teaspoon sugar

2¼ cups warm water

3 cups all-purpose flour, and more as needed

2 teaspoons salt

2 tablespoons olive oil

TO FINISH

¼ cup tomato sauce

1 pound fresh mozzarella cheese, sliced into ¼-inch slices

1 pound pepperoni, sliced thin

1 large onion, sliced thin

8 basil leaves, chopped

½ cup grated Pecorino Romano cheese

¼ cup olive oil

Fresh black pepper to taste

For the dough:

Add the yeast and sugar to the warm water in a small bowl. Let dissolve. Combine the flour and salt in another bowl. Stir to mix. Make a well in the center of the flour. Pour in the dissolved yeast and oil. Stir with a wooden spoon or fingers until the dough forms. Turn the dough out onto a floured board, and knead 10 to 15 minutes, adding flour as needed to prevent sticking, until the dough is smooth and elastic. Place the dough in a lightly oiled bowl, turn to coat all sides, and cover with a damp cloth. Place the bowl in

SHUT UP AND EAT!

a warm, draft-free spot for 2 hours, or until the dough doubles in bulk. Punch down the dough, and turn out onto a floured board. Knead lightly.

To finish:

Preheat oven to 400 degrees. Roll the dough with a rolling pin into a large circle and place onto an 18-inch pizza pan. Spoon tomato sauce onto dough, leaving about a 1-inch space around the edge. Place mozzarella over the sauce. Place the pepperoni and onion all over the pie, making sure not to touch the 1-inch edge. Bake for 8 to 10 minutes. Remove from oven and dress with basil, grated cheese, olive oil, and black pepper, and serve.

SERVES 4

LOMBARDI'S WHITE PIZZA

COURTESY OF LOMBARDI'S
32 SPRING STREET
NEW YORK, NY 10012
212-941-7994

■

FOR BASIC PIZZA DOUGH

1 package active dry yeast

1 teaspoon sugar

2¼ cups warm water

3 cups all-purpose flour, and more as needed

2 teaspoons salt

2 tablespoons olive oil

TO FINISH

¼ cup olive oil

1 pound fresh mozzarella cheese, sliced into ¼-inch slices

1 pound fresh ricotta cheese

3 cloves garlic, diced

Salt and fresh black pepper to taste

8 basil leaves, chopped

½ cup of grated Pecorino Romano cheese

For the dough:

Add the yeast and sugar to the warm water in a small bowl. Let dissolve. Combine the flour and salt in another bowl. Stir to mix. Make a well in the center of the flour. Pour in the dissolved yeast and oil. Stir with a wooden spoon or fingers until the dough forms. Turn the dough out onto a floured board, and knead 10 to 15 minutes, adding flour as needed to prevent sticking, until the dough is smooth and elastic. Place the dough in a lightly oiled bowl, turn to coat all sides, and cover with a damp cloth. Place the bowl in a warm, draft-free spot for 2 hours, or until the dough doubles in bulk. Punch down the dough, and turn out onto a floured board. Knead lightly.

SHUT UP AND EAT!

To finish:

Preheat the oven to 400 degrees. Roll the dough with a rolling pin into a large circle and place onto an 18-inch pizza pan. Drizzle dough with olive oil, making sure not to touch the edges with the oil. Place mozzarella all over the dough, leaving a 1-inch space on the edge. Place tablespoons full of ricotta cheese all over the pie, and top with the garlic. Sprinkle with a little salt and pepper and place in the oven for 8 to 10 minutes. Remove from oven and top with basil and grated cheese.

SERVES 4

BURT YOUNG

MY FAMILY CAME a long way from their original hometown of Bari, Italy, to their new home in America, in Corona, Queens, where I grew up. I've been to Bari and really enjoyed myself. They don't eat a lot of meat there but eat more fish, which is a local specialty, probably because they are located on the Adriatic Sea. I didn't like fish when I was a kid, and the only fish I would eat as a child was swordfish, because there are no bones in it. I'd rather grab some bread, dip it in some tomato sauce, and wolf it down. You could say that I'm a big, sloppy eater.

As I look back, my grandmother was a wonderful cook. She used to make a pasta dish with chicken, and the sauce would come out very light. We would all gobble it up. My mother would make the greatest baked chicken in the world with quartered potatoes, onions, and carrots. She still does!

I left my neighborhood and went into the marines at fifteen and a half years old. Quite a bit later, I came back to New York and studied at Lee Strasberg's Actors Studio and got on the path of acting. Back then, I spent a lot of time downtown at restaurants in Little Italy and uptown at Rao's and at other great Italian restaurants in the Bronx.

I eventually moved out to California for my acting career. It was definitely not an easy transition because it didn't feel like New York. It didn't have that tight-knit family atmosphere like the neighborhoods of New York City. However, I did try hard to instill our Italian heritage in my daughter, Anne. When she was growing up, whether it was winter or summer, I would have a sauce going on the stove so that when she came home from school, the house would have an Italian aroma of its own. When my daughter was a child, she didn't like vegetables, so I would disguise the vegetables in my homemade tomato sauce. I would put in peas, asparagus tips, and all kinds of healthy vegetables. She never realized that these vegetables were there. I tried very hard to make all of our dishes healthy. I rarely gave her candy or soda—only once in a while as a treat.

Today, I still take the time to prepare a homemade tomato sauce. I cook it with sausage and pork and keep it on the stove for quite a while. Sometimes, I'll cook a sauce at three in morning. I especially love to have the smell of garlic permeate throughout the house. A few times, I actually woke up my girlfriend at 3 a.m. to ask her to taste it. She would plead, "I'm sleeping and I have to be at work in the morning." I would reply, "I know, but please just taste the sauce and tell me if you think it's good." I love the aroma of a fresh homemade sauce. Making it gives me a wonderful feeling, and that smell can bring back a lot of great memories. I also love a nice glass of wine with an Italian dinner. But the vineyard people would throw me out because I usually put ice in my wine. I like it cold. What can I say?

I have had some major fun with food in some of the movies that I've been

Burt and his lovely daughter, Anne

in. I ate some great calamari in a scene in *The Pope of Greenwich Village*. I was in *Amityville II*, supposedly set in Long Island and definitely not an Italian movie. However, it was produced by the great Italian film producer Dino De Laurentiis. We went to Mexico City to film, and they made it look like Long Island. In one of the scenes, I was eating a plate of pasta with the family. My character gets violent in the script, so I threw the plate of pasta right out of the set window. All of a sudden, one of the crew, a Mexican fellow, stuck his head through the window and had spaghetti all over himself. I felt so terrible, but it was funny. I also really enjoyed appearing in *Mickey Blue Eyes*, which had a lot of food scenes, including the Italian-American wedding scene. It had a great cast, people like Hugh Grant, Jeanne Tripplehorn, and my friend James Caan. Jimmy is a great guy and comes from a wonderful New York family. I also loved working in *Vendetta: Secrets of a Mafia Bride* with Eli Wallach. He is a super actor and a wonderful man who always has a twinkle in his eye. When I worked on the miniseries *The Last Princess*, we initially shot in Italy, and then we traveled to India to finish up. The Italian crew that worked on the movie brought their own Italian food with them, so they didn't have to go around looking crazily for the Italian ingredients. Our crew enjoyed cooking the pasta and sauce themselves. They were smart because it is so easy to carry the staples to make some great Italian dishes. The movie set became a home away from home.

My idea of a good restaurant is when it feels like an extension of your own home. I like to go to a place and feel welcome. New York City has the best creative chefs in the world. It is the mecca of good cuisine. I love Rao's, where

SHUT UP AND EAT!

the Italian food is wonderful. I also like Ray's Original Pizza. The original owner is my close friend and he has a place in Manhattan in Little Italy.

I also love to cook. To me, cooking is like giving affection to others, as well as back to yourself. You are going a step beyond just buying a dinner for guests at a restaurant. To me, cooking is very personal and something I really enjoy doing. My brother and I usually push each other out of the way in the kitchen, because he is a great chef too. We usually cook at my daughter's house when the whole family gets together. It is always a warm and wonderful time.

Now, I want to be completely honest because I've also cheated in the kitchen. Here's what I mean. One night, I was supposed to cook a meal for my family, but there were a couple of prizefights on television and I really didn't want to cook. So, I ran out to the store, bought some baked chicken, potato salad, and tomato salad. I quickly took it out of the packages and threw away any evidence. They ate it and thought I was a genius. That was a real exception because I do love to cook. That's why I want to give you two of my favorite recipes. First is my hearty tomato sauce and second my favorite fish dish. Enjoy!

A MULTITALENTED actor and writer, Burt Young has enjoyed an illustrious career spanning over thirty years. Early on, he appeared in classic films like *China-town, Across 110th Street, The Gambler,* and *The Killer Elite.* However, it was his performance as Paulie in the hit film *Rocky* that catapulted his career to a new level. In fact, Young was nominated for an Academy Award for Best Supporting Actor for his stellar performance in that film. He has gone on to appear in four more *Rocky* installments as well as other hit movies like *Once Upon a Time in America, Back to School, Betsy's Wedding, Mickey Blue Eyes,* and the list goes on and on. As a writer, his credits include motion pictures like *Uncle Joe Shannon* and television episodes of hit series like *Baretta.* Burt Young is a truly versatile actor. He credits his training at Lee Strasberg's Actors Studio as an important influence on his career.

ITALIAN RAGU
(Sunday Sauce)

½ cup extra-virgin olive oil

1 medium onion, finely diced

2 cloves garlic, peeled and left whole

1 carrot, diced

1 stalk celery, diced

2 quarts plum tomatoes, peeled and passed through
a food mill or processor

Salt and freshly ground black pepper to taste

12 to 15 fresh basil leaves

1 pound ground beef

1 pound ground veal

3 slices of day-old bread, crust removed, and cut into pieces

¼ cup milk

2 eggs

3 cloves garlic, finely minced

1 tablespoon finely chopped Italian parsley leaves

⅓ cup grated Parmesan

2 pounds Italian sweet sausage with fennel seeds

4 chicken thighs

1½ pounds lean pork, chopped

8 spareribs

2 pounds rigatoni

In a large sauce pot (8-quart size minimum), heat ¼ cup of the olive oil on very low heat. Add the onion and cook slowly until it has turned translucent. Do not brown the onion, but allow it to almost melt away. Add the carrots and celery and then add the garlic cloves and very lightly cook them in the oil until golden before adding the tomatoes and all their juices. Add salt, pepper, and the basil leaves, and set the heat on low. Allow the tomatoes to cook at very low heat for at least 2 hours before adding the meat.

SHUT UP AND EAT!

To make the meatballs, begin by mixing the ground beef and veal together in a large bowl. Combine the bread and milk and mash together to form a paste; add the bread to the ground meat. Add the eggs, garlic, parsley, cheese, salt, and pepper to the meat mixture. Combine all the ingredients using your fingers to mix uniformly, but do not overmix, or the meat will dry out when cooked. Pick up 2 tablespoons of the mixture, and roll it into a ball shape using the palms of your hands. Do this until you have used all the meat. This should yield approximately 24 meatballs.

Place the remaining ¼ cup olive oil in a heavy skillet and heat over medium heat. Add the meatballs in one layer and brown on all sides before removing. Do this to the remaining meatballs until all are browned. After all the meatballs have been browned and removed from the skillet, add the sausage links and brown well. Brown the chicken, pork, and spareribs. When all the meat is browned, add to the tomato ragu, which has been cooking for 2 hours, and cook an additional hour. Serve the tomato ragu over rigatoni pasta. Serve the meats on another plate as a second course.

SERVES 8

RED SNAPPER WITH VEGETABLES

1 (1- to 1½-pound) red snapper
½ teaspoon salt
¼ teaspoon pepper
1 whole fresh tomato, chopped
1 potato, sliced and preboiled
1 small zucchini, sliced thin
1 small celery stalk, chopped
1 small carrot, shredded
1 onion, sliced thin
1 clove garlic, chopped
1 bay leaf
3 whole sprigs Italian parsley

Preheat oven to 375 degrees. Wash red snapper in cold water and remove fins that might be left by your fishmonger. Cut a piece of tinfoil big enough to hold the snapper and all the vegetables. Place red snapper onto the tinfoil and place all the vegetables and the parsley around the red snapper. Sprinkle with salt and pepper and close the aluminum foil so as to keep all the ingredients tightly inside. Place into preheated oven for 20 minutes. Serve by opening the foil with a knife, making a slit down the middle.

SERVES 2

Dan Grimaldi

I WAS FORTUNATE TO have a lot of extended family around me during my youth. We would all get together often to eat and enjoy each other's company. My mother and my aunt did the cooking. The food was basic Italian fare, but always homemade and always made fresh daily. That was essential. There was a rule in my house that if the food was bought that day, then it was cooked that day. I have carried on that wonderful tradition throughout my life.

When I was a kid, we basically knew what day it was by what we were eating. For example, on Sundays and Wednesdays, we always ate pasta. Monday, it was usually soup, and my favorite was Italian chicken soup, prepared by both my mother and aunt. My mother would buy a fresh chicken at a poultry market, then skin it, and cook it with carrots and celery. Finally, it was served with rice or angel-hair pasta, whichever you preferred. We also ate escarole and minestrone soups. On Tuesday, we always ate veal cutlets. You could eat them plain, breaded, or covered with mozzarella cheese. My house was like a restaurant because you could have the dish prepared any way you liked. On Fridays, we would alternate between fish and pizza. Then, on special holidays, my mother would make homemade ravioli. The dough would be made from scratch, then spread out on the dining-room table. Then portions of ricotta cheese would be placed on it before another sheet of dough was put on top. My job as a kid was to walk around the table with a glass and shape the ravioli. That was a lot of fun! We also had homemade manicotti, lasagna, and baked ziti, which was my favorite. I liked it with a lot of mozzarella cheese. The more the better! Also, on Sundays, we would have fresh pastries, which were bought at the local Italian bakery. My favorite was, and still is, cannoli.

My Italian heritage is very important to me. I was born in the Dyker Heights section of Brooklyn and always dreamed of going to Italy. Luckily, I have been to Italy on four different trips. My family is from Avellino, a region outside of Naples. Unfortunately, I don't have any family still living there. I have to say this, and it's not just because I'm Italian, but Italy is one of the most beautiful places in the world. Also, not only is it beautiful, but it is impossible to eat a bad meal there. The wine is always delicious, and, trust me, there's nothing like drinking real espresso in a piazza in Rome. It's a wonderful experience and something everyone should have the opportunity to do at least once. Also, eating "real" Italian gelato at an ice cream shop in Rome is like heaven on earth. Nothing compares to it! In fact, chocolate is my absolute favorite flavor. I am looking forward to going back to Italy very soon. I love Venice, Lake Como, Sienna, Florence, Rome, the Almafi Coast, and Naples. However, Rome is my favorite city.

SHUT UP AND EAT!

(Left to right) Vince Curatola, Dan Grimaldi, and Joe Ganniscoli, stars of The Sopranos

I feel that visually and emotionally, Italy's the best destination in the world. The pace of life there is much slower and oriented to enjoying life, rather than always working. Hey, who wouldn't enjoy that?

Fortunately, for me, Italian food has often played into my acting career. On *The Sopranos*, we eat wonderfully prepared Italian cuisine all the time. However, since you're working many, many hours on the set, you have to remember to not eat too much at one sitting or you won't be able to make it through the rest of the shoot. Let me tell you, it can be very hard when the food tastes that good. I once did a commercial for Polly-O cheeses and I had to eat baked ziti. I couldn't stop eating it. I must have eaten half a tray of baked ziti by the time the shoot was over! However, when I'm acting in theater, I don't eat for four hours before a performance. I believe in maintaining a very hungry psychology on the stage, both physically and emotionally. I think it makes my performance stronger. Part of the fun of being onstage is going out for a big meal afterwards with your friends, family, and fans. Having a big meal, drinking, laughing, and enjoying the experience that you just had are some of the benefits of live theater. My off-Broadway play, *Six Goumbas and a Wannabe*, was a pleasure, and my fellow actors and I ate many memorable Italian meals after performances. It was always fun.

Speaking of fellow actors, if I could eat one-on-one with one actor, I would love to eat with one of the greatest Italian-American actors of our time, Al Pacino. I loved his work in *The Godfather, Scent of a Woman, Donnie Brasco, Sea of Love*, and *Serpico*. I respect Pacino as an actor and as a person. I think he brings a tremendous sense of intelligence, intensity, and extreme love of his craft to the profession of acting. I admire his work and his ability to continue to excel with his gifts. Dining with Pacino would be the ultimate Italian eating experience!

The world-famous Patsy's Restaurant

I really enjoy cooking Italian food. My favorite is a very simple, but healthy, fried zucchini and pasta dish. It's fairly light, and yet great comfort food. When I am not cooking, I love to go to the world-renowned Patsy's Italian Restaurant in New York City. (This is appropriate because Patsy is the name of my character on *The Sopranos*.) Patsy's is still at its one and only location, 236 West Fifty-Sixth Street in New York City, where the legendary Frank Sinatra used to dine and hang out. The executive chef and co-owner, Sal Scognamillo, makes Italian dishes that are as pleasing to the eye as they are to the taste buds. The atmosphere is very theatrical and the owners are extremely pleasant hosts. They love all people, not just ones from the entertainment industry. Patsy's regular menu, as well as the nightly specials, are always prepared to perfection! I also like the restaurant because it's just like eating at your own home. It's that welcoming, no matter who you are or where you're from.

BORN AND bred on the streets of Brooklyn, Dan Grimaldi has always been proud of his Italian heritage. He graduated from P.S. 201, Xaverian High School, Fordham University (BA), New York University (MS), and City University (Ph.D.), before pursuing a career in acting. Grimaldi credits his mentor, Lee Strasberg, with his love for the craft of acting. He is a lifetime member of the renowned Actors Studio and has always been committed to the New York stage. His performances in various plays include *Six Goumbas and a Wannabe* (opposite Joe Maruzzo and Kathy Narducci), *At the Bottom* (with Tatum O'Neal), *Half-Deserted Streets* (with Michael Imperioli), and *Union Street* (with Armand Assante). During his movie career, Grimaldi has appeared in many popular films including *The Yards* (starring James Caan and Mark Wahlberg), *Men of Respect* (starring Rod Steiger and John Turturro), and *Mortal Sins* (starring Anthony LaPaglia and Brian Benben). He has been equally successful on the television screen, appearing in popular TV shows like *Dragnet, NYPD Blue, Law & Order, New York Undercover, Another World, All My Children,* and *As The World Turns,* and, of course, in his recurring role as mobster Patsy Parisi on the critically acclaimed HBO series *The Sopranos.*

FRIED ZUCCHINI AND PASTA

3 tablespoons olive oil
3 tablespoons clarified butter
3 medium zucchini
2 cloves garlic, sliced
1 cup chicken stock
¼ teaspoon salt
⅛ teaspoon pepper
1 pound pasta (suggest linguini)
1 cup fresh parsley, chopped
Grated Parmesan cheese (optional)

Combine olive oil and clarified butter in a sauté pan over medium-high heat. Slice zucchini into ¼-inch medallions, and fry until golden brown on both sides. Remove zucchini and place into a clean dish. (You may want to use paper towels or napkins on bottom of dish to absorb some of the oil.) Sauté garlic until golden brown. Remove pan from heat and add chicken stock. Be careful as it may sizzle and/or splatter. Return to heat, and add salt and pepper. Let simmer. In another pot, boil salted water and cook pasta according to instructions on box. When pasta is cooked and drained, add to sauté pan with the simmering ingredients, and add fresh parsley and stir. Place the fried zucchini on top and serve with grated Parmesan cheese, if desired.

SERVES 4

Cook's Note: If it looks on the dry side, add more chicken stock and stir.

ASPARAGUS PARMIGIANO WITH BASIL

COURTESY OF PATSY'S ITALIAN RESTAURANT
236 WEST 56TH STREET
NEW YORK, NY 10019
212-247-3491
EXECUTIVE CHEF AND CO-OWNER: SAL J. SCOGNAMILLO

■

1½ pounds asparagus, washed and trimmed
2½ tablespoons butter
½ teaspoon salt
¼ teaspoon freshly ground pepper
¼ cup minced fresh basil
⅞ cup freshly grated Parmigiano-Reggiano cheese

Preheat the broiler.

Place the asparagus in a large skillet in one layer. Add water almost to cover and bring to a boil. Lower the heat to a simmer, cover, and cook asparagus until crisp tender, approximately 5 to 10 minutes (time will depend on freshness and thickness of asparagus). Remove asparagus from skillet and place in a baking pan with ¼ cup of the cooking water.

In a small saucepan, melt the butter over low heat. Drizzle the asparagus with the melted butter, season with salt and pepper, and top with the basil and Parmigiano-Reggiano. Broil for 3 to 5 minutes, or until all ingredients are hot and the cheese is lightly browned.

SERVES 4

SHUT UP AND EAT!

CALAMARI SALAD

COURTESY OF PATSY'S ITALIAN RESTAURANT
236 WEST 56TH STREET
NEW YORK, NY 10019
212-247-3491
EXECUTIVE CHEF AND CO-OWNER: SAL J. SCOGNAMILLO

■

2 pounds cleaned calamari, cut into ½-inch rings
⅓ cup olive oil
Juice of 2 lemons
2 ribs celery, cut into ½-inch slices
20 gaeta or kalamata olives, pits removed
2 garlic cloves, minced
2 tablespoons finely minced fresh basil
Salt and freshly ground pepper to taste

Bring a large pot of water to a boil, and cook the calamari rings for 20 to 25 minutes, or until tender. Drain and place in cold water to cool for 15 to 30 minutes. Drain and set aside.

In a large bowl, combine the oil, lemon juice, celery, olives, garlic, and basil. Add the cooled calamari rings and mix thoroughly. Season with salt and pepper, and refrigerate for at least 1 hour to infuse the flavors. Serve chilled or at room temperature.

SERVES 4

SHUT UP AND EAT!

Pat Cooper

THE ITALIAN CUISINE we eat today in restaurants is considered gourmet dining. We ate the same thing at the time when I was a kid and we considered ourselves poor. We ate peas with pasta, and today it is thought of as eating a gourmet meal. As a child, I used to eat broccoli rabe made with garlic and oil, with onions, sometimes without onions, with spinach, sometimes without spinach, with meat, sometimes without meat, with lemon, sometimes without lemon. I ate so much broccoli rabe I wanted to kill myself! (Now, it's considered gourmet.) Even Chinese restaurants serve it; they put broccoli rabe in the wonton soup. Can you believe that? What we ate years ago was healthy food. We didn't need all the pills and vitamins people seem to need today. We ate the food that our mothers put on the table, and we were all as strong as horses and had a great time. These older Italians who originally came from Italy to America are a wonderful breed of people. They know how to support and feed their families right. I'm an Italian with Italian intestines, and they're just waiting for Italian food to come down there. My father never said, "Let's go get a taco." I believe that's why so many of us are unhealthy today. In one day we are eating Mexican, Chinese, and Polish. If you're of Italian descent, you should eat Italian food, and you'll live to be one hundred years old.

Pat Cooper (left) and Tony Lip at the world-famous Copacabana nightclub in New York City

My mother's side of the family is from Naples; my father's side is from Bari. Italy is a beautiful country and the people there know how to live. I grew up in South Brooklyn, New York. Everybody was Italian and many were dock-workers. They worked their asses off and were great people. The people who came to America from foreign lands and settled here are the backbone of food and culture in this country. When we were kids, if we didn't want to eat what our mothers prepared for us, we were told to go to bed. People today say that they don't want their kids to go through what they went through. What did they go through? We were raised with good homemade food and love. Today you have to practically beg your kids to take out the garbage. When I was a kid, if my dad had to even ask me to take out the garbage, I went out the window with it! Back then, we thought something was terribly wrong with our parents. They were too overbearing. However, I realize today that they were the best thing that ever happened to us.

SHUT UP AND EAT!

When I go out to eat, I always say to myself that my mother made the dish better than the chef at the restaurant. Nowadays, you watch these chefs on TV and everyone thinks they are so great. Your mother and father were great cooks. Did your parents ever have a band in their kitchen? Did your mother have forty-five pots and pans? Did your mother have a guy to clean the dishes afterwards? No! My mother had one knife, one fork, and one spoon, and she made huge Italian dinners. On Christmas, she was up at 4:00 in the morning cooking for twenty people. These guys get up at 3:00 in the afternoon and ask if the garlic has been sliced and if the fish has been cleaned.

I love to cook and I do it exactly the way I saw my mother and father cook. I love to make chicken cacciatori, marinara sauce, broccoli rabe—all the classic dishes. I like anything with spaghetti. I buy a whole fish, clean it, and then save the head and make stock out of it. How many guys do you know who do that? Remember, you do need to have good music on when cooking Italian food. Good Italian music is very important. It gives me a great feeling inside and it makes me proud to be Italian. You should always drink a glass of wine with your food. It is very good for you. Wine is one of the best medicines in the world. Garlic is another one of the best medicines in the world. Once in a while for dessert, I like a nice piece of Italian cheesecake. Really though, my all-time favorite is Italian lemon ice. I am talking about the real McCoy, the type of lemon ice that they used to sell on the street.

I am going to give you my meatball recipe. As I was growing up, every time we came home from church on Sundays, we would have meatballs. My mother made two or three dozen of them. They were delicious, hearty, and healthy. Remember, the meatball is the backbone of the Italian family!

BORN IN Brooklyn, New York, with the name Pasquale Caputo, Pat Cooper has performed stand-up comedy for almost half a century. His subject matter is usually his Italian-American background. Cooper has also frequently appeared in feature films and television shows. His movie credits include *Uncle Scam, Analyze This, Analyze That, Code of Ethics,* and *This Thing of Ours.* Cooper has performed stand-up on the *Tonight Show* many, many times and was a panelist on fellow comedian Colin Quinn's show, *Tough Crowd with Colin Quinn.*

SHUT UP AND EAT!

POLPETTE DI CARNE
(Meatballs alla Pat Cooper)

1 cup soft bread crumbs

3 tablespoons milk

1½ pounds lean ground beef, minced

3 sprigs Italian parsley, finely chopped

2 eggs, lightly beaten

½ cup grated Parmesan cheese

Salt and black pepper to taste

1 garlic clove, finely chopped

4 tablespoons vegetable shortening

½ cup flour

1 cup olive oil, for frying, plus ¼ cup

1 small onion, sliced

1 (16-ounce) can tomato sauce

Moisten the bread crumbs with the milk. Put the meat, bread crumbs, parsley, eggs, Parmesan cheese, salt, pepper, garlic, and vegetable shortening in a bowl, and knead until thoroughly blended. Break off small pieces of the mixture and shape into round balls. Roll them in flour. Deep-fry the meatballs in 1 cup of hot oil, a few at a time, until golden brown. Take from the pan with a slotted spoon and drain on paper towels. Put the meatballs aside, but keep them warm.

In a sauté pan, heat the ¼ cup olive oil, and sauté the onion until it changes color. Add the tomato, salt, and pepper, and simmer for 45 minutes. Drop the meatballs into the tomato sauce, and cook them gently for 10 minutes to let them absorb the flavor of the sauce.

SERVES 6

SONNY GROSSO

ORIGINALLY IMMIGRANTS FROM Naples, Italy, my family always ate authentic Italian food in our household. I was born and raised in East Harlem on 115th Street, right around the corner from Rao's, the legendary Italian restaurant and one of my personal favorites to this day. The neighborhood was very Italian back then and there were a lot of Italian restaurants. However, there was and is only one Rao's.

As far as family life, I remember we would always go to church on

Sundays. Then, the first thing I would do when I got back home was to head into the kitchen, spear a meatball, and eat it. It would tide me over until I ate dinner with the rest of my family. One of my favorite dishes was pasta fagiole, which is macaroni and beans. My mother would cook it in a big pot, and we would eat it a couple of times a week. It definitely wasn't what the rich people were eating, but I loved it. Back then, it was considered "peasant" food. My father died when I was a kid and I had three sisters. So things were tight for us. We ate a lot of macaroni because it was inexpensive. We had macaroni and beans, macaroni and peas, and macaroni and lentils. We had macaroni with everything! My mother also made lots of salad and prepared everything fresh. It never, ever came out of a can. Today, I marvel at all of the things you can buy at the supermarket that you can just stick into a microwave and cook in a couple of minutes. I think if my mother was alive to see that, she would jump out of a window. I'll never forget going to school and seeing my friends' lunches. The Irish guys would have their peanut butter and jelly sandwiches in clean brown bags. My bag would always have an oil stain on it and everybody used to look at me. I would feel kind of ashamed and embarrassed. However, when the kids would have a taste of what I was eating for lunch, all they wanted to eat was my lunch.

I'll never forget the first time when I was old enough to go to Rao's. The very first occasion that I walked in there was when I was nineteen years old. I took my first date to Rao's when I was a young man, still almost a kid. After I became a New York City cop, I went there more and more often. They served great steaks then and they still do now. When Vinny Rao was alive, God rest his soul, I would go there quite often. One time, Vinny asked me, "What do you want to have?" I said, "What are you having?" He answered, "You don't want to have what I'm having, because I'm having pasta fagiole." I said, "Give me a dish of that." Vinny look puzzled and responded, "I don't even know what to charge." I quickly retorted, "Well, charge me what you would charge me for a steak." Vinny said, "You're kidding, right?" I answered, "No, I'm serious." Pasta fagiole reminds me of my childhood and that is why I still eat it to this day. When Rao's started putting pasta fagiole on the menu, it really was a true indication that no matter how much money you make or what station you are at in life, good food is good food.

When I go into Rao's now, it's almost like re-creating my childhood. When I was a kid, I didn't fully realize how important those family meals were; naturally, I'd rather hang out with my friends. Today, I try to re-create those family meals. I have a table every Monday

Sonny Grosso confers with producer Phil D'Antoni on location for The French Connection

night at Rao's, no matter how crowded it is. And since the tables every week go to the same people, you know everybody eating at the restaurant, just like you know everybody in your very own home. When I walk into Rao's, it's truly like coming home and it's a very comfortable feeling. The calmest, safest, and most extraordinary times in my life were sitting with my father, my mother, my sisters, and my aunts and uncles and having a big Italian meal. I guess that Rao's gives me that same feeling of safety and calmness today. I can go to other great restaurants and eat great food, but I can't get that unique feeling and atmosphere. Rao's is special.

There's another beautiful restaurant called Manducatis in Long Island City that has a warm, wonderful atmosphere. When I am not in Rao's, I am eating there. It is a family-owned and family-operated business. The owners are Vincenzo Cerbone and his wife, Ida. They are the cutest little couple you ever want to meet in your life. In fact, Ida is in the kitchen every night preparing the food herself. She is an amazing chef who has won many, many awards. Their four kids even work as waiters and in other capacities in the place. How I first got turned on to the restaurant was when I shot a television series called *Johnny Garage* across the street. The show was about a friend of mine who owned a gas station in Harlem. It was a comedy starring Ron Silver. Ron was the little guy in the TV show *Barney Miller.* His character always wanted to be a detective. Anyway, we went across the street to have something to eat at Manducatis on the first day we were there and I never ate on the set anymore. I enjoy going there because of the family atmosphere and because the food is absolutely fabulous. Ida makes an eggplant appetizer that is truly incredible. Then, for a main course, I will eat salmon. The salmon is always fresh and delicious. Honestly, at the restaurants that I go to, I don't order any food. The food just comes. I've been going to these same restaurants long enough so that I just go in and sit down and they bring me food. It's like coming home. If I have to spend money, I'd rather spend it some place where I know the people than where I don't know the people. There's a little bit of a family-like ritual that goes on when you walk into a place where people know you and welcome you. So, it's just like coming home. To me, if I'm going to go out and have dinner, and I do that a great deal of the time, then I want to be around people that I know and like and enjoy being in their company.

SONNY GROSSO has made the amazing transition from his early career as a respected New York City police officer to becoming one of the busiest and most successful motion picture and television producers in the world today. From a simple, unassuming start as an imaginative Italian-American kid in East Harlem, Sonny never let his humble beginnings prevent him from moving upward in the entertainment industry. His exciting police experiences became the basis for the hit movie *The French Connection,* which garnered Gene Hackman an Academy Award. It was also Grosso's first acting job. His other appearances in front of the cameras include *The Godfather, The Seven-Ups, Report to the Commissioner,* and *Cruising.* However, Grosso's true forte was to be the prolific producer of highly successful motion pictures, television series, and made-for-TV movies. In addition to producing well-rated television miniseries like Dashiell Hammett's *The Dain Curse,* starring James Coburn and Jean Simmons, for network TV, he's produced various series such as *Night Heat* for CBS. Sonny Grosso has the distinction of being the television producer of the works by worldwide top-selling mystery author Mary Higgins Clark. Acclaimed Clark best sellers, like *While My Pretty One Sleeps, Moonlight Becomes You* and *Lucky Day,* have all been produced as television movies under the aegis of Sonny Grosso.

NEAPOLITAN-STYLE EGGPLANT APPETIZER

COURTESY OF MANDUCATIS
1327 JACKSON AVENUE
LONG ISLAND CITY, NY 11101
718-729-4602
EXECUTIVE CHEF AND CO-OWNER: IDA CERBONE

■

8 plum tomatoes, chopped

3 fresh basil leaves

Salt and pepper to taste

1 eggplant

2 eggs, lightly beaten

1 cup extra-virgin olive oil

1 teaspoon parsley, chopped

2 cloves garlic, chopped

¼ cup Parmesan cheese, freshly grated

Place tomatoes, basil, salt, and pepper in a saucepan and bring to a boil. Lower heat and simmer for 20 minutes while you fry the eggplant.

Slice the eggplant very thin. You should get 12 slices from one average-size eggplant. Dip eggplant into egg and then fry in olive oil until golden brown. Place eggplant on paper towel to drain.

Preheat oven to 400 degrees. When the sauce is finished, place 1 tablespoon of sauce in the center of each piece of eggplant, and fold in top and bottom. Place into a baking dish, and put a small amount of sauce over the folded eggplant. Sprinkle on Parmesan, and bake for 10 minutes.

SERVES 4

SALMON ALLA MANDUCATIS

COURTESY OF MANDUCATIS
1327 JACKSON AVENUE
LONG ISLAND CITY, NY 11101
718-729-4602
EXECUTIVE CHEF AND CO-OWNER: IDA CERBONE

■

4 (½-pound) salmon pieces
2 tablespoons bread crumbs
Salt and freshly ground black pepper to taste
1 cup sliced shitake mushrooms
1 cup sliced scallions
2 tablespoons olive oil
½ cup dry white wine

Place the 4 pieces of salmon into a baking dish and salt both sides. Broil salmon 3 to 4 minutes (depending on thickness). Sprinkle the bread crumbs, salt, and black pepper on top. Spread the mushrooms and scallions on the salmon pieces. Splash the olive oil and white wine on top of the salmon. Brown for 2 more minutes under the broiler.

SERVES 4

*Ida and Vincenzo Cerbone,
owners of Manducatis*

SHUT UP AND EAT!

VINCENT PASTORE

WE DIDN'T HAVE much food in my house when I was a child because we were very poor. But my mother, God bless her soul, made sure we were fed right. I was born in the Bronx and then we moved to New Rochelle, New York. I went into the navy at a young age and then afterward came back home to New Rochelle and ran nightclubs for quite a while. Then, I decided to give acting a try by first getting involved in community theater. I gave up the nightclub business completely, got a job as a limo driver, and went all-out to achieve my dream of becoming a professional actor. My first film role was in a movie called *True Love,* starring Annabella Sciorra. Then I appeared in many films and TV shows over the years. Of course, after playing Big Pussy on *The Sopranos,* things in my career really took off.

Nowadays, when I am not acting, I love to cook. In fact, I came up with the recipe for my Pastore's Pasta one day when I was just foolin' around in my kitchen. It's a great fish and pasta combination. In fact, I like fish with almost anything! Hey, do not accept any fugazis. Get the real thing! The genuine Pastore's Pasta can only be made with the ingredients that I've personally listed. This dish is great with a nice fresh Caesar salad. As far as wine is concerned, you gotta have this dish with a chilled white Pinot Grigio. I also enjoy a hearty Merlot or Cabernet, depending on what type of meal I'm eating.

Like most actors in this book will tell you, we work long hours, so I often eat out at my very favorite restaurant in New York City, which is, not surprisingly, Rao's! The food is second to none, believe me. For dessert, you've gotta head downtown to Ferrara's in Little Italy for Italian pastries that are out of this world!

When I think about food in the movies, my favorite Italian food scene is the one from *Goodfellas* featuring Martin Scorsese's real-life mother, Catherine, cooking for her son (played by Joe Pesci) and his mob pals in her home in the middle of the night. I like that scene because there is a great mix of realistic dialogue and humor. But I still think that the most realistic portrayals of food are in *The Sopranos.* They've got it down absolutely right! I personally love to act and I love to eat Italian. So to do both on-screen and get paid for it is a dream come true!

BORN IN the Bronx, Vincent Pastore, who is best known for his unforgettable role as Salvatore "Big Pussy" Bonpensiero on *The Sopranos*, started his professional life in the nightclub business in New Rochelle, New York. Pastore successfully ran and owned nightclubs from 1967 to 1987. When he decided to pursue acting, Pastore studied at HB Studio for about two years and, later, studied with Tommy Waits from the Actors Studio. Like all aspiring actors, he had the usual array of jobs to support himself as he went on auditions, including being a limo driver. Pastore worked hard at his craft, persevered, and made an impact in a variety of roles. Whether it's parts in feature films like *Mickey Blue Eyes* (starring Hugh Grant and James Caan), *Made* (with Jon Favreau and Vince Vaughn), and *Serving Sara* (Matthew Perry and Elizabeth Hurley) or TV films like *Gotti* (Armand Assante), *The Last Don* (with Danny Aiello), and *Witness to the Mob* (with Nicholas Turturro and Tom Sizemore), Pastore has always turned in memorable performaces. His most recent film credits include *This Thing of Ours, A Tale of Two Pizzas, The Cookout,* and *Shark Tale,* plus TV roles on hit shows like *The Practice*. In early 2004, Pastore launched his radio program, *The Wiseguy Show*.

PASTORE'S PASTA

1 pound linguini (Ronzoni brand preferable)
1 pound fresh codfish
½ cup olive oil
4 tablespoons anchovies, chopped
2 teaspoons fresh parsley, chopped

Cook linguini according to package directions, drain, and keep hot. Meanwhile, cut cod into large chunks. Heat skillet until it's hot and add oil. Then sauté anchovies and cod on high heat for 3 to 4 minutes. Do not stir the cod (it will fall apart). Turn down heat and simmer for another 5 to 10 minutes. Pour seafood mixture over pasta. Sprinkle with parsley and serve.

SERVES 4

DIANE VENORA

WHAT I LIKE most about cooking is that it brings people together. When my guests come over to eat, there's an understanding that they have to help in the kitchen. One person will chop the lettuce, someone else will make the dressing, someone else will chill the wine, another guest will open and pour the wine, and so on. Everyone has to be a part of the preparation because that's where the best conversation actually happens. Making food is always about family, love, and conversation. The center of the family is always around the meal. Growing up, we never ate alone, but always ate as a family. My father insisted that nobody eat dinner until he was home from work. Today, when people just grab something quick to eat, they miss the heart of what life and family are about. The kitchen is my favorite room in the house. When I have a house built, I always make the biggest room the kitchen.

I stayed with my grandparents often as I was growing up. They are both from Italy and believed in eating well. I grew up in Hartford, Connecticut, but my grandfather built a beautiful home in Bloomfield, Connecticut. At my grandparents' Connecticut home, they had a farm and raised all of their own vegetables, chickens, and livestock. My grandfather grew olives and even made his own wine. My grandmother prepared everything home-made, including her own pasta. She made linguini, lasagna, and spaghetti — all cut by hand. She would cut the spaghetti using a sharp knife and then dry it on racks, just like they did in the old country. Today, we have pasta machines, but we didn't back then. I remember watching my grandmother make that pasta for hours. My grandfather wouldn't tolerate any food that my grandmother didn't make. In my grandparents' house nothing was bought in a store, except toilet paper.

The women in our family have a strong musical tradition. My aunt Rose sang at the Metropolitan Opera and my aunt Lee sang at the New York City Opera. All the women sang. My grandfather didn't approve and often said, "Everybody in Italy sings. What is so special about that?" Grandpa was from the old school and believed that you have to do something in life so that you could survive if there was a war. He felt that singers don't survive. So his children became bricklayers, electricians, and hairdressers. (Like if there was a war, people would rush to get their hair done!) My uncle Dan was drafted by the Brooklyn Dodgers, and Grandpa would not let him play. He was very talented and one of the first draft picks. My grandfather thought you were being a little kid if you played ball your whole life. I wanted to be a hairdresser, but my father wouldn't let me. He wanted me to go to college. I said, "Why do I have to go? Nobody else in our family went to college." He replied, "I know, and that's exactly why you're going." I went to college and somebody suggested I audition for the acting school at Boston Conservatory. I did, was accepted, and went for a year and a half. I liked drama and a friend told me at the time that Juilliard was the best school for drama. I applied to Juilliard and was fortunate to receive a scholarship.

I come from a large family, so holidays have always been glorious events. When I was a kid, on Thanksgiving there were about forty people in the dining room! You started out with a pastina soup made out of turkey broth. Then came the antipasto with peppers, meats, olives, etc. Next, we would have some of my grandfather's homemade red wine, which I always thought tasted like it was going to kill you. Then Grandma brought out some fried baccala and after that we would have a pasta course. Finally, we would have the bird with all the stuffing and trimmings. After that, we would eat every Italian dessert you could think of—cannoli, tiramisu, cheesecake, sfogliatelle. We would also have Easter bread, which was a tradition. Then we would wash it down with a coffee, espresso, cappucino, amaretto, and grappa. After that, you would be sick and lie down.

Right now, here in Southern California, I have an Italian family from Sicily that I am with all the time. The parents are Vincenza and Joe and I met them because their son, Anthony, was my gardener. I was very ill one year and Vincenza came to my home with her homemade chicken soup from Sicily. She didn't speak English very well, but she sat next to my bed and fed me this soup and got me well. From that time five years ago, she became my friend for life. I am with her through illnesses, marriages, and birthdays, and she is the best! Vincenza's like my mother, grandmother, angel, and confidante all rolled into one. I can tell her anything because she is real and is very religious. She goes to church and prays and has been married to the same man for fifty years. I adore her. My Italian heritage is so important that when I found this family, I felt right at home. I say to Vincenza, "Please don't die; please don't die. Where will I go then to feel like I'm home?" I go to her house when I have problems in my life and she always says to me, "You may cry today, but joy comes in the morning." She gives me a little salad and soup and she tells me to eat because it will make me feel better. And you know what? It does.

SHUT UP AND EAT!

I want to give you my recipe for Vincenza's chicken soup, which I promise will make you feel better no matter what the trouble or ailment is! I am also going to give you my recipe for chicken cutlets, Italian-style. Now, I want to tell you something important that I learned from my grandfather. He was a very generous man. When a family came over from Italy, he would give them big bushel baskets of eggplants, peppers, tomatoes, and pasta. He had huge beautiful roses growing in the backyard. He would give them roses as well as carnations, mums, and whatever beautiful flowers were growing at the time. I remember my grandmother would say to my grandfather in Italian, "Why do you give so much away?" He replied, "If you give away, you will never be without." So, remember to always give.

DIANE VENORA was born and raised in Hartford, Connecticut. After studying drama and graduating from the world-famous Juilliard School, Venora went on to a career on the stage. She performed in numerous Shakespearean productions, and in 1983 she had one of the lead roles in John Papp's production of *Hamlet* at the New York Shakespeare Festival. Venora received a Golden Globe nomination for her role as Chan Parker in Clint Eastwood's film *Bird*, the biographical feature about the jazz genius Charlie Parker. She has appeared in a steady stream of top films during her career like *The Cotton Club*, *F/X*, *Ironweed*, *Romeo & Juliet*, and *The 13th Warrior*. In acclaimed director Michael Mann's hit film *Heat*, Venora played Al Pacino's wife and gave a very powerful performance as a woman caught in a troubled marriage. She worked with Mann again on *The Insider*, starring Russell Crowe and Al Pacino. Diane Venora is a member of the Ensemble Studio Theatre and the Circle Repertory Company.

CHICKEN CUTLETS, ITALIAN-STYLE

6 organic chicken cutlets

2 cups all-purpose flour

2 eggs, beaten

1 cup panko bread crumbs (very fine Japanese bread crumbs)

Kosher salt to taste

Freshly ground pepper

1 cup olive oil

½ stick unsalted butter

1 (26-ounce) jar of your favorite marinara sauce

Fresh grated Parmigiano cheese

Pound the chicken cutlets between plastic wrap until very thin. Set up 3 bowls, one with the flour, one with the eggs, and one with the panko bread crumbs seasoned with salt and pepper. Take 1 chicken cutlet and place into the flour on one side and then the other; shake off excess flour. Place the chicken cutlet into the egg and then into the panko bread crumbs.

Heat the olive oil and butter on high heat until butter melts, and then lower heat to medium. Wait a few minutes for the oil to cool, and then place 3 cutlets at a time, or as many as will fit, into the frying pan. Fry on one side for 2 minutes and then on the other side for 3 minutes. Take chicken cutlets out of the pan and place onto paper towels to let the excess oil drip out. When all the cutlets are finished, heat your marinara sauce, place each cutlet onto a plate, and put a couple of spoonfuls of the tomato sauce on top of the chicken cutlets. Add the Parmigiano, and serve with your favorite pasta.

SERVES 6

VINCENZA'S CHICKEN SOUP

6 quarts water
1 whole chicken, cut into 8 pieces
6 carrots, cut into ½-inch pieces
1 bunch Italian parsley, chopped
1 white onion, chopped
8 to 10 stalks celery, chopped
Pinch dried oregano
3 leaves fresh basil, chopped
Salt and pepper to taste

Fill an 8-quart pot with the water, add the chicken, and bring to a boil. When the scum from the chicken comes to the top, skim it off. Place the carrots, parsley, onion, celery, oregano, and basil into the pot and bring to another boil. Add salt and pepper. Reduce heat to low and let simmer for 1½ hours. The soup can be served by itself or over small pasta shells or rice.

SERVES 8

TONY SIRICO

I CAME FROM A poor Brooklyn family of Italian descent. We may have been poor when it came to money, but we were rich as far as love goes. Because of our financial situation, my family was more peasant fed. I ate a lot of pasta fagiole, lentils and macaroni, and I loved it. I love those dishes to this day, and it seems that a lot of other Italian Americans love them too. Eating a good home-cooked meal was important to me, and, believe me, my mom made a great sauce. On Sundays, it was macaroni with the meatballs and braciole. I couldn't wait for those Sunday meals!

I grew up in the Midwood section of Brooklyn on Coney Island Avenue between Avenue J and Avenue K. Woody Allen used to live around the corner from me on Fourteenth Street and he used to play baseball with us. He played second base for the older guys of the neighborhood. Believe it or not, Woody had a good glove. He was a fine ballplayer with a very quick hand. It was a sincere pleasure to have acted in numerous Woody Allen films before I got cast on *The Sopranos*.

Food on holidays was always wonderful. My mom did the big dinner on Christmas day with lasagna and other good things. Everything was delicious and very much like the traditional holiday menus of most other Italian families from my neighborhood. On Christmas eve, we would have fish. I loved lobster. I also was a crabber and enjoyed providing crabs for those holidays. I would crab for blue claw and then I would bring them home to eat. If I didn't catch any, we would buy some crabs at the market. I only ate the claws when I was a kid.

Michael Imperioli and Tony Sirico taking a stroll

SHUT UP AND EAT!

I'm glad that I've been part of some classic Italian food scenes in *The Sopranos*. I've done some food scenes where I have actually filled my plate many times over because the prop food was that good. In one *Sopranos* dinner scene, I stuffed myself with braciole so much that every time I had to say a line, I lifted my face up and my cheeks were stuffed like a chipmunk's. I was busy chomping away on the food, which was so outstanding, that I'd get preoccupied with what was on my plate.

I don't really remember a lot of food scenes from the other movies that I've appeared in. However, I do recall killing a lot of people! But, there are some great food scenes in other movies. I remember watching *Goodfellas* when the guys were cooking up a storm in jail. They had mozzarella and lots of delicious meats and Paul Sorvino's character was cutting the garlic with a razor blade. It was great to see that those guys had a sense of their freedom and humanity, through their food, even though they were serving time. They spent a few dollars here and a few dollars there, got a little creative, and it was like a meal they would eat at home. Hey, they even had a bottle of wine to boot! These guys were relaxing in their robes and slippers just like they were in their own kitchens. They even cooked the steaks in pans because they didn't have a broiler. Those guys were inventive.

I think I got my love for cooking from watching my mom cook for all of those years. Then, when I moved out and lived by myself, I started experimenting in my own kitchen. I don't know if it's in the genes, or if it's from me just watching Ma at the stove and loving the way the food tasted. Whatever it was, I still love to cook to this day. In fact, I cook every day. I like it better than eating out because I truly like the taste of my own food. Occasionally, I will eat out. When I do, I like to have a steak in one of the nice New York City steakhouses that take pride in quality food. My favorite is called the MarkJoseph Steakhouse on Water Street in the South Street Seaport area of Manhattan. They serve the greatest steak. They also serve five or six lamb chops prior to the steak that taste so delicious that you think you died and went to heaven! I was there a few weeks ago with John Franco from the Mets and a few other guys and we had a great meal, as always. On occasion, I will have dinner here in New York at Il Cortile in Little Italy, Campagnola on the Upper East Side, or Rao's on 114th Street. These three restaurants have a lot of the "Italian peasant taste" in their food and that is close to my heart. It is plain and simple, but very delicious. The chef at Il Cortile is terrific. I suggest that you go there in the afternoon on a sunny day because they have a skylight that allows the sun to shine right into the middle of the room. Go and enjoy yourself!

The recipe that I'd like to offer is my marinara sauce. I call it Sirico's Sauce and it is positively delicious. I love it with a nice dish of spaghetti. Some people use wine when preparing their tomato sauce, but I don't. Here's what I like to do. I usually start by frying some garlic in olive oil until the garlic gets a little brownish. Then, I pour just a little bit of balsamic vinegar in and let it absorb right into the garlic and the oil. About two seconds after that, I pour it in the pot and then I put my sauce in. I stir that a little bit. Then, I spread some nice, fresh whole basil on top. Combine those ingredients with the balsamic vinegar and it's pure magic. You follow my recipe exactly, and, believe me, you'll thank me for the rest of your life.

BORN IN New York City, Tony Sirico has brilliantly portrayed "Paulie Walnuts" on the Emmy Award–winning television series *The Sopranos*. In a career spanning over thirty years, he initially appeared in *Crazy Joe,* starring Peter Boyle, in 1974. Sirico has frequently been cast as a supporting actor in various Woody Allen movies, including *Bullets Over Broadway, Mighty Aphrodite, Everyone Says I Love You,* and *Celebrity.* Sirico succeeded in parlaying his gritty screen persona into an extensive acting career, with featured roles in major motion pictures like *Goodfellas, Cop Land,* and *Mickey Blue Eyes.*

SIRICO'S SAUCE
(Simple Tomato Sauce)

2 tablespoons extra-virgin olive oil

5 cloves garlic, chopped

2 tablespoons balsamic vinegar

1 (16-ounce) can Italian imported plum tomatoes

1 tablespoon salt

1 teaspoon freshly ground black pepper

8 basil leaves

Place olive oil into a saucepan and bring to high heat. Place garlic into pan and sauté until lightly golden brown. Add vinegar and sauté for 1 minute. Put all the other ingredients, except the basil, into the pan and bring to a boil. Then lower heat and simmer for 20 minutes. Just before serving, add basil leaves. Serve with your favorite pasta.

SERVES 6

JOSEPH R. GANNASCOLI

WHEN I WAS a kid, Sundays and Wednesdays were always pasta nights. My mother cooked some good Italian meals, but she was not a chef by any means. However, I did become a professional chef. I'm not sure what originally made me get into the field of cooking, but I've always enjoyed it. As a chef, I am self-taught. For approximately the last twenty-five years, I've been involved with the food and restaurant business in some capacity. My first job was at a restaurant called Manhattan Market, where they served French-American nouvelle cuisine, which was all the rage in the early 1980s. I worked at numerous restaurants in Manhattan, doing prep work in the kitchen, before I left my hometown of Brooklyn and moved to New Orleans, where a friend of mine was living. I got a job at Commander's Palace, one of the most famous restaurants in New Orleans. World-famous chefs like Paul Prudhomme and Emeril Lagasse got their starts there. I was in that environment, working and living for two years, until I decided to come back to my New York roots. When I returned, I got a chef's job in Brooklyn at a restaurant called Nightfalls. Then, I decided to open a few of my own restaurants in the Bay Ridge section of Brooklyn. Following that, I ceased my restaurant endeavors and moved to Los Angeles to pursue acting.

You would think that a big guy like me would be considered unique lookswise in Hollywood, but that wasn't the case. There were a lot of slugs walking around who looked just like me. However, I was definitely unique personality-wise and that's what separated me from the pack. Actually, I didn't give up the restaurant business completely or my love of cooking altogether when I moved to Los Angeles. In fact, I worked in a few restaurants in LA as a cook so I could pay my bills while I was trying to make it as an actor. However, the acting part of my life was not moving as quickly as I would have liked. I was working with a guy who acted as my agent, but I quickly realized that he wasn't sending me out on enough casting calls. I would stop by his apartment and look at the TV and film breakdowns (the list of upcoming auditions), and I got upset when I saw good roles that I should have been sent to audition for. Since he wasn't on the ball, I had to make my own plan. I knew that he got the breakdowns delivered to his apartment very early in the morning. So I would show up there at the crack of dawn after they were delivered. I would take them, make photocopies, and then drop the breakdowns back off at his place before he even knew they were missing. Then I would submit myself for acting jobs. I'd also follow up with bogus phone calls, posing as my own manager. Much to my surprise, I started getting myself many auditions. In fact, I became so successful that I even started doing it for my friends. That's how I got my first few acting roles.

SHUT UP AND EAT!

Sopranos stars Federico Castelluccio and Joe Gannascoli

I was in Los Angeles for four years before deciding to return to New York. I continued to act in New York and started getting some good television and movie roles, eventually landing a solid gig on *The Sopranos*. However, I haven't had the opportunity yet to cook in any acting scene. I would really like to do it because I have some good chopping skills. When I watch a movie or TV show and there is a cooking scene, I pay very close attention to it. I can tell right away if an actor or actress is a cook by the way he or she chops and sautés the food. It's hard for an actor or actress to do it correctly if he or she hasn't practiced it for quite some time. It truly takes practice. A dream of mine is to do a "food movie," and do it right in the same vein as *Eat Drink Man Woman; Babette's Feast; The Cook, The Thief, His Wife & Her Lover;* and a few other very select films of this genre. Those were beautiful movies and captured food correctly.

I love going back to my old Brooklyn neighborhood. I grew up on Gravesend Neck Road and Avenue U. It was a very Italian neighborhood with some great Italian pork stores and cheese stores. Joe's of Avenue U is still around and makes the best vastedda, which is a true Sicilian specialty. There are only a couple of places in all of New York that make this. It's basically the meat of a cow spleen baked on a roll, with ricotta and grated cheese. I grew up around the corner from Joe's and I am glad it's still there. Joe's prepares all genuine Sicilian specialties. When I was growing up, a vastedda sandwich used to be thirty-five cents; now it is $2.75, which is still reasonable. I like eating that particular sandwich because it brings back so many memories from my childhood. In fact, I want to give some special recipes for this book that will create great food memories for everyone reading it. The first recipe is for a delicious appetizer I recently came across when I hosted a party for the final episode for the fifth season of *The Sopranos*. We had the food catered from a fine Staten Island restaurant called Marina Café. The appetizer was an Italian egg roll, which is very unique. The egg roll was stuffed with risotto, broccoli rabe, sausage, and roasted peppers. It was delicious. Everybody really liked it. The next two recipes are signature pasta dishes of mine. I helped start a restaurant in 1990 called 101 in the Bay Ridge section of Brooklyn. In fact, the restaurant is still up and running and the rigatoni dish that I created is still the number one dish on the menu. It is rigatoni pasta with prosciutto, shitake mushrooms, arugula, smoked mozzarella, onions, garlic, olive oil, and white wine. I created the dish completely off the cuff. The next pasta dish that's great at 101 is a spinach fettuccine with roasted peppers, asparagus, and grilled chicken, all combined in a delicious marsala cream sauce. My forte happens to be making sauces and I really like doing it. It comes from my background in French cooking. I think the varied colors in both of those pasta dishes are really nice and the dishes are a lot of fun to make.

BORN AND raised in Brooklyn, Joe Gannascoli went from being a chef and restaurant owner to becoming an actor. After working in top restaurants in various cities in the United States, Gannascoli pursued his dream of becoming an actor with his own special brand of inventiveness and determination. Television audiences across the world know him from his recurring role as mob guy Vito Spatafore on *The Sopranos*, but he also has many top feature films to his credit. Gannascoli appeared in *Ed Wood* (directed by Tim Burton and starring Johnny Depp), *Basquiat* (with Jeffrey Wright and Benicio Del Toro), *Mickey Blue Eyes* (with Hugh Grant, James Caan, and Jeanne Tripplehorn), and television productions like *Law & Order*.

ITALIAN EGG-ROLL

COURTESY OF MARINA CAFÉ
154 MANSION AVENUE
STATEN ISLAND, NY 10308
718-967-3077
EXECUTIVE CHEF: MICHAEL PELUSO

■

1 cup olive oil, plus a little for frying the sausage
1 pound sausage, casings removed, and chopped
2 cups chicken stock
1 cup Arborio rice
1 bunch broccoli rabe, washed 3 times in cold water and chopped
½ pound sun-dried tomatoes, chopped
1 cup diced onion
Salt and pepper to taste
12 squares egg roll dough (can be purchased at your local market)
1 egg, beaten

Add a bit of olive oil to a frying pan and sauté sausage on high heat, until brown on all sides, about 10 minutes. After sausage is cooked, remove with a slotted spoon and set aside.

In a pot, bring chicken broth to a boil and add rice. Constantly stir the rice with a rubber spatula until it has a creamy texture.

Cook broccoli rabe in 1 cup of boiling water until soft, about 15 minutes.

Place sun-dried tomatoes into the pot with the broccoli rabe and cook for another 5 minutes. Add rabe, sausage, and onion to the rice and mix well. Add salt and pepper.

Take the egg roll dough and place on a board dusted with a little flour. Put a bit of rice mixture along the side of each square, making sure to leave space on the top and bottom. Roll the dough over once lengthwise; then fold in the top and bottom. Continue rolling lengthwise, like a cigar. Brush some egg along the edge and press gently to seal the roll. Place 1 cup of olive oil in a skillet; fry the egg rolls 3 or 4 at a time until golden brown on both sides.

SERVES 6

SHUT UP AND EAT!

RIGATONI ALLA GANNASCOLI

COURTESY OF 101
10018 FOURTH AVENUE
BROOKLYN, NY 11209
718-833-1313

■

1 cup olive oil
3 cloves garlic, chopped
1 cup prosciutto, chopped
6 ounces shitake mushrooms, sliced
1 bunch arugula, chopped
1 pound rigatoni, cooked according to package directions
Salt and freshly ground black pepper to taste
1 cup cubed smoked mozzarella

In a sauté pan, heat olive oil, and sauté garlic until light golden brown. Add prosciutto, shitake mushrooms, and arugula and sauté for 3 minutes. Add rigatoni to the sauté pan. Mix on high heat for 3 minutes, adding salt and pepper. Portion out on plates, and add some of the smoked mozzarella to each plate.

SERVES 6

SPINACH FETTUCCINE

COURTESY OF 101
10018 FOURTH AVENUE
BROOKLYN, NY 11209
718-833-1313

■

1 stick unsalted butter
1½ cups heavy cream
8 ounces chicken, chopped
1 cup chopped onion
1 bunch spinach, washed 3 times to remove sand, chopped
2 ounces finely diced roasted red bell peppers
1 cup Marsala wine
Salt and freshly ground black pepper to taste
1½ pounds fettucine, cooked according to package instructions

Place ½ stick of unsalted butter in a sauté pan over high heat, and melt. Take pan away from heat, add heavy cream, and cook down for another 10 minutes, stirring the cream into a thick sauce. Lower heat.

In another sauté pan, place ½ stick of butter and melt on high heat. Add chopped chicken and sauté for 5 minutes. Add onion, spinach, and roasted peppers. Sauté for 5 minutes on high heat. Take pan away from heat and add Marsala wine, and then put pan back onto high heat and cook wine down for 5 minutes. Season with salt and pepper.

Add fettuccine to cream sauce, then add chicken and vegetables, and mix well.

SERVES 6

JAMES RUSSO

THERE'S A FAMILY story about when my father was coming to the United States from Naples, Italy, as a young boy. My dad was five years old and my grandfather was holding him up as they were boarding the ship in Naples. Then, all of a sudden, a donkey bit him right in the chest. Can you imagine that! Although the trip started off badly, my father loved America. My uncle and aunt, my father's brother and sister, spoke Italian now and then, but my father did not really embrace his heritage. Maybe it was partly because of the prejudice against Italians at that time, but my father wanted to be American more than anything else. When I was a kid, Italian was not spoken in my house although I do remember that Frank Sinatra was constantly playing on the hi-fi. When I was preparing to play Sinatra in the television movie called *Stealing Sinatra,* I would listen to a lot of his music and it was a real flashback to my childhood.

Growing up, we would eat a lot of spaghetti, meatballs, and sausage. My mother was not Italian, but she adapted to that type of cooking. My father was 100 percent Italian and was a salesman for Pabst Blue Ribbon beer. I grew up in Flushing, Queens, and it was a real melting pot back then — mostly German, Irish, Jewish, and Italian. Now, it's all Korean. There was a pizza place on Main Street in Flushing called Gloria's and the pizza was incredible. To this day, if I think hard enough, I can still taste it. On holidays such as Thanksgiving, we would often go to other people's houses, and we would eat the traditional turkey. But, at some point during the meal, the pasta would eventually come out. It's impossible not to have it with an Italian holiday meal. I don't care if it's Easter, Christmas, Thanksgiving, or New Year's, the pasta always makes an appearance.

I went to a Catholic elementary school, but outside of school I was friends with kids of many religions and races. When I went to high school in Manhattan, I was surrounded by a real diverse bunch of students. But, it wasn't until I moved out to the West Coast in 1985 that my horizons really expanded. I had never had Mexican food until I moved to LA. I fell in love with the West. I loved the open space. It wasn't congested like New York City. But, to be honest, the first thing I realized when I moved to LA was that the pizza sucks!

If you look at the seventy or so movies that I've appeared in, I have only played seven Italians and acted in only one mob movie, *Donnie Brasco.* However, everyone automatically thinks of me as an Italian-American actor. I consider myself lucky to say that I worked with the two acting kings, Al Pacino and Robert De Niro. How many actors can say they acted in scenes with those guys? When I was going to New York film school, they were *it*. They were the actors whose films we studied and spoke about in depth during class. I also have a lot of respect for Robert Loggia. I admired Loggia in the film *Somebody Up There Likes Me*, which I saw as a kid. It had a big effect on me and he really stood out. Then, I loved Loggia in *An Officer and a Gentleman* and *Scarface*. I eventually acted in a Western film with him. Can you imagine that for two Italian Americans from New York? The movie was *Bad Girls* and he played my father. I remember that they had trouble casting my father in *Bad Girls*. Finally, they announced Robert Loggia for that part and I was very happy. He was also fabulous on *The Sopranos*.

Being able to work in Italy is always fun. I was working in Florence a few years ago, acting in a movie called *Sicilian Mission* with the late Vincent Gardenia. Gardenia was a very talented actor who loved to cook. In fact, he would have been great in this book. I actually could live in Florence. It is a breathtaking city and the food and people are amazing. The pizza they make just melts in your mouth. Now, I am five foot ten and usually weigh 155. However, during the course of shooting that film, I put on twenty pounds over a seven-week period! The film was shot out of sequence and in some scenes my face looks a lot fuller than others. It's pretty funny. I ate like a pig because the food was so damn good. We had huge lunch breaks with wine, pasta, fruit, cheese, and freshly baked breads that were out of this world. I ate like an animal. I really enjoyed eating with Gardenia because he told a lot of great stories. If I could sit down and eat with a few Italians from history, they would have to be Joe DiMaggio, Rocky Marciano, Da Vinci, and Michelangelo. It would be amazing to have the five of us at the same table. Now, that would be some hell of a meal!

My father's name was Daniel, but my uncle always called him Dom. I would ask my father, "Why does he call you Dom?" but he would never explain it to me. I do remember hearing vague stories about a baby in our family who was named Daniel and died of meningitis three days after he was born, but it wasn't something talked about openly. It was many years later that I found out my father's birth name was Dominic. Apparently, my father was about twelve years old when he took the name Daniel, because he wanted to carry on the baby's name out of respect. I only found out about this story when I was an adult and I decided to name my son Dominic. The dish that I am giving you the recipe for is called Dominic's Pea Pasta. I named it that because my son loves it. It is a simple dish that is made quickly, but kids really love it.

AFTER STUDYING film at New York University, James Russo moved to Hollywood with aspirations of becoming an actor. His first film break came in 1982 when he was cast as a convenience store robber in *Fast Times at Ridgemont High*. He won a Theater World Award in 1983 for his stage role as Joe in the play *Extremities*. In 1986, *Extremities* was brought to the big screen starring Russo and Farrah Fawcett. Russo has about seventy feature films to his credit, including *Beverly Hills Cop* (1984), *We're No Angels* (1989), *Dangerous Game* (1993), *Bad Girls* (1994), *Donnie Brasco* (1996), *No Way Home* (1996), *The Postman* (1997), *The Ninth Gate* (1999), and *Open Range* (2003). Russo also portrayed mobster Victor Mura in TV's short-lived *Falcone*. In 2003, James Russo offered a penetrating performance as Frank Sinatra in the made-for-TV movie *Stealing Sinatra*.

DOMINIC'S PEA PASTA

10 ounces frozen peas, defrosted
3 garlic cloves, chopped
½ cup olive oil
1 cup vegetable broth
Salt and freshly ground black pepper to taste
1 pound angel hair pasta
½ cup grated Parmesan cheese

In a sauté pan, lightly toast the peas and the garlic for 1 minute. Then add olive oil and sauté until peas and garlic are soft. Add the vegetable broth, salt, and black pepper to taste. Cook angel hair pasta according to the directions on the package. When the pasta is ready, drain and portion it out onto 4 plates, and add the peas and some grated Parmesan on top. It is a nice light dish.

SERVES 4

TONY DARROW

MY FAMILY IS from a small town called Polezano, located just out-side of Palermo, Sicily. I have been back there and really enjoyed myself. My son is seven years old, and when he gets a little older, my wife and I are going to take him to Italy to explore his roots.

The food in Italy was definitely outstanding. However, my mother was the "queen" of the Italian cooks in my neighborhood, and my fondest memories of food are from my own childhood. I grew up in the East New

York section of Brooklyn. That was where the real-life "goodfellas" came from. While it was 90 percent Italian, there were some Jewish, Black, and Irish people living there. But, if you lived there, the neighborhood was decidedly "your neighborhood," and it was very well protected by its own people. No matter who you were, if you lived in that neighborhood and had a problem, it was everyone's problem. No one locked their doors. My grandmother and mother used to take the Sutter Avenue bus to do their shopping in Brownsville, which was the next section over. They would come back at midnight with packages and no one would ever bother them. That was the kind of safe neighborhood it was. I also remember that there were pushcarts, filled with all kinds of fruits and vegetables lining the streets. It was a great place to get fresh produce.

While I was growing up, my grandfather used to make homemade Italian wine and then sell it. When we would eat, he would give all the kids, including me, a little glass of wine and put Coca-Cola in it because we were not allowed to drink the wine straight. Grandpa used to make the wine right in our basement and store it in barrels. He would often take breaks from making the wine and sit outside our house on Sutter Avenue and smoke his pipe. Whenever I would see my grandfather, I would give him a kiss. Even if I saw him fifteen times in a day, I would give him a kiss every time, because I loved him so much. My grandfather would have to take the pipe out of his mouth, wipe his mouth off, and give me a kiss back. One day he told my mother in Italian, "Tell him not to kiss me so much. Don't get me wrong, I love the kid, but he should just kiss me once because every time he kisses me, I have to take my pipe out of my mouth." Anyway, one day a friend of mine and I very quietly went down to the basement where my grandfather made his wine. We decided to break into where he kept his delicious Italian red, and we got so drunk that I thought I was going to die! I was only fifteen years old at the time. Then, another time, we even lit up one of his stogies. My cousin passed it to me and I put the lit end of the cigar in my mouth and burned myself badly. The crazy things kids do!

Food scenes are always fun in gangster movies. One of the favorite roles that I've played in my career was the part of Sonny Bunz in *Goodfellas*.

In the film, I owned a club called the Bamboo Lounge. In fact, twenty years before that, I had worked for the real Sonny Bunz, because I used to sing and do comedy in the original Bamboo Lounge on Rockaway Parkway in the Canarsie section of Brooklyn. Ironically, I wound up playing the same guy. Those great coincidences are special and you never forget them. In fact, it was in those early days of my stage-performing career when I first met Tony Lip. Tony Lip and I go back a long way to when I used to go to the Copacabana nightclub. He was a big shot there and has always been a great guy and a gentleman. Tony deserves all the success that he can enjoy in life. Eating on and off the set with your fellow actors like Tony and others is fun too. When Chazz Palminteri and I were acting in *Analyze This*, we would pick out a different restaurant in Queens and eat out together every day. Chazz has great taste in food.

As far as great Italian restaurants go, when I was younger and staying in Los Angeles, I enjoyed going to Matteo's, where Frank Sinatra used to eat. In Vegas, I used to eat at the Leaning Tower of Pizza. In New York City, my hometown, I love Rao's. I also like Il Mulino on Third Street between Thompson and Sullivan Streets and Villa Mosconi on MacDougal Street, as well. Another favorite is a restaurant called 2 Fifteen Cucina Napoletan in Brooklyn on Columbia Street. At 2 Fifteen, they don't just cook northern or southern Italian cuisine. They cook whatever you want. They also prepare great fish dishes. I love calamari, soft-shell crab, and blowfish the best. I also love linguini with white or red clam sauce and I can eat a pound of pasta myself. Following my meal, I like a nice Italian pastry. As far as wine, I drink only Italian red wine. What can I say? I love everything Italian!

I personally enjoy Italian home cooking the best. That's probably because that was all I grew up on and it brings back some wonderful childhood memories. We would have pasta three days a week when we were kids. One day, we would have it with sauce and then on the other days, we would have it with vegetables. On Saint Joseph's Day, my mom would always make baccala. I have many fond memories of that dish and that is why I am going to share the recipe with you. I also love to make linguini with red and white clam sauce. It's very basic, but wholesome and delicious. I hope you enjoy my recipes. However, to be honest, I don't enjoy cooking as much as I enjoy eating!

TONY DARROW grew up in the East New York section of Brooklyn, a neighborhood known for its tough guys, wiseguys, and "only the strong survive" ethos. His background placed him in perfect stead to play in Martin Scorsese's *Goodfellas*. For many years, Darrow built a reputation as one of the most entertaining acts in show business, singing at top clubs in Las Vegas and Atlantic City. In the past several years, he has been cast in various Woody Allen films such as *Sweet and Lowdown*, *Deconstructing Harry*, *Mighty Aphrodite*, *Celebrity*, and *Small Time Crooks*. Darrow has guest-starred on such popular television shows as *New York Undercover*, *The Cosby Show*, and *Law & Order*. He is also proud of his roles in smash-hit mob movies like *Analyze This*, with Robert De Niro and Billy Crystal, and *Mickey Blue Eyes*, with Hugh Grant and James Caan. Darrow is also a philanthropist and puts on a celebrity golf tournament every year for the benefit of United Cerebral Palsy of New York. Last year, Darrow raised a total of $225,000 in one day for the children with this popular event.

BACCALA ALLA MILANESE

2 pounds baccala, cut (make sure you get the kind in water, not dried)

1 small onion, chopped

3 sprigs Italian parsley

2 lemons

2 eggs

5 tablespoons all-purpose flour

2 tablespoons olive oil, plus ½ cup

Drain the fish, skin and bone it, then cut into 6 pieces, each about 2 to 3 inches square. Make sure no bones or bits of skin are left. Put the squares into a pan of water with the onion, parsley, and ½ a lemon. Cover the pan and bring to a boil. Let it boil for 1 minute, then remove it from the heat, and leave covered for 15 minutes.

Meanwhile, prepare a batter: beat the eggs and gradually add the flour and enough water to make a fairly thick, smooth batter. Stir in 2 tablespoons of olive oil and leave the batter to rest for 30 minutes.

Heat the ½ cup of olive oil in a deep frying pan until smoking hot. Drain the cod and dip the pieces into the batter. Drop these, one by one, into boiling oil and fry on both sides until golden brown. Drain the fritters on paper towels and serve hot, garnished with wedges cut from the remaining lemons.

SERVES 6

LINGUINI WITH WHITE OR RED CLAM SAUCE

2 dozen littleneck clams

2 tablespoons olive oil

½ medium onion, chopped

5 cloves garlic, minced

1 (28-ounce) can crushed tomatoes (only if you are making red clam sauce)

1 teaspoon red pepper flakes

2 cups white wine

4 tablespoons (½ stick) unsalted butter

1 pound linguini

¼ cup finely chopped Italian parsley

Scrub clams in cold water, and set aside.

In a large saucepan, heat the olive oil, and sauté the onion and garlic over medium heat until the onion is very soft and translucent, about 10 minutes. If you are making red clam sauce, add the crushed tomatoes. Add the red pepper flakes, clams, wine, and butter and bring to a boil. Cook just until all the clams have opened, 5 to 7 minutes. Discard any clams that did not open.

While the clams are cooking, boil the linguini according to package directions, until tender yet still al dente. Drain the pasta and toss into the pan with the clams. Stir gently to mix. Add the parsley, pour into a warm serving bowl, and serve.

SERVES 4

AIDA TURTURRO

I WAS EXPOSED to my Italian heritage when we went to my grand-mother's for Sunday dinner or to my cousin's house on the holidays, because they were all very Italian. On holidays, my family and I ate big Italian feasts, especially at Christmas and Easter celebrations. Christmas is very special to me and is my favorite holiday. At family gatherings, we usually ate antipasto and lasagna, followed by fantastic seafood — baked clams, lobster, even linguini with a lobster sauce. Oh, my God! It was unbelievable. My grandmother on my mother's side did most of the cooking on those wonderful holidays when I was growing up. Believe me, my grandmother made the best eggplant in the world.

I was born in Brooklyn, but we moved to the Lower East Side of Manhattan when I was four. The Lower East Side wasn't Italian at all when I was growing up. It was predominately a Black and Hispanic neighborhood at that time. On my father's side, the Turturro family is originally from Bari, Italy. Bari is located on the Adriatic Sea on the eastern coast of Italy and it's the capital of the province of Puglia. I recently traveled to Italy for the first time to visit my roots. It was an amazing trip. I was there for a total of nineteen days. Unfortunately, I had just lost my father. So, as fate would have it, he didn't get to go and never saw Italy. However, he was there with me every step of the way in spirit. I went with a close friend who helped me translate because I don't speak Italian. She and I went to this town called Giovinazzo, just outside Bari. That was where the Turturros were born. In fact, there are still Turturro family members in the town. Italy is beautiful. However, going there to see my family and having them welcome me with such warmth and open arms was the most beautiful thing about the trip. First of all, the Turturros in Italy all look like us. Their homes and their hearts were open to me and there was so much genuine love. It was one of the best times in my life. My great-aunt, who is the only one still alive from that original Turturro generation of my father, took me to the cemetery to see my great-grandparents' grave site. It was a meaningful bonding experience that I will never forget.

The food in Italy was just delightful. Every time I ate, the food was totally fresh and delicious and the portions were just right. Also, they don't overdose you with sauces. They also present you with the right balance of vegetables, meat, and not too much pasta. I ate a lot of artichokes and they were prepared to perfection. I thoroughly enjoyed eating in Capri, Tuscany, and Rome. However, my favorite place to eat in Italy was in our family's home area of Bari. Since it is right on the Adriatic, the seafood was incredibly fresh—literally, right off the boats.

Back here in the United States, I am extremely close to my cousins. I think the significance and meaning of "family" is when you truly want to be close to them. I especially love the time when we all bond together as a family around a dinner table and eat a great meal. It's all about talking, eating, drinking, and thoroughly enjoying each other's company. I really enjoy entertaining. Recently, one of our talented directors from *The Sopranos*, Tim Van Patten, came to my house, and a bunch of us had a great Italian meal. However, I appreciate dining with various friends from many different professions. My life isn't all about acting, and the friends that I enjoy entertaining do not have to be Italian. I like hanging out with my friends, whatever nationality they may be. Yes, you can cook for a group of friends or you can make it more intimate with just one other person, because cooking can be very romantic. I'm a firm believer that you can totally seduce somebody with delicious food. The evening can be so very sexy if the food, wine, and atmosphere are just right.

As far as my character, Janice, on *The Sopranos*, she is the worst cook. She's lazy and doesn't want to cook, but is always in the kitchen cooking. Janice is probably more unlike the real me than any character that I've ever portrayed during my acting career. I am a much better cook in real life. In fact, I want to give you two recipes for my favorite appetizers. One is my seafood bruschetta, which is comprised of clams, mussels, and delicious red sauce on top of Tuscan bread. It's pretty amazing. The other appetizer is my stuffed mushrooms. It's made with delicious stuff like fresh bread crumbs, garlic, onions, and Parmesan cheese. It is so good! I hope that you enjoy these appetizers with your friends and family!

AIDA TURTURRO graduated with a degree in theater from the State University of New York at New Paltz. In 1992, she appeared on Broadway in *A Streetcar Named Desire* with Jessica Lange, Alec Baldwin, and James Gandolfini. Turturro has had a solid film career working with some of the top directors in Hollywood like Martin Scorsese (*Bringing Out the Dead*), Woody Allen (*Celebrity* and *Manhattan Murder Mystery*), and her cousin John Turturro (*Illuminata* and *Romance & Cigarettes*). Other film credits include *Mickey Blue Eyes* (starring James Caan and Hugh Grant), *Deep Blue Sea* (Samuel L. Jackson), and *Sleepers* (Brad Pitt, Robert De Niro, and Dustin Hoffman). For her role as Janice Soprano on the hit show *The Sopranos*, Turturro was acknowledged for her skills by being nominated for an Emmy Award.

STUFFED MUSHROOMS APPETIZER

24 large white mushrooms
½ cup plain bread crumbs
½ cup Parmesan cheese
2 cloves garlic, diced
6 sprigs Italian parsley, chopped
1 tablespoon basil, chopped
Salt and freshly ground black pepper, to taste
½ cup olive oil

Preheat the oven to 400 degrees.

Boil mushrooms in water for 10 minutes; then run under cold water until cool.

Mix the bread crumbs, Parmesan, garlic, parsley, basil, salt, pepper, and 2 tablespoons olive oil in a bowl and blend.

Drizzle 2 tablespoons of oil onto a heavy, large baking sheet. Spoon the filling into the mushroom cavities and arrange on the baking sheet, cavity side up. Drizzle remaining oil over the filling in each mushroom. Bake until the mushrooms are tender and the filling is heated through and golden on top, about 20 minutes.

SERVES 8

SEAFOOD BRUSCHETTA APPETIZER

6 tablespoons olive oil

1 (16-ounce) can of plum tomatoes

5 cloves garlic, minced

1 onion, chopped

1 teaspoon crushed red pepper

Salt and freshly ground black pepper to taste

12 littleneck clams

2 dozen mussels, washed and debearded

1 loaf good Italian bread or French baguette, cut into 12 ½-inch slices

2 cloves garlic, lightly crushed

6 sprigs Italian parsley, chopped fine

Preheat oven to 375 degrees.

Place 3 tablespoons of olive oil into a large skillet and bring to high heat. Put tomatoes in a bowl and crush tomatoes with your hand before putting into skillet. Add garlic, onion, red pepper, salt, and pepper. Bring to a boil, add clams and mussels, and sauté until clams and mussels open. Discard any shells that do not open. Let cool slightly.

Meanwhile, toast bread in oven until lightly brown and crisp, about 3 minutes. Remove bread and rub at once with crushed garlic and then brush lightly with salt and pepper.

When clams and mussels are cool enough to handle, remove from shell. Return to pan and discard shell. Spoon fish and sauce onto bread and sprinkle with parsley.

SERVES 6

JOE RIGANO

THE SECTION OF East New York in Brooklyn where I grew up was a totally Italian neighborhood. My area was called Ocean Hill, a small community within East New York. I would venture to say that my neighborhood was the toughest in all of New York City. This is not to downgrade the other neighborhoods that had reputations for being tough. Ours was just a notch tougher, though. The guys from my neighborhood didn't back down from anybody. In fact, my neighborhood was where the gang known as Murder, Incorporated originated. There was nobody in that neighborhood who you could single out and say, "He was the toughest." We were all tough. There were guys from my area who could have been professional prizefighters if they weren't so screwed up in the head.

However, there was also another side to life there. My friends and I had a lot of fun growing up. We would play games like punchball—which is hitting a rubber ball with your fist and running bases—and football, right in the street. As far as playing football, we had to be creative because nobody had enough money to buy a real football. So we used to tie a newspaper together and use that as a football. During the summertime, we would go swimming at a city-owned pool not far from my house. For ten cents admission, you could swim all day long. For a total of twenty cents, you also got a locker.

I would say that 85 percent of the guys I grew up with had a nickname that was more familiar than their real name. If you asked anyone where my friend Sal Grillo was, they would scratch their heads and ask, "Who is Sal Grillo?" If you called him by his nickname, Bucky, then they would know exactly who you were talking about. My late brother, Jerry, may he rest in peace, was called Jerry Rags. He was called that because everyone would mispronounce our name as "Ragano," instead of Rigano. Recently, I wrote down all of the nicknames for the guys from my neighborhood, and I came up with a total of 275 nicknames!

Whenever I was done playing with my friends, I would go home for a nice home-cooked meal made by my mother. She was a great cook. We were a family of five boys and no girls. I grew up during the Depression years, so we were very poor. However, my mother and father always made sure that we had fresh, healthy Italian food on the table. My mother even made her own homemade macaroni. Her family back in Foggia, Italy, was originally in the bakery business. (My father's side of the family is from Messina in Sicily.) My mother would make a very different type of homemade pizza, which I loved! The pizza was not served hot. After she took it out of the oven, she would put it in the hallway or on the bed to let it dry out and get cold. Then we would eat it about an hour later. Sometimes it felt like the whole world was coming over to join our family to eat it. That's how popular my mom's pizza was in our neighborhood. I swear that you could eat that pizza for three or four days on end. The bakers in my mother's family taught her very well. She could make delicious cookies from water, eggs, and flour. My mom was extremely talented in the kitchen!

Holidays were always big feasts, especially Easter and Christmas. First, you dressed up in your suit and went to church. Afterwards, you would come back home for a huge Italian meal with the whole family. In fact, we went to church every Sunday. This was the 1930s and 1940s when everyone was wearing their "Sunday best," especially when going to church on Sunday. Today, when you go to church, people are dressed so informally that they are even wearing shorts in the summer. When I was young, it was a dress shirt and tie, with no exceptions. It was so great to have that tradition of church followed by a big home-cooked Italian meal right after the service. I am very proud of my Italian-American roots, especially that phase.

I have had the good fortune of acting in many movies with some great Italian-American actors. Prior to my acting career, which started kind of late in life, I worked for the City of New York for thirty years. I was a chief highway inspector for the Borough of Queens. I started in 1963 as an inspector and retired as a borough coordinator in charge of thirty-five inspectors with an office staff of twelve people. In 1995, I got into the movie business. In fact, I got involved in acting on a dare. One of my fellow members at the Sons of Italy Lodge had gone on a casting call for the Martin Scorsese film *Casino*, which starred Robert De Niro and Joe Pesci. When he came back from the audition, we started talking and he told me about it. I said, "If I was thirty-five years younger, I would try to get into acting." He then answered, "What are you talking about? The casting office was filled with a bunch of old bastards." He challenged me and told me that I didn't have the balls to do it. I said, "Give me the damn phone number." First I got called by the casting agent who was doing the background casting for *Casino*. Then another casting director, Ellen Lewis, called a week later and told me that Robert De Niro and Martin Scorsese wanted to meet with me. I went to Scorsese's office, met them, and read for the part, and they thanked me. A week later I got a phone call from Las Vegas, where they were filming *Casino,* and I was told that they'd like to have me in the movie as one of the crime bosses. I flew out to Vegas and the rest is history.

Interestingly, when I was making *Casino,* De Niro and Scorsese both told me, "Joe, for the part you're playing, you're a natural. You have the looks. You have the background. Don't try to act. Just be yourself." What I do as an actor—the way I curse and how I carry myself—is not really an act. This is actually how I've been my whole life. It's common behavior in the area of New York City that I grew up in. Yes, I am a character actor and I'm very satisfied with that. You see my photo, you hear my voice, and you get an immediate impression. Would you put me in bed with a twenty-one-year-old girl? Let's get real! The casting people know exactly what I can do and what I'm capable of.

It's still the best part of my day to come home to my wife's homemade Italian cooking. She makes really great dishes. My wife is the only child from a Sicilian family and was taught to cook at a very early age. I think she makes the greatest meatballs in the world. However, I personally learned how to cook from my mother. Today, I can definitely hold my own in the kitchen, but in no way can I cook as well as my wife. Here are two of her Italian recipes and you can be the judge. I promise you won't be disappointed!

SHORTLY AFTER his retirement from New York's Department of Highways, Joe Rigano began a new career as an actor. Since 1995, he has appeared in some fifteen films. Rigano's signature raspy voice and natural acting style initially attracted the attention of renowned director Martin Scorsese. Following his big-screen debut in Scorsese's *Casino,* Rigano went on to appear in major motion pictures such as *Analyze This, Mickey Blue Eyes, Hollywood Ending, The Crew,* and *Coffee and Cigarettes.* Joe Rigano has also appeared with fellow Italian-American actor Vinny Vella in twenty-five commercials for ESPN.

RIGANO'S PASTA

5 tablespoons olive oil
1 whole eggplant, cut into 1-inch-square chunks
1 tablespoon salt
1 teaspoon black pepper
1 pound angel-hair pasta
3 tablespoons grated Pecorino Romano cheese

Place olive oil in a 12-inch sauté pan and bring to high heat. Add the eggplant and sauté for 5 minutes. Add salt and pepper, and sauté for another 2 minutes on high heat. Take eggplant out of sauté pan, and drain on paper towels.

Prepare angel hair pasta according to directions on the box. Angel hair pasta cooks quickly, so don't overcook or it will stick together. When pasta is done, drain all the water out. Put pasta and eggplant back into the sauté pan and sauté for 2 minutes. Sprinkle grated cheese on top of each serving.

SERVES 4

PORPETTE DI UVI
(Egg Patties)

2 tablespoons olive oil, plus 2 cups for frying
2 cloves garlic, chopped
3 (12-ounce) cans crushed tomatoes
1 teaspoon salt
½ teaspoon freshly ground pepper
3 leaves basil, chopped
2 cups seasoned bread crumbs
1 small onion, diced
3 tablespoons grated Pecorino Romano cheese
6 eggs

Place 2 tablespoons olive oil into a sauté pan and sauté the garlic. When garlic is golden, remove the pan from heat, and add the crushed tomatoes, salt, pepper, and basil. Bring heat up to high until sauce starts to boil. Lower heat and simmer for 20 minutes.

Meanwhile, in a bowl, mix the seasoned bread crumbs, onions and cheese. Beat 6 eggs and place them into the bread crumbs and mix well. If batter gets too thick, add a little milk or water. If batter is too thin, add more bread crumbs. Batter should be thick enough so that when you make it into patties, they don't fall apart. Place the 2 cups of olive oil into a 12-inch frying pan, and let it get very hot. Using a tablespoon, scoop out the batter, form it into a patty about 3 inches in diameter, and place it into the frying pan. Don't put too many into the pan at a time; make sure the patties aren't touching each other. The batter should yield 12 patties. When the patties are a light golden brown, take them out of the frying pan and place on paper towels to remove excess oil. Place patties into the tomato sauce and simmer for 45 minutes.

SERVES 6

Vincent Curatola

BOTH MY GRANDMOTHER and my mother were fabulous cooks. They were businesswomen and didn't have all day to cook. However, when my mother and grandmother got home at 5:30 p.m., it literally took only about a half hour before the place was filled with delicious food. My favorites were chicken with lemon and garlic, always cooked to perfection in our family's broiler. We ate this as an appetizer. That was usually followed by a main course of stuffed breast of veal, which literally melted in your mouth. I'm going to give you that very same recipe later.

Vince and his lovely wife, Maureen

My grandmother emigrated from Sicily to the United States as a young girl and wound up settling on the Lower East Side of Manhattan. She quickly became quite an accomplished cook. The word got out about her skills in the kitchen, and, as a young teenager in New York, she enjoyed the distinction of cooking for Mayor Fiorello LaGuardia and the great opera singing legend Enrico Caruso. Food was a tremendous part of my upbringing as well as my family's pride, and I was blessed with that.

Growing up, I have to admit that my first love was great Italian food, but my second love was to watch my favorite actors portray "tough guys" on the screen. I always admired actors like Edward G. Robinson and Fredric March. In truth, my favorite gangster movie of all time is *Al Capone* starring Rod Steiger. Even though he was not of Italian descent, if I could sit down with any classic mob-movie actor, one-on-one, and enjoy an Italian dinner

SHUT UP AND EAT!

with him, I would have to pick Rod Steiger. He was a great actor and I had the pleasure of meeting him once at Elaine's restaurant in New York City. I hope to meet up with him in the hereafter and share a meal with him.

My favorite food scene in a movie is from (what else?) *The Godfather*. Ironically, it is not a scene where they are eating Italian food. There is a particular scene in the film where they are waiting for a call to find out where Michael Corleone is going to meet the character called Sollozzo, "The Turk," and they're eating Chinese takeout. The reason I love this scene is because they're all chomping down on the food and are so focused on how good the takeout is that they have completely blocked out the fact that in an hour there is going to be a huge meeting where someone is going to die. No worries, just the thought of, "Hey, can you believe how good this lo mein is?"

I've found that food scenes in *The Sopranos* have almost become legendary with the viewers. The scenes have developed as vital parts of our story lines. The most important meetings between my character, Tony Soprano, and Carmine, my late fictional mob boss, have been conducted over food. It seems to be a primal urge in fictional mob life to make a decision on a full stomach. I remember once, we were filming a scene for an episode in the fourth season. When the final take was done, I counted that I had consumed six orders of baked clams and drank down many, many glasses of Welch's grape juice, which we used on camera to look like wine. I was eating all day!

Working alongside Tony Lip, my mob boss Carmine, was great. He fits the profile of a true mob-movie actor. When you sit down with this guy, either in a scene or away from work, you feel like you are really in the presence of someone who knows a lot of things he is never going to tell you. It is mysterious and entertaining at the same time.

There is really only one Italian restaurant that my wife and I go to, and that is Il Cortile on Mulberry Street in New York City. The food is unbelievably good and so well flavored. I generally avoid other Italian restaurants or restaurants in general because when I walk in, they usually want to know if I am a real-life tough guy. Nowadays, I love to cook at home. The recipes you are going to see here are some of my favorites and favorites of my wife (whom I love to watch cook even more). My loving wife,

Maureen, is of Irish descent, but she is an incredible Italian cook because she learned from my late grandmother. Nothing beats a home-cooked Italian meal. There are actually some Italian dishes that are so elaborate that I don't think the kitchen in our present house is big enough to handle them, and that's the main reason that I'm buying another, larger house. We love to cook, so what can I say?

VINCENT CURATOLA was born and raised in Englewood, New Jersey, a town just across the Hudson River from New York City. He always loved the entertainment business and proceeded to study filmmaking at New York University. After studying at NYU, Curatola pursued other careers but becoming an actor still interested him. He then started appearing in off-Broadway theater productions, playing such memorable roles as Harry Roat, the villain in *Wait Until Dark,* and George in *Same Time Next Year.* However, his Italian roots helped him successfully play mob parts in television movies-of-the-week like *Gotti* and, of course, portray the definitive mob underboss on *The Sopranos.* Curatola has also appeared on the long-running TV series *Law & Order* and *Third Watch.* When he is not busy acting, Vincent Curatola is busy supporting charities like HeartShare Human Services of New York, which provides services to people living with mental and physical disabilities.

LINGUINI DIAVOLO

1 tablespoon extra-virgin olive oil

1 large onion, chopped

3 cloves garlic, minced

3 (15-ounce) cans of crushed tomatoes

2 tablespoons Worcestershire sauce

3 fresh basil leaves, chopped

1 teaspoon oregano

5 drops Tabasco sauce

1 dozen medium-size shrimp, shelled and deveined

1 dozen littleneck clams

2 dozen mussels

1 pound linguini

Heat oil in a large saucepan and sauté onion and garlic until golden, 5 to 10 minutes. Add remaining ingredients, except for seafood and pasta, and simmer 20 minutes. Add seafood and simmer 10 minutes more (or until shells of clams and mussels have opened). Discard those that do not open.

Meanwhile, cook linguini according to package directions, drain, and keep hot. Serve seafood mixture over pasta.

SERVES 6

STUFFED BREAST OF VEAL

1 (4- to 5-pound) breast of veal (have butcher cut pocket for filling)
Salt and black pepper to taste

FOR STUFFING MIXTURE
1 cup Italian bread crumbs
1 cup grated Romano cheese
3 eggs, beaten
2 tablespoons chopped fresh Italian parsley
½ cup black raisins
2 tablespoons pignoli nuts

FOR BASTING MIXTURE
2 cloves garlic, minced
½ cup balsamic vinegar
1 teaspoon oregano
3 tablespoons extra-virgin olive oil

Preheat oven to 400 degrees. Salt and pepper breast of veal inside and out and set it aside. To prepare stuffing mixture, combine all ingredients until mixture has a moist consistency (add a tablespoon of water if mixture is too dry). Stuff mixture into the pocket of the breast of veal, and place in a shallow roasting pan. Salt and pepper the outside of the veal. Put in the oven for 15 minutes. Reduce temperature of oven to 350 degrees, and cook for 40 to 45 minutes more or until a thermometer reaches 140 degrees.

Combine ingredients for basting mixture. Reserve some of the mixture for serving. During the last half hour of roasting, baste the breast of veal every 10 minutes.

Let the roast sit for 10 minutes before slicing. Pour the reserved basting mixture over slices.

SERVES 8

SHUT UP AND EAT!

LOUIS GUSS

WHEN I WAS born, World War I was ending, so I probably have a much different perspective of the Italian-American lifestyle than most of the younger actors and actresses who've told their stories for this book. I was born on the Lower East Side of Manhattan, but then we moved to the East Bronx. My new neighborhood wasn't really Italian, but the Italian section of town was only a short bus ride away for us. So, if my family and I wanted a nice Italian meal out, we would hop on the bus and go to one of the two Italian restaurants we really liked. We would also get our fresh cheeses and breads from the local stores in that same Italian neighborhood.

I am actually half Italian; my father was from Ferrari, located in northern Italy. However, my mother did most of the cooking, and she was Jewish, so the cuisine wasn't always Italian. She did cook Italian food from time to time to please my father, so we enjoyed an international table of food, just like many other New Yorkers.

When I was growing up, one of the things I loved, besides a good meal, was watching Western movies. In fact, so did everyone else from my generation. Eventually, the Western was replaced in popularity with the gangster film. The gangster actors I loved from that era were Edward G. Robinson and James Cagney. Later, *The Godfather*, which I acted in, set the pace for the gangster movie. It was wonderfully written and amazingly well performed. Even though many of the characters in that film were murderers on-screen, audiences loved the characters. I think that the great writing and performances were what really appealed to people.

I also enjoyed being in *Moonstruck*, which, of course, was not a gangster film. However, it was one of the greatest "slice of life" movies about Italian-American culture of all time. I got the wonderful opportunity to eat in scenes with fellow cast members like Cher, Nicolas Cage, the late Vincent Gardenia, and Olympia Dukakis. I was lucky enough to also eat off camera with fellow cast members like Cage and Gardenia, which was so much fun. We exchanged a lot of great stories. I really enjoyed sharing stories with another actor on the film, who is half Italian like me. The old man in *Moonstruck*, played by the late Feodor Chaliapin, was of Russian and Italian ancestry. His father, Feodor Chaliapin Sr., was a very famous Russian basso opera singer and is regarded as perhaps one of the greatest operatic performers who ever lived. His mother was an Italian ballet dancer who danced in Russia and that was how his parents met. Feodor was a very fascinating and interesting character with wonderful stories. In fact, he had been an extra in movies here in the late 1920s, before sound films were introduced in the United States. That is the best part about breaking bread with people in this business. Many actors and actresses have had such colorful histories.

Today, I live on the West Side of Manhattan and there are many great Italian restaurants that I frequent in my neighborhood. I love Carmine's in midtown Manhattan, where the food is wonderful. It is a family-style restaurant with large portions. You usually need to go there with a group of people because the portions are so huge. I love their chicken scarpariello because it just melts in your mouth. Another restaurant I like is Don Giovanni, where I usually get the veal marsala with fettuccine pasta. The food is always good and the prices are reasonable.

I also like to cook for myself sometimes. I have always found that it relaxes me. I love pasta dishes and I can cook some pretty good ones. For openers, I definitely love to start a meal with a nice bowl of soup. My favorites are my potato leek and minestrone soups. My minestrone recipe is the best. It's very healthy with lots of vegetables and beans. I am now in my eighties and still acting, so maybe minestrone is one of the keys to youth and longevity!

STILL ACTING after close to a half century of performing in movies and on television, Louis Guss made his debut in the 1950s in the hit New York–produced TV cop series *Naked City*. Guss has a list of credits that seemingly never ends. Earlier in his career he appeared in classic films like *Crazy Joe* and *Lucky Lady* and guest starred on high-rated television shows like *Taxi*, *CHiPs*, and *Kojak*. After his appearance in the 1987 Italian-American themed comedy *Moonstruck*, as Raymond Cappomaggi, at age seventy, Guss entered one of the busiest phases of his career. He proceeded to divide his acting time between parts in top-rated television shows like *Law & Order*, *Chicago Hope*, and *100 Centre Street* as well as roles in motion pictures such as *Original Sin, Night Falls on Manhattan, Girlfight,* and *The Crew.*

MINESTRONE ALLA MILANESE
(Milanese Vegetable Soup)

1 (26-ounce) can white cannellini beans
¼ pound salt pork
1 clove garlic, chopped
3 sprigs Italian parsley, chopped
1 onion, thinly sliced
½ pound mild bacon, cut into thin strips
3 large potatoes, peeled and cubed
3 carrots, diced
3 stalks celery, sliced and diced into ½-inch pieces
2 zucchini, thinly sliced
2 ripe tomatoes, peeled and chopped
1 teaspoon salt, plus 2 tablespoons
1 teaspoon black pepper
1 small cabbage, shredded
1 (10-ounce) box frozen green peas
1 pound ditalini pasta
4 teaspoons finely chopped basil
Grated Parmesan cheese to taste

Rinse the beans in cold water to remove brine, then set aside. Finely chop the salt pork, and sauté with garlic and parsley in a very large pan over moderate heat until the fat begins to run. Add the onion and let cook until soft but not brown. Add the bacon, beans, and all the vegetables except the cabbage and the peas. Cover with plenty of water—about 12 cups—add salt and pepper, and bring to a boil. Lower the heat and let the soup cook gently for 1½ hours. Then, add the cabbage and the peas. Cook for another 15 minutes.

Meanwhile cook the ditalini pasta in 5 quarts of water with 2 tablespoons of salt until al dente. Strain and add to soup. Serve soup with a sprinkle of basil and cheese.

SERVES 6

SHUT UP AND EAT!

ITALIAN LEEK AND POTATO SOUP

12 average-size leeks

3 tablespoons olive oil

4 large potatoes, cut into 1-inch cubes

1 teaspoon salt

1 teaspoon freshly ground black pepper

1 sprig fresh thyme, finely chopped, or ½ teaspoon dried thyme, crumbled

2 (14-ounce) cans chicken or beef broth

⅓ cup cognac

1 tablespoon lemon juice

3 sprigs Italian parsley, chopped

Leeks need to be cleaned thoroughly because of the sand and dirt that get trapped between the tight layers of leaves. First trim off the root and all but an inch or so of the green top and rinse well under cold water, spreading the leaves as much as possible. You'll probably find it necessary to make a slit in the top with a sharp knife in order to separate them. Cut leeks into small pieces. You should have about 2 cups when you are done.

In a large soup pot, add the olive oil and bring to high heat. Add the leeks and potatoes, and let brown. Add salt, pepper, and thyme. Add broth, bring to a boil, and then reduce the heat. Cover and let simmer until the leeks and potatoes are just tender, about 15 minutes. Add the cognac, let the liquid come to a boil again, and simmer for 2 to 3 more minutes. Sprinkle with a few drops of lemon juice and garnish with chopped parsley.

SERVES 4

KATHRINE NARDUCCI

LIKE MANY OTHER Italian Americans of my generation, I grew up in East Harlem, New York, which was heavily Italian at the time. In fact, it's the section of New York City where many Italians first moved to when they came off the boat from Italy. Italians came to Harlem first and then they eventually moved to places like the Bronx, Brooklyn, and the Little Italy neighborhood of Lower Manhattan. My family is originally from Caserta, which is about twelve miles north of Naples. Many of my relatives still live there, and they reside on a street called Via Narducci.

East Harlem was a wonderful place for me to grow up because of all the Italian families and their deep ties to our heritage. I lived right around the corner from the famous Italian restaurant Rao's. However, we hardly ever went out to eat because my mother was a gifted cook. She made every traditional Italian dish you can think of and she cooked them well. In fact, my mother taught me how to cook. I recall that back in those days, they cooked dishes on the heavier side. Today, I prepare every dish my mother made, but I make them healthier. For instance, when she would make her meatballs, she would use fatty beef. Today, I use extralean chopped meat. Also I don't fry the meatballs; I bake them. When my mother was making her gravy on Sundays, she would put in sausage, pork, beef, and braciole. Today, I make a much lighter marinara sauce on Sundays, which is fat free.

I have very fond memories of my mother cooking in the kitchen. I would sometimes watch her cooking without her noticing and I could tell that she was very happy—content in her own world. In the kitchen, my mother was her most pure, her true organic self. You could see the happiness in her angelic face. When my mother cooked, she sang; she loved music just as much as she loved food. If she wasn't singing, she was listening to music. In fact, I don't think she ever cooked without music. My mother really enjoyed listening to Barbra Streisand. It could have been a regular Sunday dinner or a Monday dinner, a holiday dinner, or any dinner for that matter; my mother just loved music and loved to cook.

I've been cooking a long time and have even been approached to write a cookbook. I was a guest on a television cooking show, and afterward the executive producers were so impressed with my knowledge of food that they wanted me to do a cooking show. However, I don't really want to do it because I cook for pure enjoyment only. Also, I don't want to be known as a professional chef because that would overshadow my true creative self. I am a professional actress and very proud of that. The story of how I started my career as an actress is an interesting one. It all started when I read an article in the *New York Daily News* that said Robert De Niro was looking for a little boy to play the part of his nine-year-old son in his feature film directorial debut, *A Bronx Tale*. There was an open casting call. So

I asked my son, Nicholas, who was nine years old at the time, to try out for the part. He agreed and so, I took him to this open call, which was more like a cattle call. There were many, many little boys there. My son was the last boy to go in to audition, and the very next part they were casting was for the role of De Niro's wife. I noticed that the women coming in to audition were all my type and in my age category. I asked the casting director if I could read for the part. She explained, "For that role, they want somebody with a little bit of acting experience." I was honest and said, "The truth is that I have never really acted before." The casting person replied, "Well, if we don't find what we're looking for today, you can call me tomorrow and I will try to get you in for an audition." I called the very next day and, luckily, they hadn't found the right woman for the part. I went down and I auditioned on videotape. Just two days later, I got a phone call explaining that Robert De Niro saw the tape and wanted to know if I could return and read with him. I thought it was one of my cousins playing a joke on me, so I hung up on the casting agent. She phoned back, thank God, and said De Niro saw the tape, loved it, and wanted me to read with him. I did that and they kept calling me back for further auditioning until I finally got the role. I beat out twenty-five hundred women for the part. It was my first movie role, and I received a lot of valuable experience working with Robert De Niro and Chazz Palminteri during the six months we shot the film. I have to add that my second favorite movie role was in a film called *Two Family House*. I played the female lead part of Estelle Visalo opposite Michael Rispoli, who played my husband. *Two Family House* won a Sundance Audience Award. The critics loved it, giving the film three and a half to four stars. The movie also did great in the movie theaters and was a wonderful experience overall.

I also want to emphasize that nothing is better than eating with your own family. I love getting together with my family to eat a big meal, especially on the holidays. We get together with all our cousins and have a wonderful Christmas holiday up in Salem, New York, where my cousin lives. My cousin has a terrific house with a big fireplace and the holidays are so much fun. We do it every year. It has become a true family tradition.

What I love the most about cooking is creating. I also take pleasure in making people happy with my food because I know people enjoy my cooking. Cooking for others is an extremely personal way of socializing; you spend quality time preparing and sharing the food. I think it brings people closer together in the truest sense. I love cooking a meal because it creates a very special bond between you and the people who are enjoying it. You're truly sharing a part of yourself by giving the wonderful gift of home-cooked Italian food to your friends and family. I hope your family enjoys my recipe for Italian baked chicken as much as my family does.

BORN AND raised in East Harlem, New York City, Kathrine Narducci's acting debut was in the hit film *A Bronx Tale*, playing the part of the wife of a hardworking bus driver, portrayed by Robert De Niro. After that role, her career took off. Narducci has frequently appeared on top television shows like *NYPD Blue, Third Watch,* and *Law & Order,* as well as acting in TV movies like *Witness to the Mob*. Narducci has had an equally successful career in theater, appearing in popular off-Broadway productions such as *Pieces of Ass* and *Six Goumbas and a Wannabe*. One of her favorite movie roles was in the hit independent film *Two Family House*, which won the coveted Sundance Audience Award. Narducci is also well-known for her recurring role as Charmaine Bucco on the hit TV series *The Sopranos*. When not busy acting, she enjoys cooking and painting.

ITALIAN BAKED CHICKEN

3 tablespoons olive oil

1 (3½- to 4-pound) chicken, cut into 8 pieces

1 tablespoon salt

1 tablespoon black pepper

1 cup water

2 onions, sliced into ¼-inch pieces

5 cloves garlic, sliced

1 teaspoon oregano

Juice from 1 lemon

Preheat oven to 350 degrees. In baking pan, pour 1 tablespoon olive oil and rub it all over the bottom and sides of the pan. Place chicken parts in the pan, with skin side down, and pour the remaining olive oil over them. Sprinkle with salt and pepper. Add the water. Place onions and garlic over the top of the chicken. Bake for 1½ hours. After an hour, turn the turn chicken over, but make sure that the onions and garlic are replaced back on top of the chicken. Then sprinkle the chicken with oregano and lemon juice. Continue to bake for 30 minutes. Before serving, baste chicken with the juice from the bottom of the pan and let stand for 10 minutes.

SERVES 4

FEDERICO CASTELLUCCIO

I'M PROBABLY ONE of the few actors in America today who was actually born in Italy. I was born in Naples, right in the heart of the city. A lot of people say that they're from Naples, but they're really from the outskirts. Not me. I lived near the National Museum of Art in Naples, also known as Museo Nazionale. Then, in 1968, when I was about three and a half years old, my family moved to the United States. Back then, Italians were emigrating to America because many of their family members were already living here. There was a U.S. government act at the time that enabled people living in the United States to bring their relatives in for visas and for green cards. So people, I guess, were taking advantage of that opportunity including my family. My family had dreams of coming to this country to build a better life for us—their children. My mother, Theresa, felt it was much more expansive and open here. Where we originally lived in Naples, it was such a tight and confining neighborhood that everybody knew each other. You could yell down the block and call your cousin instead of using the phone. My family wanted a change.

I came to America with my mother, my sister, and two brothers. My father, Leonzio, came about eight months to a year later due to the American immigration rules at that time. The mother would have the chance to invite her husband over later after she got her family established with the support of her existing family already here. Even though I was young, I have a vivid memory of coming to America because for a three-and-a-half-year-old, moving from one country to another was very traumatic. You don't know what's going on and suddenly you're going into an airplane, and moving to a very strange place. I have vivid memories of people crying around me—not just my own family—because they were also leaving their friends and family in Italy.

We moved to a neighborhood called People's Park in Paterson, New Jersey. It was very Italian with many Italian cafes, shops, and grocery stores. Today, it's definitely diversified and a lot of the Italian shops have moved as the Italian-born residents moved to other areas. I go back to that Paterson neighborhood every once in a while, just out of nostalgia. However, it's really a changed place. Back then, during my childhood, it was so Italian that you could get by without speaking English. My mother, one of my brothers, and I did not speak any English at all. My sister and my older brother did know some English because they studied it in school in Italy. Since my mother did not know English, she worked as a seamstress. My father worked with colors as a dyer. My artistic genes come mainly from my father, but also in part from my mother's side because there were artists on her side of the family. So, I got the best of both worlds in the artistic genes department. I find that most Italians are generally art conscious. Whether it's with regard to their clothes, paintings, or food, Italians are pretty savvy and usually conscious of quality things and good art. I was exposed to art at a young age and I am thankful for that opportunity.

Italian food in my house was always a big deal. My mother has always been an extremely gifted cook and the food was always fresh. Believe it or not, I was about fifteen years old when I ate my first McDonald's hamburger! When I went to school, all the other kids were eating peanut butter and jelly sandwiches and lunches like that. I came to school with exotic Italian lunches. The variety of things that I would have for lunch would make the other kids' jaws drop. Sometimes, my mother made this delicious potato with peppers meal for dinner. She would put the extra potato and peppers on bread and make it a sandwich that I could bring to school for lunch the next day. Overnight, the potatoes and peppers would soak into the bread, and by the next day it tasted unbelievable. My mother also made an incredible eggplant parmigiana. The kids looked at my eggplant parmigiana sandwich at lunchtime and wondered what the hell it was. They said, "That looks great, but what is it?" I taught them a lot about Italian cuisine. In fact, all of my friends would love to come over to my house because they knew they were going to get an outstanding meal.

My father cooked for our family too. He prepared some great Neapolitan dishes. It seems that if you're from Naples, you naturally are able to sing, paint, play an instrument, and cook. That has been my experience with people who come from Naples. In fact, my father makes his own wine to this day and has been doing it since he lived in Italy. My father actually crushes all the grapes himself. He doesn't buy the juice preprepared. When people say, "I make wine," they usually go and buy the juice. They just ferment it and then say they made it. That is not really making your own wine. My father starts from scratch. He makes red, white, and a rosé. It tastes great and doesn't hit you over the head. However, if you drink a lot of it, it'll definitely catch up to you.

One of my dreams was to have a meal with the great Italian-American director Francis Ford Coppola. I got the opportunity to do it at Gracie

Mansion in New York City at an event hosted by another great Italian American, former New York City Mayor Rudy Giuliani. I talked to Coppola for quite a while. Ironically, this was at the time he was closely viewing *The Godfather* trilogy once again. They were transferring the movies to a new DVD set, and he had to do commentary for them. Coppola hadn't seen the films for many, many years. We got to speak in depth about the movies, which was a big thrill for me. It was great because we talked on a one-on-one basis. In fact, it wasn't like an actor speaking to a director. It was more like speaking on a very personal level, which was fabulous. Coppola owns a California vineyard and he's a real wine connoisseur. In addition, Coppola is also a very accomplished photographer. We talked extensively about art, and it was a great experience to meet him.

One Italian movie director that I never ate with, but would have loved to, was Federico Fellini. He's intrigued me forever. I feel so cheated that I never got a chance to actually meet him and talk to him in person. He's gone now, but Fellini had a vision that was unique and was very singular compared to so many other directors. Fellini was also a painter and did his own storyboards for his films. He was just a phenomenally talented person, all the way around. In fact, my own production company is called La Strada, named after one of my favorite Fellini films. It starred his wife, Giulietta Masina, and the great Anthony Quinn. I love Anthony Quinn. I've always admired him because not only was he a talented actor, but he was a painter as well and a sculptor too. Quinn wasn't afraid to express himself in different artistic ways. So eating with Fellini and Quinn would be an amazing fantasy meal. I know it would be a long meal too, because we would have a lot to talk about—painting, sculpting, acting, directing, cooking, and more.

As far as cooking is concerned, there's definitely an art to it, and my mother is one of the best cooks I know. I am going to provide you with a recipe for a simple but classic Italian meal of meat and peas that I have always loved. It's a very basic dish that I ate often growing up. It's just fantastic.

FEDERICO CASTELLUCCIO was born in Naples, Italy, and at the age of three and a half, he along with his family emigrated to Paterson, New Jersey. From an early age, Federico had dreams of becoming an artist. Having a unique talent for drawing and painting, Federico was awarded a full scholarship to the School of Visual Arts in New York City. He went on to do a portrait of the legendary comedian George Burns, who was so impressed by his work that he introduced him to executives at PBS, ABC, and the other television networks. Castelluccio was then hired by several of them, becoming an award-winning illustrator. He also had an interest in acting. After studying for several years, he began doing showcase plays. Soon, Castelluccio moved on to do summer stock theater, off-off-Broadway, and Shakespeare festivals. He's appeared in productions of *A View from the Bridge*, *Twelfth Night*, and *Goodnight Desdemona*. He then made the transition to film, appearing in movies like *Made,* starring Jon Favreau and Vince Vaughn; *Fire,* featuring Robert Klein; and *18 Shades of Dust*, starring Danny Aiello. His television credits include the critically acclaimed HBO-TV series *The Sopranos,* where he portrayed Neapolitan enforcer Furio Giunta. When not acting, he is busy supporting numerous charities like Project Sunshine (which benefits the families of terminally ill children and the children themselves), Project ALS, and the Michael J. Fox Foundation for Parkinson's Research.

MEAT AND PEAS OVER RICE

¼ cup olive oil

3 cloves garlic, chopped

1 small onion, sliced

1 box frozen peas, defrosted

1 pound chopped sirloin

1 (28-ounce) can crushed tomatoes

2 dried whole bay leaves

3 basil leaves, chopped

3 sprigs Italian parsley, chopped

Salt and pepper to taste

2 cups uncooked rice

½ cup grated Pecorino Romano cheese

Put the olive oil in a sauté pan and bring to high heat. Add the garlic and onion and sauté for 2 minutes until light golden brown. Add the peas and continue to sauté for about 3 minutes. Add the chopped meat and stir until it turns brown. Add the crushed tomatoes, bay leaves, and basil, and bring to boil. Add parsley, salt, and pepper and simmer for 20 minutes.

Meanwhile, prepare rice according to instructions on package. When rice is ready, mix in the cheese, and then add the meat and peas (remove bay leaves) and serve.

SERVES 6

Steven R. Schirripa

MY BELOVED GRANDMOTHER was an excellent cook, originally emigrating here from Calabria, Italy. In fact, she was recognized as a great cook in our neighborhood of Bensonhurst, Brooklyn, where there were tons of fine Italian cooks. Thirty-five years ago, she used to cook in the kitchen of the local Italian deli in our neighborhood. The deli would freeze her food, put their own brand name on it, and sell it in the store.

On Sundays, I would always get together with my grandfather and grandmother and eat my grandma's delicious homemade Italian dishes. For Italians, every Sunday is like Thanksgiving. The wives are in the kitchen cooking up a storm, while the guys are watching a ball game on TV. The kids are usually running around the house. Italians have been doing that religiously on Sundays for over fifty years here. Maybe longer! A friend of mine was recently reflecting on his own Italian-American childhood and said, "On Friday nights, I would go to my mother's parents' house to eat. On Saturday nights, I would go to my father's parents' house to eat. On Sundays, everyone would eat together as one big family." So that's something that a lot of Italian Americans have in common. I think Italian cuisine tends to be a more "family bonding" style of cuisine than any other. Hey, if you started eating Italian food as young as I was at those family get-togethers, you'd feel the same way. Food is a big part of Italian culture, plain and simple. When two Italians want to meet up, they don't say, "Let's meet at Starbucks for a cup of coffee." No, Italians say, "Let's go meet for something to eat and have a glass of wine." That's how Italians do business.

There can also be humor when it comes to Italian food. In fact, you might think what I am about to tell you is funny, but at the time, I didn't. Well, I had just started dating a girl and she invited me to her parents' house for Thanksgiving. I was meeting her mother and father for the first time and, of course, wanted to make a good impression. In fact, all of her relatives were there. We were eating salad and I picked up the Italian salad dressing bottle off the table. I thought the top was on tight, so I shook it up over my head. Well the top wasn't on tight enough and the dressing went all over the curtains, the table, and the walls—a total mess. Oil and vinegar everywhere! I have never been more embarrassed in my life. Italians may like oil and vinegar, but, trust me, they don't like it on their curtains!

When I first moved to Las Vegas to work in 1979, it was a tough transition going there from New York City because Italian food in New York is the best. In Vegas, the food was not like the food from my childhood Italian home in Brooklyn. That's putting it mildly. There are so many different kinds of Italian Americans living in Las Vegas. They migrated from places like Buffalo, Chicago, Cleveland, and so forth, so you get all different kinds of

Italian-style food. I definitely prefer the "New York Italian" type of cuisine. People would recommend an Italian restaurant to me in Las Vegas, and when I'd go there, the sauce would look like chili. I would ask, "What the hell is this?" Ten years later, and by the time I was settled in my job as entertainment director of the Riviera Hotel, there were many Italian restaurants in Vegas that had good food.

I like wine with an Italian meal. When I am at a restaurant, I order a nice Pinot Grigio, usually Santa Margarita. It is light and that's what I drink almost all the time. Other people could be ordering two-hundred-dollar bottles of wine, but that's not what I usually like to drink. In the winter, I like red wine, but only when it is cold out.

If I could have a fantasy dinner, a one-on-one Italian meal with anybody, it would have to be with the late Frank Sinatra. I was at a dinner with him once, but we were with a large group. (There were about twenty of us at a restaurant in Las Vegas.) However, I was able to be at the same table with him and that's a special night to remember. It would have been really interesting to talk with him one-on-one, but that wasn't to be on that particular night. Sinatra was one of our greatest Italian Americans and it's unfortunate that he passed on, but what a life he led and what a legacy he left!

My character, Bobby Baccala, on *The Sopranos* is generally in scenes with food and I'm happy to report that the food is always excellent on the set. Here's a story that will give you some idea of how these food scenes work. One time, while James Gandolfini and I were shooting a scene, we started eating chicken cacciatore at 7:00 a.m. For the next seven hours, while they were filming, that was all we ate. In fact, I think we ate so much chicken that at one point I heard Gandolfini clucking like a chicken! Seriously though, I love chicken cacciatore, but hey, enough is enough! It was great to meet Tony Lip through *The Sopranos*. He played a very interesting character on the show. I remember seeing him act in *The Pope of Greenwich Village* and many other fine films over the years. Let me assure you that Tony's not just a terrific character actor, he's a great guy as well.

When I'm in New York City shooting the show, I love to dine at Il Cortile on Mulberry Street in Manhattan's Little Italy. Somebody had first

*The flag outside
Il Cortile Restaurant*

recommended that I try the place, and I have now actually become close friends with the owner. It is one of the best Italian restaurants in New York City. Everything you eat is 100 percent fresh. They also have people who are cleaning the place twenty-four hours a day, so it's spotless. Dominic Chianese got married recently and we had his bachelor party at Il Cortile. When a few of the characters have gotten killed on *The Sopranos*, that's where we've taken the cast members for a sort of "prewhacking party." I also had my book party at Il Cortile. Michael Imperioli's family and my family often eat there together. The restaurant has a great family atmosphere combined with really outstanding Italian food. I'm going to give you one of their recipes called Las Vegas–Style Lobster. They also make a homemade Sunday sauce completely fresh, but only on Sunday mornings. Speaking of sauce, one of my favorite food scenes in a movie is from *The Godfather* when the character Clemenza was teaching Michael how to make a Sunday sauce. Even in *The Godfather*, it wouldn't have been a Sunday without it!

I also like to cook a few dishes myself. I make a shrimp oreganato on Christmas Eve

Il Cortile Executive Chef Michael DeGeorgio

SHUT UP AND EAT!

that my father used to make and I follow his tradition. I ate it when I was a kid and I cook it for my kids today. I think tradition is important and I'm proud to continue instilling the Italian food heritage and traditions in my own family. My wife is not Italian, but she enjoys cooking Italian dishes. We have two little girls and I enjoy passing along my Italian heritage to them.

AFTER GRADUATING from Brooklyn College, Steve Schirripa decided to move from New York to Las Vegas. He worked many jobs while he was there, including gigs as a bouncer. After working as the entertainment director of the Riviera Hotel and booking acts like Ray Romano, Denis Leary, and Drew Carey, Schirripa got the itch to perform, himself. He has acted in various feature films such as *Casino* (starring Robert De Niro and Sharon Stone), *Fear and Loathing in Las Vegas* (with Johnny Depp and Benecio Del Toro), and *Joe Dirt* (starring David Spade). However, audiences worldwide know him as Bobby Baccala on the hit TV series *The Sopranos*. Schirripa has also hosted a new television show for the Discovery Channel, entitled *Mob Scene*. An accomplished book author, Schirripa wrote the national best seller *A Goomba's Guide to Life* and the follow-up book, *The Goomba's Book of Love*. His third book, *Nicky Deuce: Welcome to the Family,* was released in September 2005. *The Goomba Wedding Planner* is set for publication in 2006.

SHRIMP OREGANATO

1 pound large shrimp (16 count), peeled and deveined
1 teaspoon salt, plus additional as needed
1 teaspoon crushed red pepper flakes
3 tablespoons olive oil, plus 1 to 2 teaspoons
1 medium onion, sliced
1 (16-ounce) can plum tomatoes, mashed
1 cup dry white wine
3 garlic cloves, chopped
¼ teaspoon dried oregano
3 tablespoons chopped fresh Italian parsley
3 tablespoons chopped fresh basil leaves

Toss the shrimp in a medium bowl with the 1 teaspoon of salt and red pepper flakes.

Heat the 3 tablespoons oil in a heavy large skillet over medium-high heat. Add the shrimp and sauté for about 1 minute, toss, and continue cooking until just cooked through, about 1 to 2 minutes. Transfer the shrimp to a large plate; set aside. Add the onion to the same skillet, adding 1 to 2 teaspoons of olive oil to the pan, if necessary, and sauté until translucent, about 5 minutes. Add the tomatoes with their juices, wine, garlic, and oregano. Simmer until the sauce thickens slightly, about 10 minutes.

Return the shrimp and any accumulated juices to the tomato mixture; toss to coat, and cook for about a minute so the flavors meld together.

Stir in the parsley and basil. Season with more salt, to taste, and serve.

SERVES 4

LAS VEGAS–STYLE LOBSTER

COURTESY OF IL CORTILE
125 MULBERRY STREET
NEW YORK, NY 10013
212-226-6060
EXECUTIVE CHEF: MICHAEL DEGEORGIO

■

2 (2½-pounds) live Maine lobsters
3 tablespoons extra-virgin olive oil
3 ounces garlic, cracked
1 shallot, minced
10 ounces shellfish broth (recipe follows)
6 ounces butter
4 tablespoons chopped parsley
12 fresh basil leaves
Salt, pepper, oregano, and red pepper to taste
1 pound linguini

Insert the tip of a sharp knife just underneath the head of each lobster and cut down, splitting each lobster in half, lengthwise. Remove and discard the heads and stomachs, and cut the rest of each lobster into eight pieces. You can have your fish market cut and clean them for you. In a large sauté pan (18-inch size) heat the olive oil. Add in the garlic and shallot. Sauté until golden brown. Add in all the lobster and sauté it for about 8 minutes, stirring with tongs. Add in the shellfish broth, butter, parsley, basil, and seasonings. Bring to a boil and let it simmer, covered, for about 8 minutes or until the broth reduces by half.

Set the lobster aside. Cook the linguini in boiling salted water until al dente. Strain linguini well. Toss with the lobster and serve. Garnish with more chopped parsley. Spicy red pepper should be added to each person's liking. The Las Vegas–Style Lobster should be spicy.

Shellfish Broth

1 quart water

6 clams, scrubbed clean

12 mussels, scrubbed clean and debearded

1 carrot

1 onion

4 celery stalks

2 sprigs each: parsley, sage, and rosemary

Salt and pepper to taste

In a large pot, add water and all ingredients. Bring to a boil, then simmer for 45 minutes and strain well.

SERVES 4

LEO ROSSI

AFTER YOU EAT a big Italian meal with the fellas, it's great to share stories. Over the years, I've been in the company of some terrific actors who are also great storytellers. I was in a movie that was filmed in Montreal, *One Eyed King*, and I was at the dinner table with Chazz Palminteri, Armand Assante, William Forsythe, and director-writer Bobby Moresco. All of these guys have colorful backgrounds. For instance, Moresco grew up in the Hell's Kitchen area of Manhattan and Chazz comes from the Bronx. After dinner, the guys started spinning stories and it was brilliant. Some younger kid in the group tried to tell a story and it didn't go over very well. After this young guy told the story, Chazz said, "You're in the major leagues of storytelling here. If you're gonna bring a story to the table, it better be in the major leagues. You're definitely down in the minors with that story." Moresco and Chazz agreed that Tony Lip is at the top of the mountain of storytellers. When he tells a story, it's almost like an offbeat type of poetry. When you hear stories from him in a steady stream, you know they're true to the core. The Lip has lived about six lives, and God bless him, he's still alive.

Food and acting can go hand in hand. One time, I was appearing in a play about an Italian family, directed by a real Italian from Sicily. Every night before our performance, this director would cook sauce on a hot plate in the back of the theater so that the whole theater smelled of fresh tomato sauce. Talk about establishing atmosphere! People who walked into the theater were in the mood right away to see a play about an Italian family. I thought that was a touch of pure genius. The director told me, "There are many ways to set the right atmosphere. I've known production people who actually adjust the climate control in the theater to create a mood. So, when you go into an Italian household, what is the first thing that hits you? Of course, the scent of Italian cooking." The smell of that fresh sauce throughout the theater put the audience right where it had to be mentally.

As an actor, when you're doing a food scene in a film, if you're a real pro, you usually keep an empty bucket off camera. You eat in the scene and when the director yells, "Cut," you spit the food into the bucket. I mean, you can't eat all night. Bobby Costanzo is a heavyset actor who was in *Honeymoon in Vegas* and also played Joey's father on TV's *Friends*. Anyway, we did a miniseries together called *Falcone* on CBS. Bobby and I had an eating scene in a restaurant. Most actors can't eat for seventeen takes straight. However, Bobby is the exception. He's a pro actor and is also a pro eater. Bobby ate everything in sight for seventeen takes. We thought he was going to explode! It was mind boggling. I said to Bobby, "What are you doing?" He looked at me and replied, "Hey, Rossi, I'm a hedonist!" That's my favorite food scene that I ever acted in, because the sheer impact of Bobby Costanzo eating so outrageously was amazing.

I am from the southern part of Philadelphia. South Philly is my home, baby! A friend of mine owns a restaurant there called Frederick's. He is a self-taught chef and puts out some dishes that defy description. Freddie makes a calamari appetizer that is mouthwatering. It's made with green and red peppers and onions. Now, let me tell you about two of the best Italian-American restaurants in Philadelphia, places that I also love. I'm referring to Tony Luke's restaurant on Oregon Avenue. Tony does twenty-two thousand sandwiches a week at his sandwich place. They have my picture up over the cash register there. Tony Jr. once joked, "Rossi, we have your photo up on the wall above the cash register because we want you to watch over the money!" Tony's kitchen at his sandwich place makes the best Philly cheesesteak and also serves delicious chicken cutlet sandwiches, Italian-style. The owners, the Lucidonio family, even bake their own bread. Tony Jr. is proud of the honors his food has received from highly respected sources such as *Gourmet* magazine and *Zagat*. Now, that's really being at the top of your game. Eating one of Tony Luke's sandwiches is like heaven on earth!

LEO ROSSI is a proud Italian American who was born and raised in South Philadelphia. A veteran character actor, Rossi has been in over sixty feature films. Some of his credits include *Halloween II* (with Jamie Lee Curtis), *River's Edge* (with Crispin Glover and Keanu Reeves), *The Accused* (with Kelly McGillis and Jodie Foster), *Analyze This* (with Robert De Niro and Billy Crystal), and *One Night at McCool's* (with Matt Dillon and Liv Tyler). Throughout his long career, Rossi has guest starred on many top television shows such as *Hill Street Blues, 21 Jump Street, Murder, She Wrote, Judging Amy, ER, JAG,* and *Frasier.* Rossi also cowrote the extremely funny movie *We're Talking Serious Money*, starring himself, Dennis Farina, and Fran Drescher.

TONY LUKE'S BELLY BUSTER

COURTESY OF TONY LUKE'S
39 EAST OREGON AVENUE
PHILADELPHIA, PA 19148
215-551-5725

■

½ cup mayonnaise
¼ cup ketchup
2 tablespoons horseradish
1 tablespoon pickle juice
2 (9-inch) crusty Italian rolls
14 ounces thinly sliced roast beef
8 slices tomato
12 slices dill pickle
1 medium-size onion, thinly sliced
8 strips bacon, cooked
4 ounces frozen seasoned curly fries

Mix together mayonnaise, ketchup, horseradish, and pickle juice, and stir until well combined.

Slice rolls. Spread a thick layer of the sauce on the bottom of each roll. For each sandwich, cover sauce with half of the roast beef. Top with (in this order) 4 tomato slices, 6 pickles, half of the onion, and 4 strips of bacon. Cook the curly fries in either a deep fryer or conventional oven until fully cooked. Mound a large handful of hot curly fries on top of bacon. Drizzle fries with more horseradish sauce.

MAKES 2 SANDWICHES

SHUT UP AND EAT!

VINNY VELLA SR.

MY MOTHER WAS born in Naples, Italy, while my father was born here in the United States. However, when he was nine months old, my dad's parents took him back to Italy to live. From what I understand, the story is that my grandparents were only planning to stay a short time in America. While they were here, my grandmother gave birth to my father, and then, nine months later, they decided to go back to live in Italy. So my father actually grew up in Bari, Italy. But, I grew up in New York

City and I'm a first-generation American. I grew up downtown in Greenwich Village on Bleecker Street, between Sixth and Seventh Avenues. I lived in an apartment over John's Pizzeria. Now I live not far away on Elizabeth Street, right off Houston Street. So, I have been in this neighborhood my whole life.

When I was growing up, my area of Greenwich Village was mostly Italian. People would sit outside their buildings in chairs at night during the summertime. They would bring out coffee and fruit and everybody would talk. In those days, it was a lot different because not only was the neighborhood mainly Italian, but it was segregated to a certain extent as far as representation from the various regions and cities of Italy. For example, Neapolitans all lived in one building, Sicilians lived in another building, Milanese lived in yet another building, and so on. Don't get me wrong. We all got along, but that was how we lived back then.

There was a lot of fresh produce and great Italian food right outside your door. You never had to leave that neighborhood. Everything you needed was right on your block. On the north side of the street, there were pushcarts where the vendors would sell fruits and vegetables. There were so many pushcarts lined up end to end that you couldn't get between to cross the street. There wasn't even enough room to crawl through. You had to walk to the corner to get to the opposite side of the street. There was also a dry cleaner, fish market, flower shop, candy store, and social club right outside our door. So you had everything right there. If I walked just two blocks away from my house, people would stop me and ask, "Hey, Vinny, what brings you over here?" Only two blocks away and they would say that! Can you believe it? Nobody ever left their block. That was how tight-knit the old Italian neighborhood in New York was.

My mother and father were the best cooks. Thankfully, I still have my mother, who is ninety years old. I lost my father in 1998 and I loved him dearly. My father owned Louie's Fish Market for fifty-one years, located at 131 Mott Street, which was not far from where we lived. I grew up eating fish. In fact, my father would get upset if he knew my mother was spending any money on meat. He used to say in broken English, "The fish is a better. I gotta the fish. Why you gotta buy the meat?" Every once in a while, before my father got home from his fish store, my mother used to go to the butcher right across the street from our apartment and buy a huge steak, which in those days cost only one dollar. Of course, my father, bless his heart, was really into fish. He could make a whole meal out of one little piece of fish. In fact, my mother had the same ability. If she only had a small box of pasta, she could somehow make a huge meal out of it. How they did it, I will never know.

Once in a while, we would buy a pizza pie. I remember when I was twelve years old, my mother sent me to John's Pizzeria. That was back when a whole pie was seventy-five cents. I went to give the guy seventy-five cents, and before I even ordered the pie, he said, "I want you to know that the pies went up in price to eighty-five cents." So I went back upstairs to get another dime from my mother for the pie, and she said, "Eighty-five cents! Forget it, I don't want a pizza pie." From that day on, my mother never bought another pizza pie again. She always made her own. My mother and father grew up during the Depression, so every extra penny they made was stashed away. They hardly spent any money. We all had nice clothes on our backs and we had a place that we used to go to in the summertime, but they never spent money frivolously.

In fact, they would never even spend the money to go to a movie. I brought them to see the Martin Scorsese film I was in called *Casino,* and it was the first movie they had seen since silent pictures. When I brought them to see the movie, my father was amazed by the cursing and violence, and that the film was actually in color. He was also surprised to see me on the big screen. My mother, on the other hand, was not affected that much by me being on the big screen. My mother wore glasses and couldn't see well. For almost half the movie, she kept rummaging in her pocketbook looking for Chiclets. I kept telling her, "Mom, watch the movie." Then, when I appeared on the screen, I said, "Mom, look, there I am." She dropped something and by the time her eyes focused back up on the screen, my scene was over and she said in broken English, "You looka nice." I said, "Mom, that's Sharon Stone." I tried to get them to go see the movie

The Godfather, because my father happened to be in the first one. They filmed in my neighborhood, right outside my father's fish market. It was the scene where Marlon Brando came out onto the street and was buying fruits and vegetables. Then some hit men came from behind and shot him. In the upper-left-hand corner of the screen, you can see my father with his back towards the camera sorting the fish alongside his store sign, which read LOUIE'S FISH MARKET. I said to my father, "Let's go see the movie." He replied, "I got to go pay to see myself?" He simply didn't believe in spending any money unnecessarily.

I really enjoyed being in the film *Casino*. In fact, it was great to act alongside Martin Scorsese's mother, Catherine Scorsese. She was an amazing cook and used to live in my building. In one of the early scenes in the movie, Catherine was making sauce in the back of this Kansas City Italian grocery store, which was owned by the mob. Believe me, she was really cooking the gravy. There was a whole huge pot of it with meatballs, sausage, and braciole. Everything was there and then they put the food in front of us to pretend like we were eating. But, I couldn't hold back and just pretend to eat because there was so much food and it tasted so good. Marty kept saying, "Vinny, don't worry about eating the food because after this scene, we're going to go to lunch." I said, "Marty, I love you with all my heart, but this tastes better than the shit the caterers are going to feed us." I just kept eating and eating and eating. Catherine was an excellent cook and a very sweet woman. When she first saw me on the set, she said, "Vinny, what are you doing here, sweetheart?" I answered, "I'm in the movie." She asked, "What movie?" I said, "*Casino*." She then asked, "Who put you in it?" I replied, "Your son." She smiled and commented, "Oh, he's a good boy." So I hung out with Catherine because I speak Italian and when I was growing up in our neighborhood, she was like a mother to me. Marty's mother and father were wonderful, wonderful people who used to buy fish from my father. Now, I want to give you one of my father's legendary fish dishes. It's called Louie's Octopus Dish con Linguini and it's absolutely delicious!

BORN AND raised in New York City, Vinny Vella is as charismatic in person as the colorful characters he portrays on the big screen. In fact, he is the subject of a sixty-seven minute documentary entitled *Hey, Vinny*. In 1995, he acted in one of his first feature film roles as Artie Piscano in Martin Scorsese's critically acclaimed mob-gambling film *Casino*. Vella has gone on to appear in an array of cult classics like *Ghostdog: The Way of the Samurai* (starring Forest Whitaker), and original films like *Kissing Jessica Stein* (starring Jennifer Westfeldt and Heather Juergensen), as well as mainstream favorites like *Analyze That* (starring Robert De Niro and Billy Crystal), and *Coffee and Cigarettes* (starring Bill Murray) and the list goes on. Vinny Vella has appeared on episodes of top-rated television shows like *The Sopranos* and *Law & Order,* as well as in twenty-five TV commercials for ESPN alongside fellow Italian-American actor Joe Rigano.

LOUIE'S OCTOPUS DISH CON LINGUINI

3 tablespoons olive oil
2 cloves garlic, sliced thin
1 teaspoon crushed red pepper
Pinch oregano
1 (6-ounce) can tomato paste
1 (28-ounce) can crushed tomatoes
2 pounds baby octopus
1 lemon
1 pound linguini

Put olive oil in a saucepot on high heat. Sauté garlic, crushed red pepper, and oregano for 1 minute. Add the tomato paste and sauté until garlic and oil mix together with the tomato paste. Add the crushed tomatoes, stir well, turn off the heat, and cover the pot. While the sauce is cooling down, prepare the baby octopus.

Clean the octopus very well and soak in 1 quart of water mixed with the juice of one lemon for 1 hour. Then, chop baby octopus into small pieces (tablespoon size) and put into saucepot. Bring sauce up to a boil; then lower heat and simmer for 2 hours. Check periodically, making sure the sauce doesn't stick to the bottom of the pot. Take a piece of the octopus out; if the fork goes in and out easily then it's ready.

Cook linguini according to the directions on the package. When the pasta is ready, strain and place portions onto 6 plates; ladle octopus over the pasta and serve.

SERVES 6

JOHN VENTIMIGLIA

M Y MOM ALWAYS cooked good, healthy food. It was always fresh and home cooked and you could feel her love in the food. I grew up in a traditional Sicilian-American home, living near my grandparents, aunts, and uncles. Both of my parents are originally from Sicily and I grew up in Teaneck, New Jersey. My parents came to America in the 1950s and, eventually, moved out of New York City and into the suburbs. Of course, my folks helped me retain our Sicilian heritage and traditions, which never changed over the years. Every night, my mother would cook great meals with pasta, vegetables, and fish. I've been to Sicily a bunch of times and they cook just like my mother did. Sicilians are not really big on eating meat. They eat a lot of fish, since it's an island and fishing is such a big industry. In fact, my grandfather was a fisherman, as well as a part-time pasta maker. He worked in a pasta factory in Italy. I remember that my family loved pasta con sarde, which features sardines, because sardines are a huge delicacy in Sicily. In fact, that's one of the recipes I'm going to provide.

Whenever we ate, there was always wine on our table. My father still drinks wine at every meal. Italians understand three things thoroughly — olive oil, cheese, and good wine. Naturally, over the years other countries have caught on to making good wine. Today, countries like South Africa, New Zealand, Portugal, and Spain make and export a lot of great wine. Also, California makes excellent wines now, whereas the better wine used to only come from Italy, France, and Spain. So, since there's a lot more competition now, the quality of the wine in the world has really gone up. I drink wine pretty regularly and I find it to be an important part of an Italian meal. I also think vegetables are very important in a meal. My family was poor when I was growing up, but my mother made sure we had fresh vegetables daily. I remember that we would eat cuccutza, which is a vegetable in the zucchini family. It is a long edible gourd, which you skin, cut in half, and remove the seeds from. Then, when it's cooked, you put it over a nice plate of pasta or rice. That's a fantastic dish and extremely healthy. I'm going to give you that recipe too.

Today, I live in Park Slope, Brooklyn, with my wife, Belinda, and our two daughters, Lucy and Odele. What's unique about where we live is that we have a garden in our backyard. I grow a lot of good things like tomatoes, basil, string beans, broccoli, carrots, corn, and more. My kids love to plant stuff with me. My wife and I probably share the cooking equally. Belinda is not of Italian descent. She's Australian, a vegetarian, and very health-conscious when it comes to food. We are members of a food co-op in Brooklyn. What you do to be part of the co-op is that you work there two and a half hours a month, and then you get a 30 percent discount off the food. It's great—a real community effort. Also, the food is unbelievably fresh. The co-op sells a lot of organic products, including the meat. It's a valuable thing to be a part of. When you have kids, you really have to make an effort to educate yourself about food. If you don't, you're not going to be giving your kids the best food that they can get. My mother made so much healthy Italian cuisine during my childhood that I can't do any less than

Vince Curatola and John Ventimiglia, familiar Sopranos faces, have a laugh at a charity event

that for my own children. I learned how to cook first from watching my mother cook and then from watching my wife, who has truly enlightened me with a new style of cooking.

Even though I love to cook, I was surprised when I got cast as the chef on *The Sopranos*. It's one thing to love food in your life, but it's another thing to reflect that love through your role as an actor. My first thought was, "The chef?" I thought I was a "tough guy" style of actor. However, in retrospect, I think that the producers used great insight in making me Artie Bucco. First of all, I really enjoy playing the part. Artie is not a gangster or a complicated character, but is more of a regular person, struggling with the day-to-day issues that he's dealing with. I really enjoy it when people come up to me and say, "Hey, you're the chef! Do you cook? Do you like to cook?" The part has brought me even closer to food. Again, I was surprised at first when I was cast in that role. However, now I fully understand their perception and the wisdom behind it. Plus, I get to cook while I'm acting, which is always terrific!

SHUT UP AND EAT!

What I enjoy the most about cooking is that when I cook, I truly know what I'm eating. Being part of the process, you are more connected to the food. The awareness and care in preparation shows love for your family and for yourself. I have a lot of pleasant memories of my mom cooking when I was a kid. I would smell her meatballs or her sauce, almost anything she made, and everything just smelled great. Also, the way she would take so much care in setting the table and presenting us with the food, I knew that my mother truly cared. She cared deeply about our family and took pride in feeding us meals that were good to eat. So there is a strong sense of pride in our family in cooking something well. When I cook a homemade meal, it's a way of showing my family that I care about them, and that means a lot to me.

JOHN VENTIMIGLIA was born and raised in Teaneck, New Jersey. He has been acting in theater, motion pictures, and television for many years. Ventimiglia has appeared in major feature films like *Bullets Over Broadway, Postcards From America, I Shot Andy Warhol,* and *Cop Land.* Who can forget his classic portrayal as the artist-mobster Johnny Graziosi in the hit comedy *Mickey Blue Eyes*? John Ventimiglia has also had a successful television career playing chef Artie Bucco on the hit series *The Sopranos*, as well as acting in featured roles on top long-running network shows like *Law & Order* and *NYPD Blue.*

CUCCUTZA ALLA JOHN VENTIMIGLIA

1 large cuccutza (or summer squash)

¼ cup olive oil

1 onion, chopped

3 cloves garlic, chopped

1 (28-ounce) can crushed tomatoes

1 pound spaghetti

2 tablespoons salt

½ cup grated Pecorino Romano cheese

Freshly ground black pepper to taste

Wash the cuccutza under cold running water. Cut the squash in half lengthwise, remove the skin, and take out all the seeds. Cut the cuccutza into 1-inch cubes. Pour the olive oil into a saucepot, and bring heat to high. Sauté the onion and garlic for 30 seconds, and then place the cuccutza cubes into the pot, and sauté until they have turned brown on the edges. Add the crushed tomatoes and cook for another 20 minutes. Meanwhile, cook the pasta al dente in salted water according to the directions on the box. Divide pasta among six plates, and place sauce with the cuccutza over the pasta. Sprinkle with cheese and pepper and serve.

SERVES 6

PASTA CON SARDE

¼ cup extra-virgin olive oil, plus 3 tablespoons
8 cloves garlic, chopped
1½ cups plain bread crumbs
½ cup Italian parsley, chopped
Kosher salt and freshly ground black pepper to taste,
about one teaspoon of each
2 (4-ounce) tins sardines, drained, boned, and chopped
1 teaspoon crushed red pepper flakes
1 pound linguini, fresh or dried, cooked in salted water, and drained

In a large skillet preheated over medium heat, add ¼ cup olive oil. Add garlic, and when garlic turns light brown, add bread crumbs. Stir bread crumbs until deep golden in color. Add parsley and a liberal amount of salt and pepper. Transfer bread crumbs to a dish and reserve.

Return skillet to heat and add 3 tablespoons olive oil. Add sardines and red pepper flakes to the pan, and sauté over medium heat, 2 or 3 minutes. Add hot, cooked pasta to the skillet and toss with sardines. Add bread crumbs to the pot and toss thoroughly to combine and evenly distribute the mixture.

SERVES 4

FRANKIE GIO

MY REAL FAMILY name is Gioseffi and my mother was born in Sicily, while my father was from Naples. I am first generation here in America and grew up in the South Bronx near where I was born on Morris Avenue and 152nd Street. That particular area of the South Bronx was almost all Italian. But if you went up farther in the Bronx, there were German and Polish immigrants. That's where Dutch Schultz and other legendary gangsters like Legs Diamond had their strongholds. But my area was all Italian immigrants. My family lived in an apartment building and the hallways always smelled of Italian cigars, which we nicknamed "guinea stinkers." Only two guys in my building smoked them, but the odor went throughout the whole place. My grandfather smoked the same cigars, but he didn't live with us. I also remember guys involved in betting and taking numbers up and down the street. Those were the memories of my neighborhood, my block.

My mother did all of the cooking—wonderful Italian food. Tony Lip and I met when we were kids and later we used to go to dances together. I lived in a tenement building and Tony lived in a private house, which to me was the luxury of living. His father even had a garden, so it seemed like he was living in the suburbs. However, Tony came to our area and loved it.

Being an Italian kid from the South Bronx, I am asked by many people how I got into acting. The way I became an actor was an accident. I was training at Stillman's Gym when I was a professional prizefighter and was asked to do a scene there for a movie about the great heavyweight cham-

Elaine's restaurant, one of Frank Gio's favorite spots

SHUT UP AND EAT!

pion Joe Louis. So I did a scene, joined SAG, and the rest is history. Now I've been in almost too many movies to keep track of. But I have to mention that when I was preparing to do a scene with Cher in *Moonstruck,* and we were looking at each other off camera, I told her, "Don't look into my eyes; you'll fall in love with me. My eyes, they are hazel and they turn green." She laughed and said, "I've had enough of you Italian guys!" I really enjoyed working with Cher. She's really down to earth.

Regarding Italian food, something I like that's different is called abonada. This is like pizza, because it features dough, but the filling is rolled up inside the dough like a jelly roll. I remember that my mother used to make it with broccoli and tuna fish, and sometimes with tuna fish alone, broccoli alone, or maybe just onions. It's really something that is very unique.

When I go out to eat, I want to go to a place where I feel at home and I always feel that way at Elaine's. Thursday night is a wonderful night to hang out there. You see actors, actresses, directors, writers—EVERYONE! Elaine's has been around forever. She used to have Colavita Olive Oil bottles on the tables. That's how far back I used to go there! When writers like Truman Capote were struggling, along with so many actors and actresses, Elaine Kaufman always managed to take care of them. They repaid her when they became well known by becoming the celebrity customers that Elaine's is now famous for. What I like to eat there is their shrimp and spaghetti dish. They make it special for me, and it is a special dish, so enjoy!

BORN AND raised in the Bronx on Morris Ave and 152nd Street, Frankie Gio started his career as a professional heavyweight boxer. Most of his professional prizefights were held at the old Madison Square Garden. One day, while training at Stillman's Gym in Manhattan, he was discovered when he was offered a small part in *The Joe Louis Story.* He went on to have a steady career in television, appearing in classic shows like *Kojak, Car 54, Naked City,* and *The Equalizer.* Gio has acted in a wide range of films such as *Once Upon a Time in America, The Pick-Up Artist, King of New York, Married to the Mob,* and *Moonstruck.* He recently played the part of Lou "The Wrench" Ragazzi in *Analyze That,* starring Robert De Niro and Billy Crystal, and was in *Assassination Tango,* starring Robert Duvall.

SHUT UP AND EAT!

PIZZA ABONADA ALLA FRANKIE GIO

FOR PIZZA DOUGH

1 package active dry yeast

1¼ cups warm water

2¼ cups all-purpose flour, and more as needed

1 teaspoon salt

1 tablespoon olive oil

FOR FILLING

2 cups broccoli florets

1 whole onion, sliced

5 tablespoons olive oil

2 (6-ounce) cans tuna fish, packed in olive oil

8 ounces mozzarella cheese, sliced thin

Salt and black pepper to taste

Add the yeast to the warm water in a small bowl. Let dissolve. Combine the flour and salt in another bowl. Stir to mix. Make a well in the center of the flour. Pour in the dissolved yeast and 1 tablespoon oil. Stir with a wooden spoon or fingers until the dough forms. Turn the dough out onto a floured board and knead 10 to 15 minutes, adding flour as needed to prevent sticking, until the dough is smooth and elastic. Place the dough in a lightly oiled bowl, turn to coat, and cover with a damp cloth. Place the bowl in a warm, draft-free spot for 2 hours or until the dough doubles in bulk.

While you are waiting for the dough to rise, sauté the broccoli and onion in a frying pan with 2 tablespoons of olive oil, until onions are translucent. Leave in pan off the heat and let stand until you are ready to use them in the dough.

Preheat oven to 400 degrees. Punch down the dough while it is still in the bowl; then turn it out onto a floured board. Knead lightly. Roll the dough with a rolling pin into a large circle. Place the sautéed broccoli florets, onion, tuna fish, mozzarella, salt, and pepper onto the dough and sprinkle 1 tablespoon of olive oil all over. Season with salt and pepper. Roll the dough like a jelly roll and seal the edges with a fork. It should look like rolled up Italian bread. Brush the dough on top with the remaining olive oil. Bake for 45 minutes or until dough is golden brown. Take the abonada out of the oven and let cool for 10 minutes before slicing into 6 pieces.

SERVES 6

LINGUINI AGLIO-OLIO WITH SHRIMP

COURTESY OF ELAINE'S
1703 SECOND AVENUE
NEW YORK, NY 10128
212-534-8103

■

2 pounds linguini (imported if possible)
2 tablespoons salt, plus more to taste
6 cloves garlic, sliced very thin
½ cup extra-virgin olive oil
36 medium shrimp, peeled and deveined
1 teaspoon crushed red pepper flakes
6 sprigs Italian parsley, chopped

Cook pasta in 8 quarts of boiling water with 2 tablespoons of salt. While the pasta is cooking, in a large sauté pan, sauté the garlic in olive oil until it starts to turn golden, then add the shrimp and salt, and sauté until the shrimp are almost done, 1 to 2 minutes. Add the red pepper flakes and the drained pasta. Toss well and add the parsley. Add more olive oil if needed; the pasta should be well coated with the oil.

SERVES 6

DENISE BORINO

THERE WAS A very big Italian influence during my childhood. To this day, we still have the traditional Sunday family dinner with maca-roni and gravy. Like many Italian Americans, my fondest food memories of my family getting together are from Christmas Eve. The whole family would join together—aunts, uncles, cousins, children, and grandchildren—and we would have seven different seafood dishes including shrimp (either fried or cocktail), baccala salad, scungilli salad, lobster, crab, and more.

Then, of course, we also had macaroni. For dessert we would have delicious strufoli, which is essentially small balls of baked dough rolled in honey and topped off with tiny multicolored sprinkles. I would fast all day, knowing that this dinner was going to be the best. In the beginning, we would always have Christmas eve at my grandparents' home, and there would be up to thirty people at their house. Today, this is still a very big tradition in my family. Four generations of Borinos meet at my cousin Gail's house and we spend a whole Sunday just making strufoli. We make enough for the whole family, and I don't mean just the Borinos based in New Jersey, where I was born and raised in Roseland. I'm talking about family members from out of state too. My cousin and my aunt go out and buy fifty pounds of flour, jars and jars of honey, gallons of oil, tons of eggs, and so on. Then we make the strufoli and ship it out. My oldest niece, Alexa, is ten years old and really loves preparing the strufoli. She appreciates being a part of the family process of making this special Italian dessert and looks forward to it. We're proud to be Italian American and feel that our tradition is very important.

I also get the wonderful opportunity to act with many talented Italian Americans on *The Sopranos*. How I landed the role of Ginny Sacrimoni, the wife of the underboss of the New York mob, Johnny Sack, is interesting. I was one of the hundreds of people who went to the open casting call that *The Sopranos* show had in Harrison, New Jersey. I didn't even want to go, but my friend talked me into it. We stood in the line for three and a half hours and that was when the cops shut it down because it was getting out of hand. The casting company gave out the address to send in head shots, so I wrote it down and sent in my photo. Then I got a phone call to come in for an audition. Afterward, I got a call from the casting office and was told that I got the part. The first time I acted on *The Sopranos* was the greatest experience of my life. The biggest thrill for me was meeting Steven Van Zandt. I love his band, Little Steven Van Zandt and the Disciples of Soul. He turned out to be the greatest guy in the world! Everyone was so nice to me. The very first scene I shot was with James Gandolfini. It is the scene when Tony Soprano comes to our home and welcomes us when we move to his New Jersey neighborhood. It is wonderful to work with Jimmy. He is a great guy. I also love playing Vince Curatola's wife on the show because Vince is such a fine person. I truly adore him. My character even prepared some Italian food on the show, which was a lot of fun.

When I'm at home, I cook every night for me and my fiancé, Luke. I usually cook Italian food. However, I honestly don't know how to cook for two people, so we usually have a lot of leftovers in my house. When you are used to cooking for a big family, you tend to make a lot of extra food because you never know who is coming over to visit on Sunday. For instance, my mother makes anywhere between two and a half to three pounds of macaroni on a Sunday. Anyway, I'd rather cook at home than just eat out because I find it to be much more personal. I make things like antipasto, eggplant parmigiana, chicken francese, and cold broccoli salad, just to name a few dishes. My fiancé makes a great linguini and clam sauce when we are in the mood for that. Cooking can be romantic! But sometimes we invite people over because I love to cook for friends too. I just love to cook, period! I love strufoli and that's why I'm going to give you the Borino family recipe for it! Normally, people just put on the little sprinkles. However, I also add crushed nuts to the strufoli before adding the sprinkles on top as the final touch. I love it! In my opinion, it is the best Italian dessert.

DENISE BORINO has been interviewed on all the popular television shows like *Extra* and *Entertainment Tonight* and on networks like E!, each wanting to know about the lucky way in which she was cast on *The Sopranos*. Borino was selected from hundreds of aspiring actresses at an open casting call in Harrison, New Jersey. She literally went from her day job as a suburban secretary to becoming a featured actress on one of the most successful television shows in the world, *The Sopranos*. Seen in over eighty nations across the globe, *The Sopranos* has brought Borino a level of audience recognition that she never expected. Considering herself fortunate to be in the company of such talented actors and actresses on *The Sopranos*, she's ready for any television or motion picture challenge that may come along in the future.

STRUFOLI

2 cups all-purpose flour, sifted
1 teaspoon salt
3 eggs
1 teaspoon vanilla extract
Oil for frying
1 cup honey
1 tablespoon sugar
1 cup chopped walnuts (optional)
Multicolored sprinkles

In a large bowl, mix flour and salt. Make a well in center of the flour, and add eggs, one at time, mixing slightly after each addition. Add vanilla extract and mix well to make a soft dough.

Turn dough onto a lightly floured surface and knead. Divide dough in half. Cover in plastic wrap and refrigerate for ½ hour. Remove from refrigerator; roll out each piece of dough to form a 1-inch-thick rectangle. Cut dough with a pastry cutter into strips 1-inch wide. Using the palm of your hand, roll strips to pencil thickness. Cut into pieces about 2 inches long and roll pieces into balls.

Put oil in a large pot several inches deep. Heat until oil is very hot but not smoking (about 360 degrees). Carefully drop in balls of dough, but be sure not to overcrowd them. Fry 3 to 5 minutes or until lightly browned, turning occasionally during frying time. Remove with a slotted spoon and drain over oil before moving the balls to absorbent paper, or place balls in a brown paper bag and shake vigorously to remove excess oil.

In a skillet over low heat, add honey, sugar, and walnuts. Heat for about 5 minutes until honey and sugar melt. Remove from heat to add strufoli pieces. Stir constantly until all pieces are coated with the honey/sugar/walnut mixture. Remove strufoli pieces with slotted spoon, and place on a large platter, arranging them into a mound. Set platter in refrigerator to chill slightly. Sprinkle with multicolored sprinkles and serve.

SERVES 8

SHUT UP AND EAT!

DOMINIC CHIANESE

IF THERE WAS ever a real Italian-American neighborhood, it would have to be the one where I grew up — 187th Street in the Belmont section of the Bronx. That's in the heart of the northern area of New York City. It was a working-class area, not far from Fordham Road. What an authentic Italian-American neighborhood! In fact, it was so Italian, you could eat it! We bought our Italian groceries from stores right in our own immediate neighborhood. My mother was a very decent cook, but her father was a true maestro—a maestro in the kitchen. He was a chef and the food he prepared was absolutely out of this world. I remember the food from my childhood being very southern Italian. The sauces were very rich and there was a lot of seafood. We ate everything that was authentic southern Italian cuisine, from fish to meats to soups. My mother even made her own homemade macaroni, a talent that is now considered a lost art.

I have always enjoyed cooking and I dabble in the kitchen today. However, when I was growing up, my mother never let me in the kitchen. It was exclusively her domain. Today, I enjoy making sausage and peppers, but my favorite dish is pasta fagiole. It is a simple dish, but when prepared correctly, it's delicious. I've loved it since I was a kid. I also love ziti al forno, Neapolitan-style. I like the pasta really well done so it's crispy around the edges. I often make this at home and eat it when I'm out. There are so many good restaurants in New York City, especially when it comes to Italian cuisine. Rao's has the best meatballs. There is absolutely no doubt about that. They are delicious, big, and hearty. It is extremely hard to get a good meatball in a restaurant these days, and, trust me, Rao's has got 'em.

I find music to be important when I am eating. Good live music can be enjoyable, making the atmosphere so very simpatico. I am a musician and singer, so music is close to my heart. However, the food and the company you're with are still the most important basic elements of life. Bonding over an Italian meal with friends and family is the greatest. There is nothing like eating around a big table and seeing the faces of the people you like and love. So, here are my observations and advice: Food alone is not going to make people like each other. That's impossible. You have to like each other first and then enjoy the food. It's a combination of those ingredients on the table and the feelings in your heart that make for the perfect meal!

My favorite part of the meal is the dessert. I like it because a perfect dessert signifies the feeling of the end of a great meal, and that's the time when everyone sits down around the table and speaks. Even the cooks who have been working all day join in the conversation. It is a great bonding time. My favorite desserts are Italian pastries, and that's why I'm giving you my recipes for sfogliatelle and Cannoli Chianese. After dessert, I enjoy a cup of espresso with a little Sambuca. I also like desserts because they represent the true warmth and heart of the old Italian neighborhood. One thing's for sure: Italian cuisine has always been special to me and it always will be.

AN ACCOMPLISHED singer and guitarist, Dominic Chianese is a graduate of Brooklyn College. His first language is English, followed by a smattering of the Neapolitan dialect (Chianese's grandparents came from southern Italy, Naples and Sorrento). Chianese did some professional stage work in the 1950s, highlighted by his stint with a Gilbert and Sullivan repertory company of singers, actors, and musicians called the American Savoyards. After attending acting classes at HB Studio (founded by the legendary Herbert Berghof), Chianese's first Broadway show was *Oliver,* and he's been busy ever since. From his initial movie role as Johnny Ola in *The Godfather, Part II*, Chianese has gone on to appear in films such as *Dog Day Afternoon, And Justice for All, Night Falls on Manhattan, The Last Capone, Gotti, and Unfaithful*. All these parts served to set the stage for his tour de force acting role as Uncle Junior on television's *The Sopranos*. A multitalented performer, Chianese can also be heard playing his guitar and singing songs from his CD at popular spots like Sophia's in New York City's Broadway theater district.

SFOGLIATELLE
(Sweet Ricotta Turnovers)

FOR PASTRY
1¾ cups all-purpose flour

7 tablespoons granulated sugar

Pinch salt

6 tablespoons unsalted butter, softened

FOR FILLING
2 cups water

¾ cup semolina

Pinch salt

1 cup ricotta cheese

¾ cup granulated sugar

1 egg beaten

¾ cup candied fruit

1 teaspoon vanilla extract

Pinch cinnamon

TO FINISH
2 egg yolks, beaten

Powdered sugar, for dusting pastries

For pastry:

Sift the flour onto a pastry board or into a bowl. Add the sugar and salt, and then work in enough cold water to make a very firm dough. (The actual quantity of water depends on the kind of flour being used and the weather.) Cut the butter into small pieces and knead into the dough. Continue kneading until the dough is smooth and pliable, roll into a ball, and put aside until needed.

(You can also use frozen pastry dough or phyllo dough for this recipe.)

For filling:

Bring the water to a boil in a small pan, and slowly stir in the semolina. Add salt, and cook briskly for 5 minutes, stirring vigorously with a wooden spoon. Turn into a large bowl and let cool.

Mix the ricotta cheese, sugar, beaten egg, candied fruit, vanilla extract, and cinnamon together, then stir into the semolina, and beat the mixture until smooth.

To finish:

Preheat oven to a moderate temperature (about 375 degrees). Break the pastry dough into 12 pieces and roll them into ovals, ⅛-inch thick. Put a little of the filling on each oval of pastry, fold over, and seal the edges firmly. Now, using a glass, cut the turnovers into perfect rounds, trimming off the excess dough neatly, and again make sure that the edges are firmly sealed.

Butter a baking sheet and arrange the turnovers on it. Brush with beaten egg yolk and bake. The turnovers should be cooked and golden brown in 15 minutes; if not, bake them for a little longer. Sprinkle with powdered sugar and serve warm or cold, not hot.

SERVES 12

SHUT UP AND EAT!

CANNOLI CHIANESE

FOR CANNOLI SHELLS

1¼ cups all-purpose flour

1¼ teaspoons cocoa

1 teaspoon instant coffee

Pinch salt

1 teaspoon granulated sugar

2 tablespoons cold butter

Approximately 1 cup white or red wine or Marsala

Olive oil for deep-frying the shells

FOR FILLING

¼ cup dried fruits, chopped

2 tablespoons grappa liqueur

8 ounces ricotta

¼ cup sugar

2 ounces (¼ cup) mascarpone

¼ cup toasted pistachio nuts, chopped

¼ cup powdered sugar, for garnish

Sift the flour, cocoa, instant coffee, salt, and sugar into a bowl. Cut in the butter and rub it into the flour. Then gradually add sufficient wine to make a firm dough. (The quantity of wine will vary slightly according to the type of flour used.) Knead the dough until smooth and elastic. Roll it out into a very thin flat sheet and cut into twelve equal-size squares, each approximately 3 x 3 inches. Place a metal tube (can be bought at a bakery supply store) diagonally onto each square and bring the two corners over to meet in the middle. Press gently to seal.

Heat plenty of olive oil (enough to cover the tubes) in a deep pan, and deep-fry the pastry-covered tubes, 1 or 2 at a time, until dark golden and crisp. Take out with a slotted spoon and drain on paper towels or, better still, on a rack over absorbent paper. As soon as the tubes are cool enough to handle, take them gently out of the pastry, and then let the pastry become quite cold.

Soak the dried fruits in grappa liqueur for 15 minutes. Combine the ricotta and sugar in a small bowl and whip until smooth. Add the mascarpone and stir to incorporate. Be careful not to overmix, or the mascarpone might separate. Fold in the pistachios and dried fruits.

Filling the shells:

Transfer filling to a pastry bag fitted with a plain tip, and pipe the mixture into the cooled cannoli shells. Do this close to serving time so the shells won't lose their crispness. Arrange the cannoli on a dish, and dust with powdered sugar. Serve immediately.

SERVES 12

INDEX

INDEX

INDEX

INDEX

PHOTO CREDITS

Cover photos: James Gandolfini © Fred Rouser/Reuters/Corbis • Drea de Matteo © Eric Robert/Corbis/Sygma • Chazz Palminteri courtesty of Chazz Palminteri • Tony Lip courtesy of Tony Lip • Pasta sauce © Laurie Rubin/Getty Images

Photos on pages 3, 4, 6, 7, 8, 10, 11, 14, 17, 18, 21, 22, 24, 25, and 174 courtesy of Tony Lip. • Photo on page 26 by Ralph Lewis. • Photo on page 27 courtesy of Chazz Palminteri • Photos on pages 33, 34, 61, 63, 69, 194, 199, 201, and 275 by Soprano Sue Sadik. • Photo on page 39 collection of AVCO Embassy. • Photo on page 45 courtesy of Michael Rispoli. • Photos on pages 53 and 55 courtesy of Joe Mantegna. • Photos on pages 77, 78, and 79 courtesy of Danny Aiello. • Photo on page 85 by Gene Gabelli. • Photo on page 93 by Katri Pyynonen. • Photos on pages 97 and 98 courtesy of Michael Badalucco. • Photo on page 105 courtesy of Lorraine Bracco. • Photos on pages 106 and 107 courtesy of Da Silvano. • Photo on page 113 by Kristina Loggia. • Photo on page 119 courtesy of Frank Pellegrino. • Photo on page 125 courtesy of Robert Davi. • Photo on page 135 courtesy of Ray Abruzzo. • Photos on pages 147 and 148 courtesy of Drea de Matteo. • Photo on page 150 courtesy of Lombardi's Restaurant. • Photos on pages 157 and 159 courtesy of Burt Young. • Photo on page 165 courtesy of Dan Grimaldi. • Photo on page 168 coutesy of Patsy's. • Photo on page 173 courtesy of Pat Cooper. • Photos on pages 177 and 179 courtesy of Sonny Grosso. • Photos on pages 182, 258 (top), and 280 by Steven Priggé. • Photo on page 183 by Jerome de Perlinghi. • Photo on page 187 courtesy of Diane Venora. • Photo on page 193 courtesy of Tony Sirico. • Photo on page 207 by Richard Wright. • Photo on page 213 courtesy of Tony Darrow. • Photo on page 219 courtesy of Aida Turturro. • Photo on page 225 courtesy of Joe Rigano. • Photos on pages 231 and 232 courtesy of Vincent Curatola. • Photo on page 237 courtesy of Louis Guss. • Photo on page 243 courtesy of Kathrine Narducci. • Photo on page 249 by Babaldi Studios. • Photo on page 255 by Susan Maljan. • Photo on page 258 (bottom) courtesy of Il Cortile. • Photo on page 263 courtesy of Leo Rossi. • Photo on page 267 courtesy of Vinny Vella Sr. • Photo on page 273 courtesy of John Ventimiglia. • Photo on page 279 courtesy of Franki Gio. • Photo on page 285 by Anthony Maddaloni. • Photo on page 289 courtesy of Dominic Chianese, taken by Adolfo Gallela.